THE PERSISTENCE OF
THE NEGATIVE

Affirmation – as a substitute for uniting – belongs to Eros; negation – the successor to expulsion – belongs to the instinct of destruction. The general wish to negate, the negativism which is displayed by some psychotics, is probably to be regarded as a sign of a defusion of instincts that has taken place through a withdrawal of the libidinal components.

Sigmund Freud

Down to the vernacular of praising men who are 'positive,' and ultimately in the homicidal phrase of 'positive forces,' a fetish is made of the positive-in-itself. Against this, the seriousness of unswerving negation lies in its refusal to lend itself to sanctioning things as they are.

Theodor Adorno

But for every tumour a scalpel and a compress.

Samuel Beckett

THE PERSISTENCE
OF THE NEGATIVE

*A Critique of Contemporary
Continental Theory*

Benjamin Noys

EDINBURGH UNIVERSITY PRESS

© Benjamin Noys, 2010, 2012

First published in hardback by Edinburgh University Press 2010

Edinburgh University Press Ltd
22 George Square, Edinburgh EH8 9LF

www.euppublishing.com

Typeset in Sabon
by Servis Filmsetting Ltd, Stockport, Cheshire, and
printed and bound in Great Britain by
CPI Antony Rowe, Chippenham and Eastbourne

A CIP record for this book is available from the British Library

ISBN 978 0 7486 3863 5 (hardback)
ISBN 978 0 7486 4904 4 (paperback)

The right of Benjamin Noys
to be identified as author of this work
has been asserted in accordance with
the Copyright, Designs and Patents Act 1988.

Contents

Acknowledgements

I would like to thank all those who have contributed to the formation of this book, often through debate and disagreement: Jon Baldwin, Jason Barker, Geoff Bennington, Lorenzo Chiesa, John Cook, Gail Day, Mark Fisher, Hugo Frey, Marc Goodman, Gilles Grelet, Peter Hallward, Graham Harman, Owen Hatherley, Diarmiud Hester, China Miéville, Reza Negarestani, Saul Newman, Gareth Payne, Nicole Pepperell, Nina Power, Simon Sellars, Steven Shaviro, Nick Srnicek, James Trafford and Alex Williams. In particular thanks are due to Mathew Abbott, Ray Brassier, Dominic Fox, Bram Ieven, Ben Roberts, John Roberts, James Tink, Alberto Toscano and Evan Calder Williams, for their comments and criticisms of the manuscript. Of course none of the above is responsible for the positions taken or errors made in what follows, which are mine alone. My greatest thanks are to Fiona Price for her invaluable intellectual, moral and practical support.

Preface

The aim of this book is simply stated: to rehabilitate a thinking of negativity through an immanent critique of contemporary Continental theory. This could appear to be a deliberately quixotic gesture. If we consider contemporary theory as polarised between the antithetical figures of Alain Badiou and Antonio Negri – an austere Platonism versus a joyous Spinozism – this apparent antagonism conceals their shared commitment to affirmation. In very different forms they both affirm the creation of unashamedly metaphysical ontologies, the inventive potential of the subject, the necessity for the production of novelty, and a concomitant suspicion of the negative and negativity. Beyond these two figures, and unnoticed in all the disputes, debates and metaphorical wars that have wracked contemporary theory, this 'affirmationism' constitutes a dominant and largely unremarked *doxa*. Outside of high theoretical positions a more dispersed affirmationist consensus operates in the contemporary humanities and social sciences. Although proclaiming its opposition to the supposed abstractions of high theory, this 'low affirmationism' does so in the name of affirming historical density, complexity and materiality – thereby simply replacing one form of affirmation and construction with another, that is supposedly more nuanced. The result is that any rehabilitation of negativity faces an inhospitable environment, in which it is at best condescended to as the sign of the last remnants of a paleo-Hegelianism, or at worst regarded as the endorsement of nihilistic destruction. Reifying negativity into *the* negative, which is treated as synonymous with what is outdated or purely destructive, these ideological mystifications serve their purpose in blocking any thinking of negativity as a practice.

We can easily adduce internal reasons for the hegemony of affirmation: the persistence of a dispersed quasi-Nietzscheanism and neo-Spinozism, a continuing fear of the supposed totalising effects of dialectical thought, and a general turn to historicism, especially the historicisation of difference. A more speculative answer also suggests itself: the politics and metaphysics of affirmationism are indicative of a response and resistance to the dynamics of contemporary neo-liberal capitalism. What Marx had identified as the dissolutive logic of capital – 'all that is solid melts into air' – has, once again, came to the fore after the brief and localised hiatus of supposed stability that was Fordism. Gilles Deleuze and Félix Guattari have provided a resonant re-statement of Marx's point in their analysis of capitalism as operating through an axiomatic of deterritorialisation – the filtering, intercep-tion and concentration of decoded flows. This 'return' of capitalism to the primacy of decoded flows has not gone unopposed: the Chiapas uprising of 1994, the emergence of what is called in Italy '*Il popolo di Seattle*' in 1999, the anti-war protests of 2004 and the experiments of 'laboratory Latin America', have all been signs of resistance, although ambiguous in terms of their success. I would argue that the affirma-tive theorisations of Badiou, Negri and others, including the continu-ing resonance of the thought of Deleuze, also belong to this cycle of contestation.

These orientations, which were formed by the anti-systemic struggles of the 1960s and 1970s (usually condensed in the figure of 'May '68'), have endeavoured to adapt to new conditions of defeat and dispersion. In particular they have sought to resist capitalism's pseudo-dialectic, in which the globalising logic of the commodity is predicated on the management and distribution of difference. Resistance to this dialectic, which found its mirror in poststructuralist theorisations of difference, has often taken the form of the affirmation of new generic forms of universality. Negri, inspired by Deleuze, insists on a superior form of difference – the monstrous multitude of immanent singularities – that exceeds any form of capitalist control. For Badiou resistance requires the thinking of an egalitarian communist politics of the 'Same', sub-tracted from capital and indifferent to socially sanctioned difference. We could also add Jacques Rancière's affirmation of an axiomatic egalitarian politics available to all, which ruptures the ordered polic-ing of social hierarchies, and Giorgio Agamben's invocation of generic *potentia* as an ontological politics of refusal of the state and capital. Despite all the differences and tensions between these theories they form an affirmationist bloc committed to affirming new points of resist-ance supposedly intractable to capitalist capture or deterritorialisation.

While I am in sympathy with this desire for resistance it is precisely the affirmation of some positive, primary and productive point, or points, of resistance that first aroused my suspicion. The mantra-like repetition of Deleuze's maxim that 'resistance comes first' by Negri and others, evaded, it seemed to me, the complexity of the question of resistance in the face of capital's powers of recuperation. The irony was that the very desire to refuse the recuperation of difference by invoking a superior power of positive difference *qua* resistance brought this thinking into alignment with the ideology of contemporary 'creative capitalism' – one predicated on invoking the inexhaustible value-creating powers of novelty, production and creativity. The same is true of Badiou's invocation of rare events as unique sites requiring affirmation, which leads to a surprisingly similar model of resistance couched in the terms of construction and production. The wider tendency in affirmationism to ontologise resistance as a perpetually occluded actuality left that resistance all too vulnerable to the cunning of capitalist reason.

Of course there is a rich alternative history of dialectical theory attuned to a thinking of immanent negativity: from Walter Benjamin and Theodor Adorno, to contemporary figures such as Slavoj Žižek, Fredric Jameson and Alenka Zupančič. While I draw inspiration from this tradition, especially such heterodox figures as Benjamin and Guy Debord, I am sceptical of its ability to fully come to terms with the problem of affirmationism. On the one hand, figures like Žižek concede too much to affirmationism by reconstituting the dialectic of negativity – the 'negation of negation' – as a superior form of affirmation. Here resistance is again couched within the terms of a discourse of production, construction and novelty. On the other hand, Adorno's mordant posing of negative dialectics courts convergence with the softer forms of affirmationism, in its embrace of weak thought, finitude and the pathos of the suffering subject. Here we have the ironic affirmation of human finitude as the essential operator of resistance. This risks not only a defanging of negativity, but also bringing negativity into alignment with the ideologies of militarised humanism and tolerated difference, which are predicated on the model of a weak and suffering humanity.

Due to my scepticism with these existing alternatives I have instead decided to contest affirmationism on its own ground. My wager is that the traversal of affirmationism offers the best opportunity to sharpen a thinking of negativity that is resistant to re-coding under the sign of affirmation, while avoiding a 'weak negativity' that leaves us unable to grapple with the ideological operations of capital. This is a local and conjunctural intervention, which aims to problematise the way in which the recourse to the affirmative has become second nature. Instead, I argue that it is only through the reconfiguration of negativity as a practice that we can develop more supple and precise forms of resistance and struggle within and against capitalism. To put it bluntly, any theoretical or political project committed to a radical egalitarian politics requires a thinking of negativity if it is to be truly able to think the conditions of possibility of the *change* necessary to achieve that politics, and the potential forms of *agency* to carry out that change.

Benjamin Noys
Bognor Regis 2009

Introduction

In his mapping of modern post-Kantian philosophy Giorgio Agamben suggests that it is divided between two lines: the line of transcendence, which starts with Kant and culminates in Derrida and Lévinas, and the line of immanence, beginning with Spinoza and passing through Nietzsche to Deleuze and Foucault.[1] The contemporary dominance of affirmationism in Continental theory can be read as a sign of the triumph of this second line of immanence, which has become correlated with the political ability to disrupt and resist the false transcendental regime of capitalism. It is the affirmation of immanence, particularly as the locus of power and production, which is supposed to deliver the re-establishment of the grandeur of philosophy and the possibility of a new post-Nietzschean 'great politics'. It would, however, be an error to understand the appearance of affirmationist theory as simply another in the regular 'turns' of contemporary theory, or as the re-tooling of the particular verities of pre-Kantian metaphysics. Instead, in this introduction, I want to argue that we can map the emergence of this high affirmationism in a more localised and politically-sensitive fashion in order to better critique it.

The emergence of affirmationist theory obeys a strange temporal logic in which this supposedly new current in fact developed in *parallel* with the more well-known theoretical orientations of the 1970s and 1980s, which are usually grouped together in the Anglophone world under the banner of poststructuralism. In fact, we might better speak of *resurgence* rather than emergence. This resurgence can be thought in terms of the Freudian temporality of *Nachträglichkeit* or deferred action, in which an 'original' trauma only emerges as a result of a 'later' activation. In this case the theoretical engagements of the 1970s provide

a retroactive 'primal scene' for supposed 'later' emergence of affirmationist theory. I want to argue that the 'original' trauma in this case is
the simultaneous attempt to actualise left-libertarian forms of political
agency coupled to an awareness of the first signs of neo-liberal capitalist counter-revolution, evident in the mid-1970s work of Deleuze and
Guattari, Lyotard and Baudrillard. Their work is a hyper-theoretical
instance of what Daniel Bensaïd calls the 'neo-libertarian current . . .
[which] constitutes a state of mind, a "mood", rather than a well-
defined orientation'.[2] In this case 'libertarian' refers to a contestation
from the ultra-left of the sclerotic forms of the groups and parties of
the traditional workers' movement. Largely ignored or sidelined in his-
tories of theory, which prefer to read this period as the time of deconstruction or poststructuralism, I will argue that this brief theoretical
moment frames an acute politicisation before the retreat of the 1980s
and early 1990s into the sheltering thought of Otherness – either in its
high form of total alterity (Lévinas, Derrida), or in the low or minor key
of localised forms of alterity expressed in particular political or cultural
identities.[3] We can locate affirmationist theory as the attempt to resist
the *via negativa* of Otherness, and as the attempt to find a different
solution to the political aporia of the libertarian thinking of the 1970s –
which found its own libertarian articulations in dangerous consonance
with new forms of capitalist accumulation.

II

The usual left narratives that consider the fate of theory first homog-
enise the series of works that developed on the unstable boundary
between philosophy and the human sciences during the 1960s in
France under the banners of postmodernism and poststructuralism.
They do so to operate a political critique, which argues that these theoretical endeavours should be read as a series of 'symptoms of political
defeat'.[4] The claim is that although initially energised by the struggles
of May '68 theory parlayed the dispersion of these political energies
into theoretical forms that validated defeat. The resulting emphasis on
difference, drift and fragmentation only mirrors the new ideological
dispensation of a triumphalist capitalism. A more sinister variant of this
narrative regards theory as having 'been mobilised to domesticate, in
institutional ways, the very forms of political dissent which those movements [of the 1960s] had sought to foreground'.[5] In this case theory
contributes to the defeat of political radicalism by providing a false
path that absorbs and recuperates radical energies – the long march
through the institutions leading to a dead end. Often these narratives

are combined together to argue that theory is a discourse that both ratifies defeat and that substitutes for true political radicalism. In all cases what is assumed is that theory merely replicates and reproduces capitalist relations. This leaves Marxism as the untouched master (of) theory – a tool of diagnosis and analysis that presumes to judge theory and find it wanting.

My approach is to be suspicious that we can so simply evade the lessons of theory and, in the words of Antonio Negri, presume 'that "isomorphism" that is so dear to the champions of the base / super-structure relation'.[6] It is not simply that theory *qua* superstructure reflects capitalism *qua* base. I want to assimilate the lesson of Negri that:

> Critical Marxism is anything but determinist. The clash between productive forces and capitalist relations of production, both in reality and in representation (theoretical and metaphysical, scientific and historiographical), is always linked to events, to relationships of forces, to the creative capacity of historical subjects.[7]

Instead of simply homogenising and dismissing theory I want to grasp it in a more nuanced fashion as a creative, if problematic, response to the political crisis of the 1970s.

Crucial to my work of political historicisation is the suggestion of Walter Benjamin that it is necessary to make a distinction between the work of the historical materialist and the cultural historian. Benjamin rejected the existent discourse of cultural history for its reliance on a 'reified *historical continuity*'.[8] Of course contemporary cultural history and cultural studies make much of their careful consideration of the fragmentation and disruption of 'historical continuity', and of their opposition to teleological master-narratives. This position of cultural history and cultural studies, however, serves a deeper narrative of historical continuity, couched in terms of the density, complexity and materiality of history; 'micro' ruptures and breaks are accepted and deployed against any revolutionary 'macro' ruptures. Therefore I would argue Benjamin's criticisms still hold good:

> In short, cultural history only seems to represent a deepening of insight; it does not present even the appearance of progress in dialectics. For *it lacks the destructive element* that guarantees the authenticity of dialectical thought and of the dialectician's experience. It may well increase the burden of the treasures that are piled up on humanity's back. But it does not give mankind the strength to shake them off, so as to get its hands on them.[9]

Contemporary cultural history and cultural studies can only project out the 'destructive element' onto the usual historical signs of catastrophe

and disaster. They fail to recognise the possibility of destructive processes that would deliberately rupture the imposed continuity of the
accumulation of history, and so miss the opportunity to perform some
necessary destruction of their own.

For Benjamin it is not only the cultural historian but also the posi-
tivists among his Marxist contemporaries who are 'alienated from the
destructive side of the dialectic'.[10] It is this double criticism that is so
vital to my reading of the politics of the affirmationist consensus: as
Benjamin critiques both conventional cultural historians and the 'official' opposition of Marxism for their shared detachment from the negative, destructive, side of the dialectic, so I will use a similar manoeuvre
against the conventions of the 'low affirmationism' of cultural history
and cultural studies and against the new oppositional currents of high
affirmationist theory. In both cases what disappears is negation and
negativity. Certainly this is another political reading, but it is one sen-
sitive to the need for greater historical and contextual precision when
analysing theoretical forms, and to the need to recognise how theoretical interventions have also functioned as forms of political practice. It is
not a new anti-theory diatribe, but rather a theoretical reading attuned
to 'the destructive side' of negation and negativity – and particularly to
the forms of agency that might condense this negativity as a point of
intervention.

III

Let us return to the history of post-68 theory with this orientation in
mind. Antonio Negri endorses the hypothesis of Michael Hardt that:
'while in the nineteenth century France did politics and Germany did
metaphysics, in the twentieth century France did metaphysics and Italy
did politics'.[11] My argument is that particularly in the 1970s France
did metaphysics as a *means* of doing politics. I want to begin by isolating a series of theoretical interventions made in the early 1970s, which
all responded to the new libertarian mood induced by May '68. The
confluence of various discourses of liberation, notably sexual liberation, produced new discourses of contestation directed against capitalism, but also against the limits of the existing left. While many on the
left responded to the rapid ebbing of the events of May with calls to
Maoist or Leninist discipline, others argued the need to pursue the
quasi-anarchist path of liberation from *all* structures of discipline –
left or right. Three works were key expressions of this tendency, and
were often grouped together, despite mutual antagonisms, as the 'philosophy of desire': Gilles Deleuze and Félix Guattari's *Anti-Oedipus*

(1972); Jean-François Lyotard's *Libidinal Economy* (1974); and Jean
Baudrillard's *Symbolic Exchange and Death* (1976). These texts all
display their authors' formation by currents of the ultra-left,[12] and each
tries to outdo the other in terms of their radicalism. In particular they
reply to Marx's contention that '[t]he *real barrier* of capitalist production is *capital itself*',[13] by arguing that we must crash through this
barrier by turning capitalism against itself. They are an exotic variant of
la politique du pire: if capitalism generates its own forces of dissolution
then the necessity is to radicalise capitalism itself: the worse the better.
We can call this tendency *accelerationism*.[14]

Whereas the Anglo-American New Left had sought out the negation
of capital in the supposedly unintegrated subjects of revolt, such as the
lumpen-proletariat, students or the peasantry, accelerationists tried
to identify new subjects of revolt as being those most radically *within*
capitalism. If, as Lyotard put it, '*desire underlies capitalism too*',[15] then
the result is that: 'there are errant forces *in* the signs of capital. Not in
its margins as its *marginals*, but dissimulated in its most "nuclear", the
most essential exchanges'.[16] What the accelerationists affirm is the capitalist power of dissolution and fragmentation, which must always be
taken one step further to break the fetters of capital itself. For Deleuze
and Guattari the problem of capitalism is not that it deterritorialises,
but that it does not deterritorialise *enough*. It always runs up against
its own immanent limit of deterritorialisation – the reterritorialisation
of the decoded flows of desire through the 'machine' of the oedipal
grid. In the face of the deterritorialising axiomatic of capital we have
'[n]ot to withdraw from the process, but to go further, to "accelerate
the process", as Nietzsche put it: in this matter, the truth is that we
haven't seen anything yet.'[17] It is the figure of the schizophrenic, not to
be confused with the empirical psychiatric disorder, which instantiates
this radical immersion and the coming of a new porous and collective
'subject' of desire. The schizophrenic is the one who 'seeks out the very
limit of capitalism: he is its inherent tendency brought to fulfilment'.[18]

Contrary to Deleuze and Guattari's faith in a subject who would
incarnate a deterritorialisation in excess of capitalism, Lyotard's
Libidinal Economy denies any exteriority, insisting that capital itself
'is the unbinding of the most insane drives',[19] which releases 'mutant
intensities'.[20] The true form of capital is incarnated in the a-subjective
figure of the libidinal 'band' – a Möbius strip of freely circulating
intensities with neither beginning nor end. The extreme results of such
a position are summarised in Lyotard's notorious statement on the
experience of the worker in the nineteenth century – the most overt
acceptance of all the consequences of an accelerationist position:

there is *jouissance* in it, the English unemployed did not have to become workers to survive, they – hang on tight and spit on me – *enjoyed* the hysterical, masochistic, whatever exhaustion it was of *hanging on* in the mines, in the foundries, in the factories, in hell, they enjoyed it, enjoyed the mad destruction of their organic body which was indeed imposed upon them, they enjoyed the decomposition of their personal identity, the identity that the peasant tradition had constructed for them, enjoyed the dissolutions of their families and villages, and enjoyed the new monstrous *anonymity* of the suburbs and the pubs in morning and evening.[21]

The Marxist concept of alienation collapses because there is nothing left to alienate – capital itself is *jouissance*. There is no longer a true or real economy of desire somehow repressed or alienated by capital, but only the flickering appearance of a disenchanted libidinal economy on the far side of capitalism.

Jean Baudrillard's *Symbolic Exchange and Death* (1976) is a more ambivalent and uneasy example of accelerationism. If Lyotard outbids Deleuze and Guattari then, initially, Baudrillard outbids Deleuze and Guattari *and* Lyotard. He argues that their collective retention of the signifier of desire leaves them all locked into a dialectics of liberation tied to the functioning of the system. As he would later put it in *Forget Foucault* (1977) the attempt 'to rediscover a phantasmal and instinctual truth of the body in desire, is still only to unearth the psychic metaphor of capital.' [22] In a critique of accelerationism *avant la lettre* Baudrillard argues that this 'compulsion toward liquidity, flow, and an accelerated circulation' is only the replica or mirror of capitalist circulation.[23] The difficulty is that Baudrillard's own catastrophising strategy comprises a kind of negative accelerationism, in which he seeks the point of immanent *reversal* that inhabits and destabilises capital. In *Symbolic Exchange and Death* this is the 'death-function', which 'cannot be programmed and localised'.[24] Against the law of value that determines market exchange Baudrillard identifies this 'death-function' with the excessive and superior form of 'symbolic exchange' which is 'based on the extermination of value'.[25] We have reached the (literally) terminal point of resistance to capitalism. The problem for this strategy, pointed out by Lyotard in *Libidinal Economy* when reacting to Baudrillard's earlier work, is that perhaps '*[t]here is as much libidinal intensity in capitalist exchange as in the alleged "symbolic" exchange*'.[26] Baudrillard's reversible point is vitiated by capital's own powers of intensity. For Lyotard, Baudrillard fails to draw all the consequences of a radically immanent thought: the abandonment of any critique or critical position. It is an irony, as we shall see, that Lyotard himself would soon return to the relative certainties of Kantian critique.

These texts trace their own pattern of acceleration and outbidding as they try to exceed each other *and* a deterritorialising capitalism. Collectively they embody a shared desire to exacerbate capitalism to the point of collapse, aiming to out-radicalise Marx and Engels's argument that capitalism liberates us from 'feudal, patriarchal, and idyllic relations' by drowning these relations 'in the icy water of egotistical calculation'.[27] Heretical as they no doubt are, and they each make much of this, we should not forget that these are *Marxist* heresies. It is probably unsurprising that this micro-sequence of theory is often regarded as a terminal point, if not as symptomatic of the excesses that come from doing theory (even Lyotard later referred to *Libidinal Economy* as his 'evil book').[28] I will not take this peculiarly anti-intellectual line, because I want to argue that this accelerationist theoretical 'excrescence' is an engagement with, and re-formulation of, the political situation of the time. Against those interpretations that argued the failure of May '68 was due to the lack of a 'Party' or equivalent form of organisational discipline, this orientation gives a hyper-theoretical and abstracted form to the libertarian impulses of that moment. This accounts for the still pertinent refusal of Lyotard to engage in the normative language of 'perversion', or the lashing out of Deleuze and Guattari against 'paranoia' as the signature disorder of domination – including for revolutionary militants.[29] The accelerationists are, however, engaged with an ambiguous situation. On the one hand, they try to stay faithful to the libertarian effects of May '68 that involved the breaking-up of pre-existent moral and social constraints, especially in education, sexuality and gender relations; on the other hand, they also try to find a liberating dynamic in the 'unleashing' of capital flows due to the withdrawal of the post-war regulative mechanisms in the 1970s. They at once accept this situation and then try to 'direct' it, we could even say 'surf' it, to libertarian ends.[30]

The difficulties are obvious. While the accelerationists maintain a figure of revolution or revolt traced along existing tendencies of capitalism, they became increasingly detached from any actual social or political agency that could actuate this politics. Where are the schizophrenics? What exactly would be the 'subject' of Lyotard's libidinal band? How can the 'dead' or symbolic exchange produce resistance? In the retreat of political experimentation during the 1970s the potential subject of this politics – what Lyotard sarcastically dubbed the 'good hippy'[31] – disappears. This then leaves only one subject: 'the *desire of capital*'.[32] At the theoretical level the more any 'outside' from capitalism is eliminated, and the less convincing any internal force of overturning appears, the more unnecessary any subjectivity appears to

be: capitalism will do the work for us. Agency disappears into a fundamental passivity – becoming agents *of* capital – which is congruent with
forms of passive market-formed agency such as the Smithian 'invisible
hand'.[33]

Accelerationism, in another unintentional irony, risks restoring
the most teleological forms of Second International Marxism. The
slogan of Bernstein's revisionism was 'the ultimate aim of socialism is
nothing, but the movement is everything';[34] the accelerationists put a
twist on this: the movement would *achieve* the aim. The un-nuanced
celebration of the supposedly emancipatory possibilities secreted at the
nucleus of capital left this orientation high-and-dry when capitalism
counter-attacked in the purity of its own desire for accumulation. As
Moishe Postone states: 'With their critical gaze fixed upon what proved
to be another passing configuration of capitalism, poststructuralist
approaches backed into a still newer configuration, a neoliberal social
universe with which they were ill-prepared to deal'.[35] While the accelerationists could offer a critique of the codified normative orderings
of welfare or Fordist capitalism, and puncture some illusions concerning representation or organisation on the left, when capitalism itself
became 'purer' these theories lost purchase.[36]

During the 1980s those who had adopted an accelerationist position
responded to this crisis by taking up more classical positions, trying to
establish relatively stable points of resistance that were not absolutely
congruent with capitalist flows. While maintaining a faith in immanence, in *A Thousand Plateaus* (1980) Deleuze and Guattari paid far
more attention to the dangers in pursuing a full-blown 'schizo' deterritorialisation of desire.[37] To produce the consistency of a body without
organs requires an 'art of dosages, since overdose is a danger',[38] and it
is not to be carried out with a sledgehammer but with 'a very fine file'.[39]
Lyotard no longer praised the capitalist enhancement of bodily *jouissance* in the environment of the factory, but took refuge in the shelter
of the Jewish (or as he preferred 'jewish') thinking that 'the Other is
the law', opposed to the Heideggerian 'Western' thinking of the Other
as being.[40] This was predicated on a return to Kant, in which the sub-
limity of the law replaced the untrammelled *jouissance* of the worker.
Baudrillard retained most fidelity to his own negative accelerationism
of an autophagous capitalism. In *The Transparency of Evil* (1990) he
figured this immanent collapse of the system through the metaphor of
autoimmune disorder,[41] but now even Baudrillard bolstered this with
an insistence on the 'Other's indestructibility'.[42]

The collapse of accelerationism under the pressure of capitalist re-
composition, coupled to the desire to preserve a point of resistance

to capitalism, tended to lead to the localisation of that point as *transcendent* to capitalism. In different forms these positions now risked re-constituting alterity as what Derrida called the '*tout-Autre*' (the totally or completely Other),[43] courting the danger that they would become functionally indistinguishable from a transcendent religious conception. This configuration actually re-connected to elements within critical theory that had undergone a rightward shift in the 1960s, such as Horkheimer's rather undialectical invocations of the 'entirely other' (*ein ganz Anderes*).[44] In both cases the search for a final bulwark against the advance of disenchantment could all too quickly lead to the mysticism of the *deus absconditus*.

I V

Affirmationist theory can be positioned as another response within the same political moment, which refuses this oscillation between the Scylla of the un-nuanced affirmation of capitalism itself as source of liberation, and the Charybdis of the appeal to a 'pure' Other. This has become particularly crucial post-1989. In the situation of capitalism rid of even its intra-systemic rival, a capitalism 'unleashed', affirmationist theory has attempted to develop a politics of immanence that is directed against capitalist deterritorialisation. It has done so through the construction of new figures of subjective revolt 'within and against' what Hardt and Negri call the 'ontological fabric' of capitalism *qua* 'Empire'.[45] In doing so it has violently reacted against the theological turn to the totally Other, and to the variant turn to more localised identitarian models of 'otherness'. These models of alterity remain consonant with, or irrelevant to, capitalist dynamics. The consoling model of Otherness as exteriority supposedly immune to capitalism neglects its generation within the theological effects of commodity exchange, while the identitarian 'otherness' of particular forms of life fits the capitalist dispersion of differential identities as sources of accumulation. In response Badiou turns to Saint Paul as the operator of a new militant conception of universal resistance to Empire.[46] For Hardt and Negri, in a similar style, it is Saint Francis of Assisi who provides the figure of a positive, constructive and innovative militancy in his denunciation of poverty and his affirmation of a joyous life against the discipline of nascent capitalism.[47] In these cases the 'religious turn' is the turn to religious *practice*, rather than theological speculation (as in Derrida or Agamben), to provide the models for an immanent and resistant universal communism.

At the core of these shifting theoretical responses we can see the attempt to grasp the function of capital as a form of 'real abstraction'. Real abstraction implies the operation of capital as the abstraction of labour – its detachment from its pre-capitalist grounding – and through the abstractive effects of the commodity, in which the law of value 'levels' equivalences. Developing these points, through a reading of Roberto Finelli and Alfred Sohn-Rethel, Alberto Toscano argues that we can analyse this real abstraction as the ontology of capital: first, the concrete articulation of reality as a series of differences, and second, the void of its absence of determinations, the lack of a historical or cultural content to capital.[48] We can see how closely this model conforms to the path of recent theoretical innovation and the impasses of the model of alterity. The appeal to concrete differences (the alterity of identity) and the appeal to a total alterity (the void of determinations) seem to pose a mediated, but fundamentally congruent, response to this situation of capitalist development.

In Finelli's words we can speak of this absence of determinations as the 'reality principle' of capital,[49] which indicates its fundamental indifference to particular historical and cultural forms. These forms become up-for-grabs through the process of abstraction. In a way, as already developed by Deleuze and Guattari in their concept of capitalism as an axiomatic, we might say capitalism itself is a directly theoretical or philosophical matter. To resist the ontological 'weight' of capital it becomes a matter, for affirmationist theory, of forming a new counter-ontology. There is not a simple separation between theoretical intervention and capitalist 'reality', but rather the fraught struggle between the capitalist production of real abstraction and the attempt to work on and against these abstractions without returning to some simple underlying reality supposedly obscured by abstraction. To put it in a lapidary fashion we might say reality itself has become abstract: this is its 'ontological fabric'.

This problem is further exacerbated by the 'financialisation' of capital in response to dropping corporate profits: the massive expansion of the Finance, Insurance and Real Estate (FIRE) sector, the development of new speculative financial products (hedge funds, junk bonds, etc.), the phenomenon of 'nomad dollars' (dollars held outside the US, especially by China), the credit 'bubble', and so on, particularly since the 1970s and the collapse of the Bretton Woods system.[50] These new modes of capital accumulation have also been particularly dependent on the development of computing power – as computers allow new and sophisticated mechanisms for charting and calculating future risk. In Fredric Jameson's words, the result is that: 'capital itself becomes free-floating'.[51] Profit is not generated through production but through the management of risk. In this way financialisation relies on the 'fourth dimension' of time, commodifying the very course of our lives in terms of investment and loss.[52] Jameson has identified 'this new colonization of the future as a fundamental tendency in capitalism itself'.[53] It was precisely this explosive 'deterritorialising' effect of financialised capital in the 1970s, and the effect of 'finance-capital spectralities',[54] which theorists of the 1970s were trying to engage and turn to libertarian ends. This is one reason why the formulations of Deleuze and Guattari seem so resonant in formalising the financialisation of capital, but at the same time problematic.

What concerns me is the effect of this 'ultimate dematerialization'[55] of capitalism on forms of agency and theory. In terms of agency we can emphasise again the fragmenting effects of financialisation along both the spatial and the temporal axes. Along the axis of the spatial we see the parcelling out whereby 'traditional' forms of working class activity and potential agency in the process of production are displaced to new sites of production (notably China and India). Alongside this there is the catastrophic effect of the creation of zones of abandoned 'monetary subjects without money' (particularly in Africa, and in the new global slums). Finally, within the core capitalist countries we see the loss of manufacturing production, the rise of the new so-called 'immaterial' and service forms of labour, coupled to the binding of individuals to finance throughout the course of life, particularly through the mechanism of the mortgage. These zones of accumulation are also policed by new forms of spatial apartheid (border controls, gated communities, exclusion zones, etc.), which materially lock people in place and leave little realisable capacity for collective articulations of resistance.

Along the temporal dimension we see the increasing rapidity of capitalist exchanges between these zones, from the use of computers to containerisation, which gives capitalism the power to evade resistance by the re-siting of production and consumption. In the case of those subject to the effects of lifetime financialisation the individual becomes 'a two-legged cost and profit centre',[56] with all agency reduced to the lifetime management of oneself as financial portfolio. Resistance to this alienation is constrained through the imperative to manage these 'investments' (read debts) throughout the life course, from student loans, to the mortgage, to pensions. As I have just traced we can analyse currents in theory during the period since the early 1970s as, in part, attempts to come to terms with these effects of the 'spectralisation' of agency. Once again this is not to set up a simple one-to-one iso-morphism between free-floating theory and free-floating capital. I see these currents of affirmationist theory as trying to produce affirmative articulations and stabilisations that can resist the void of capitalism's real abstractions, and grapple with the fragmentation of the spatiality and temporality of subjectivity as it becomes alienated through these effects of displacement, delay and deferral.

The credit crunch, credit crisis, or financial crisis, which began in 2007, indicates both the power and vulnerability of real abstractions, as well as throwing into stark relief their effects on agency. The crisis was the result of a 'toxic combination'[57] of factors: financial deregulation, an asset bubble (notably in housing), new securitisation technologies, and the switch to financialisation in the search for profits. This caused a catastrophic chain-reaction, which may yield further disastrous results as it washes through global financial markets. The New York fiscal crisis of 1975 signalled the shift from Keynesianism to neoliberalism (although a covert Keynesianism remained for corporations and the rich);[58] it remains unclear whether this new crisis will signal a new financial 'regime change' or a patching-up to allow 'business as usual'. Certainly the struggle of capitalist managers, politicians and ideologues to re-start, or to save, the regime of financialisation and to mitigate its potentially disastrous effects have indicated the constraints and limits of agential interventions into that ultimate real abstraction: 'the economy'. Slavoj Žižek has pointed out how the collapse disables agency because of a crisis of prediction and confidence – the market depends on a delegated agency of anticipated trust in which we rely on what we predict others to do.[59] This disabling of agency is also produced by the very spectrality of the crisis, as Alain Badiou has insisted we are left watching a 'crisis-film' in the manner of a Hollywood disaster epic.[60] Crisis does not simply expose spectral abstraction, but also redoubles it.

This spectral dimension does not imply a quasi-Baudrillardian simulacral capitalism of pure speculation detached from any referent. Badiou's analysis of the spectacular dimension of the crisis argues that the 'real essence' of the crisis is a housing crisis,[61] while Robin Blackburn has noted that the crisis rests on poverty – those unable to pay off their sub-prime mortgages and the low wages of Chinese workers.[62] The difficulty still remains in articulating this 'real essence', which precisely lies in the appearance. This is why, as Geoff Mann insists, it is essential to return to the analysis of real abstraction, which takes place in reality – the abstractions of the value-form are 'as real as real can be'.[63] These abstractions are what create the fragmentation and fracture of the spatio-temporal coordinates of capital, and what constitute 'living labour' as the condition of the capitalist value-form. It is only by studying the articulation of the reality of these abstractions that we can articulate the 'real essence' of the crisis. Even in crisis the baroque complexity of the new forms of financialisation easily rival the most technical forms of poststructuralist theory. What I want to suggest is that the crisis is revelatory of the ontology of capital, at once spectral and real, empty and material, voided and differential. It is only *through* real abstraction that we can trace the possibility of the destruction of this ontology as the destruction of the value-form.

V

Affirmationist theory is one of the strongest and most developed attempts to provide a solution to articulating agency in the context of an ontology of capital that operates through the voiding of content and the distribution of differences. It challenges the notion of difference as constituting a possible counter-ontology to capital, insisting on the need for a positive point of orientation to truly disrupt the void or absence of determinations at the heart of capitalism. The solution offered is a new positive thinking of the 'Same', or of a superior 'Difference', irreducible to conventional social differences, on the one hand, or absolute alterity, on the other. It is this solution to the problem of thinking revolutionary subjectivity that I wish to contest through thinking the persistence of the negative, but without returning to the negative theology of the *tout Autre*. I aim to excavate a negativity that is not simply congruent with the capitalist void, which is not the negativity of capital, but negativity as the condition for re-articulating a thinking of agency. To articulate this thinking of negativity I insist on the traversal of affirmationist theory, rather than its dismissal.

It is essential to note, however, that the tendency to affirmation has not passed uncontested. The debate has particularly been focused around the work of Gilles Deleuze, subject of my second chapter. A number of recent works – Alain Badiou's *Deleuze: The Clamor of Being* (1997), Slavoj Žižek's *Organs without Bodies* (2004) and Peter Hallward's *Out of this World* (2006) – have posed politico-philosophical critiques of Deleuze. While inspirational to this work they have tended to offer their own 'affirmative' alternatives to the Deleuzian vitalism of life: Badiou's subtractive thinking of the event that leads to the construction of a new positive politics, Žižek's argument for a subjectivisation and positivisation of negativity through the 'repetition' of Leninism, and Peter Hallward's insistence on an affirmative voluntarist politics of the will.[64] Each of these works has provided me with resources for re-thinking the concept of negativity, but I wish to break with their tendency to replace one form of affirmationism with another. This tendency is, for me, one of the signs of the hegemony of affirmationism. It is also evident in Diana Coole's *Negativity and Politics: Dionysus and Dialectics from Kant to Poststructuralism* (2000). Her work parallels my argument by attempting to recover a reading of contemporary theory in terms of negativity, and is particularly astute on the possible interconnections between the dialectical 'tradition' and the seemingly anti-Hegelian 'Dionysiac' reading of negativity departing from Nietzsche. The difference is, again, that Coole finally re-codes the 'celebration of negativity' as affirmation.[65]

A more stringent attempt to contest affirmationism by a thinking of negativity, made in the context of Italian post-autonomist thinking, is Paolo Virno's *Multitude: Between Innovation and Negation* (2008). He argues for a 'nondialectic[al] understanding of the negative: [as] ambivalence, oscillation, [and] that which is perturbing'.[66] Such a manoeuvre is to be welcomed, especially in terms of Virno's suggestion that anti-capitalist and anti-state politics require 'no positive presupposition to be vindicated'[67] – a central thesis of this work. I am unconvinced, however, by his grounding of this negativity within the undifferentiated subject-form of the multitude, and more particularly in linguistic and bio-historical human capacities.[68] While Virno claims that the capitalist subsumption of humanity is revelatory of its bio-linguistic capacities, and gives them new weight, the vagueness of his specification of how these capacities are to be articulated against the value-regime of capital is striking. Negativity is posed in this most general of forms, largely in the register of the linguistic, but then little account is given of the actualisation of negativity, except in a discourse of displacement and flight. The result is a weightless concept of negativity, lacking any substantial sense of the *activation* of negativity as a practice of the necessary destruction of existent positivities.

Finally, a true anomaly to affirmationism is Ray Brassier's *Nihil Unbound: Enlightenment and Extinction* (2007). This work offers its own highly technical and speculative deduction of a 'being-nothing' – a non-dialectical negativity – to produce a rigorous nihilist naturalism. Brassier robs philosophy of any affirmationist role by deducing it as an anti-humanist organon of extinction, through the resources of Laruelle's non-philosophy, neurophilosophy and a nihilist reading of contemporary theory. In this case, to use a term of Badiou's, Brassier's deduction cuts a 'diagonal' across the usual tendencies of affirmationism. Again, although inspirational, I consider Brassier's inquiry problematic: I am wary of his tendency to naturalism, inscribed through very different neuro-scientific resources to that of Virno, and also the lack of specificity of how this philosophically radical nihilism might be articulated with a political radicalism. Brassier appears to favour a nihilist accelerationism, in which neuro-scientific interventions re-figure a post-humanist, and possibly post-capitalist, 'subject'. Once again, this seems to signal a dependence on a disabused faith in the *negative* dynamics of contemporary capital – its indifference to cultural and political contents – to dismantle the ideological props of the capitalist order.

VI

The chapters that follow are based on a selection, which is not intended to be exhaustive, of the leading theorists of affirmationism. This selection is guided by my attempt to contest affirmationism on its strongest ground, with each of these thinkers providing key and highly influential articulations of affirmative thought. In each case I will assess their construction of affirmationist theory through the prism of the traces of irreducible negativity that mark their work. These readings function as discrete chapters, and can be read as such, but they also link together in terms of a narrative of the *return* of this effect of negativity.

In Chapter 1 I argue that the thought of Jacques Derrida, often regarded as instantiating perpetual delay and prevarication, is actually better understood as a form of 'weak affirmationism'. In this way he broaches this new consensus, but we can also trace in his work an anguished negotiation with negativity that allows us to begin to grasp the rudiments of a new political practice of negativity. Chapter 2 deals with *the* central figure of contemporary affirmationism: Gilles Deleuze. Here I trace the persistence of Deleuze's affirmative orientation but, at the same time, his direct and continual engagement with the political problems of the present. Contesting Deleuze from within, we can see the intermittent flickering of a strategic thinking of negativity coordinated with capacities for political intervention and agency. Chapter 3 deals with Bruno Latour, who, as a sociologist and no political radical, seems to be an exception to affirmationist theory. It is Latour's insistence on an anti-revolutionary conception of the dense material network of relations that actually makes him emblematic of a generalised 'low affirmationism' in the humanities and social sciences. Latour is an ideological test case for my claims concerning the necessity for a thinking of the praxis of negativity. In Chapter 4 I consider Antonio Negri as the thinker most resolutely committed to founding affirmative ontological and communist politics on the radical subordination of negativity. It is Negri's subordination of negativity, I will argue, that leaves his conception of radical agency vulnerable to capitalist recuperation. Finally,

Chapter 5 is devoted to Alain Badiou. He is a crucial figure for my work because although he insists on his own affirmationist bona fides – he even coins the term affirmationism as a positive description – we can also locate him as figuring an exit from affirmationism. To do so I read Badiou's historicisation and formalisation of the negative, which tends to subordinate it to affirmationism, against the grain. While agreeing with Badiou's claim that we are witnessing a 'crisis of the negative', my solution is to push for a stronger conception of the practice of negativity against any subordination.

My procedure in this book obviously runs the risk of what Žižek identifies as 'the standard procedure of philosophical rejection':[69] we totalise the field we are rejecting by a caricatural procedure that falsely unites a 'set' of thinkers, while disavowing our own position as somehow 'external' to this field. Certainly my construction of an affirmationist bloc does involve a necessary element of caricature, provocation and polemic. I write without heeding Gilles Deleuze's (affirmationist) warning that: 'No book against anything ever has any importance; all that counts are books *for* something and that know how to produce it'.[70] (It should be noted Deleuze himself did not consistently obey this injunction.) This is, I would argue, an acceptable cost to gain a polemical purchase on the orientation of contemporary theory. At the same time the precise point of my immanent critique is that affirmationism in no way exhausts these thinkers' work, individually or collectively.

VII

It may be worthwhile to offer an initial orientation to two of the key terms that will be unpacked at length in this book: negativity and agency. First, negativity here is articulated against the tendency of models of dialectical negativity to subordinate or idealise negativity, especially when they cast negativity in the form of a superior affirmation. Such models create, as Derrida had noted, an *economy* of negativity that tends to reappropriate it and put it to work,[71] or, as Negri puts it, the 'sublimation of the negation.'[72] In the current context, tropes of production, construction and development, even if cast in the form of the production of struggles, seem suspect to me in their concession to capital's own affirmationism. Of course, Derrida, Deleuze and Badiou all, in different ways, attempt to articulate a non-dialectical conception of negativity – one not subject to contradiction or synthesis – primarily through a re-conceptualisation of difference *qua* negativity that is presumed to exceed dialectical coordination. Belonging to a longer tradition, which also includes Bataille and Blanchot, the risk courted in abandoning the dialectical tension of contradiction for the play of differences is that we will only be left with what Deleuze calls 'respectable, reconcilable or federative differences'.[73]

It is the departure from the tension of dialectical difference that seems to result in a fatal slackening of thought. Deleuze's answer to this problem, which I will argue is shared by Derrida, Badiou and Negri, is that difference requires the 'proper degree of *positivity*' to release 'a power of aggression and selection'.[74] Negativity is 'freed' from dialectical subordination, only to be made subject, finally and fatally, to affirmationism. In this way negativity is 'rescued' from the threat of being merely idle and abstract negativity. The hegemony of this strategy is brought home by the fact that Slavoj Žižek, a thinker who insistently begins from negativity, also finally re-codes negativity in terms of affirmationism, insisting on the congruence of his thought with that of Badiou.[75] Once again, the wholly understandable political desire to produce a truly resistant and powerful thought that can match the globalising ontological power of capital seems to lead inevitably to affirmationism. It is just this inevitability I wish to question.

Part of the attraction of this strategy is that the alternative, to embrace negativity, seems to lead to a different form of weakening – negativity being correlated with the suffering pathos of the subject. In rehabilitating negativity I wish to avoid this false choice between affirmationism and a 'synthesis' of negativity with finitude. Although often carried out in the name of an anti-synthetic negativity, as in Adorno's 'negative dialectics', or in various forms of post-deconstructive 'weak thought', this model sutures negativity to the *incapacity* of the subject.[76] The inscription of negativity in the subject, usually in the form of its constitutive finitude, is taken as the sign of what allows the subject to always escape or exceed capitalist capture. We have a symmetrical affirmation and ontologisation of resistance to high affirmationism, simply re-cast in different terms. This deflationary concept of the subject, however, leaves mysterious the processes by which the failure of the subject will be converted into active and successful resistance. The magical moment of reversal, in which weakness becomes a new source of power, evades the precise nature of the political valence of negativity as a practice.

Against both high affirmationism and this 'weak negativity' I wish to trace such a political reading of negativity, stressing it as a practice of the destruction of existent positivities through the performance of immanent ruptures. Therefore, negativity is not intended to function as a replacement ontological principle to affirmation, whether that be coded as an absolute or total negativity in which we can dwell in disabused certainty, or as some intrinsic and fading 'weak negativity' with which we must always come to terms. Instead, negativity only operates in the expropriation of positivities as a relation of rupture.

To refine this sense of negativity as a *practice* I have preferred the term 'agency' over the usual theoretical terms of 'subject' or 'subjectivity'. This is because those latter terms tend to ontologise or substantialise agency as a capacity of the subject – whether that be taken as superior power or as intractable weakness. David Harvey points out that such theories tend to posit agency in terms of a 'residual' or 'surplus' moment that escapes the crushing logic of social processes, and that this reification of agency generates the suspicion that what is being proposed is more the way out of a particular theorisation than an actual process of social change.[77] In contrast he argues, and this is also my proposal, that agency results from 'leverage points within the system',[78] leading us to the work of identifying forms and possibilities of agency. 'Agency' is not, however, a magical solution. Perry Anderson has noted that it replicates the ambiguity of the term 'subject' in alternating between senses of activity and passivity; we speak both of 'free agents' and of 'agents of a foreign power', for example.[79] This semantic slippage is at ideological work in the continual conflation of the sense of 'free agent' with 'market-agency', in which being an agent of the market is taken as the only acceptable form of freedom. My aim is to wrest away the concept of 'free agent' from market-agency, precisely through setting out the conditions for a collective practice of negativity. The question is how to articulate this collective political agency in the contemporary conjuncture?

It is true that affirmative conceptions of the subject and subjectivity also try to contest this reduction of our freedom to market freedom. In their inflation of the powers of the subject, however, they tend, ironically, to capsize back towards senses of passivity and unintended consequences that leave them perilously close to capitalism's valorisation of the power of the subject to dispose of her labour power and her income. The result is that agency is attenuated in the name of agency. Obviously, the deflation of the subject is no better solution, but merely another form of attenuation. My political reading of negativity tries to indicate more specific forms of agency that are more apparently modest, but, I would argue, more effective in their precise disruption of existent positive forms of ideological subordination. There is no doubt that negativity and agency cannot be some theoretical 'magic bullet' that would simply fill the gap of the relative absence of agency. I do want to argue that they can better pose the problem. In particular, as

Anderson makes clear, to truly grasp a concept of collective political agency that can wrest freedom from necessity requires a coordination of will and knowledge, rather than a voluntarism which supposes the 'will' alone as able to break structural constraints.[80] This work is intended as a contribution to this coordination, which requires, I will argue, the bending of the stick to negativity to escape the deadening constraints of the present.

NOTES

1. Agamben, *Potentialities*, p. 239.
2. Bensaïd, 'On a Recent Book', p. 170.
3. See Badiou, *Ethics*.
4. Eagleton, *The Illusions*, p. 19.
5. Ahmad, *In Theory*, p. 1.
6. Negri, *The Political Descartes*, p. 320.
7. Ibid. p. 321.
8. Benjamin, 'Edward Fuchs', p. 342.
9. Ibid. p. 360–1; my emphasis.
10. Ibid. p. 358.
11. Negri in Casarino and Negri, 'It's a Powerful Life', p. 154.
12. Although Deleuze did not have a particularly 'activist' left formation, Félix Guattari was a militant in the Trotskyite group *Voie Communiste* (1955–1965) and later involved in the student activism of May '68. Jean-François Lyotard was a member of the ultra-left group *Socialisme ou Barbarie* from 1954 until 1964 when he became a member of the break-away group *Pouvoir Ouvrier*, leaving that group in 1966. He was later involved in the May '68 events (for Lyotard's own analysis of his political history, see 'A Memorial of Marxism' in *Peregrinations*, pp. 45–75). Baudrillard's thesis was supervised by the radical thinker Henri Lefebvre, associate of the Situationists, and he later worked at Nanterre, the trigger point of the May '68 events.
13. Marx, *Capital vol. 3*, p. 358.
14. A. Kiarana Kordela makes a similar, although more narrowly focused, point when she critiques postmodern 'neo-Spinozism', notably Hardt and Negri's *Empire*, for the assumption 'that replicating and reinforcing the structures of capital, far from supporting it, amounts to accelerating the advent of its end as an exploitative, oppressing system' (*$urplus*, p. 3).
15. Lyotard, *Libidinal Economy*, p. 106.
16. Ibid. p. 110.
17. Deleuze and Guattari, *Anti-Oedipus*, pp. 239–40; See Garo, 'Deleuze, Marx and Revolution', p. 611.
18. Deleuze and Guattari, *Anti-Oedipus*, p. 35.
19. Lyotard, *Libidinal Economy*, p. 138; trans. mod.
20. Ibid. p. 214.

21. Ibid. p. 111; see also Lyotard's comments on this passage in *Duchamp's Transformers*, pp. 14–19.
22. Baudrillard, *Forget Foucault*, p. 26.
23. Ibid. p. 25.
24. Baudrillard, *Symbolic Exchange*, p. 126.
25. Ibid. p. 1.
26. Lyotard, *Libidinal Economy*, p. 109.
27. Marx and Engels, *The Communist Manifesto*, p. 222.
28. Lyotard, *Peregrinations*, p. 13.
29. Deleuze would later demonstrate his frustration with the limits of this binary opposition between (good) schizophrenia and (bad) paranoia when he remarked, in 'Letter to a Harsh Critic', that: 'Real and pretend schizophrenics are giving me such a hard time that I'm starting to see the attractions of paranoia. Long live paranoia' (*Negotiations*, p. 3).
30. The metaphor of 'surfing' is Brian Massumi's, from an interview with Mary Zournazi, 'Navigating Movements', and is perhaps derived from Deleuze and Guattari's *What is Philosophy?*, when they endorse the aim 'to turn the thinker into a sort of surfer' (p. 71).
31. Lyotard, *Libidinal Economy*, p. 108.
32. Ibid. p. 110.
33. Bull, 'The Limits', pp. 34–6.
34. Bernstein, *Evolutionary Socialism*, p. 202.
35. Postone, 'Critique', p. 56.
36. See Timothy Brennan's *Wars of Position: The Cultural Politics of Left and Right* (2006).
37. Jérémie Valentin remarks that Deleuze regarded *Anti-Oedipus* 'as a total failure' ('Gilles Deleuze's Political Posture', p. 188).
38. Deleuze and Guattari, *A Thousand Plateaus*, p. 160.
39. Ibid. p. 160.
40. Lyotard, *Heidegger and "the jews"*, p. 89.
41. Baudrillard, *The Transparency of Evil*, pp. 60–70.
42. Ibid. p. 146.
43. See Derrida, *The Gift of Death*.
44. Slavoj Žižek has explicated this tendency in critical theory to produce a denial of determinate negation:

    The idea is that, with the 'dialectic of Enlightenment' which tends towards the zero-point of the totally 'administered' society, one can no longer conceptualize breaking out of the deadly spiral of this dialectic by means of the classical Marxist notion according to which the New will emerge from the very contradictions of the present society, through its immanent self-overcoming: the impetus for such an overcoming can only come from an unmediated Outside. (*In Defense of Lost Causes*, p. 337)

45. Hardt and Negri, *Empire*, p. 354.

46. See Badiou, *Saint Paul*.
47. Hardt and Negri, *Empire*, p. 413.
48. Toscano, 'The Open Secret', p. 276.
49. Ibid. p. 277.
50. Giovanni Arrighi, in his article 'Hegemony Unravelling II', has argued, by drawing on the work of Fernand Braudel, that financialisation is a recurrent cyclical dynamic of capital. This is important for drawing attention to the long-term dynamics of capitalism, and the possible crises of these dynamics. Therefore financialisation is not 'new' as such, although its depth, penetration and scope do appear to mark a qualitative shift. This shift, combined with the dynamic of real abstraction, poses particularly acute questions for the status of theoretical and critical work that has to engage, whether it likes it or not, with this 'ontology' of capital.
51. Jameson, *The Cultural Turn*, p. 142.
52. Blackburn, 'Finance', p. 39.
53. Jameson, *The Cultural Turn*, p. 185.
54. Ibid. p. 188.
55. Ibid. p. 154.
56. Blackburn, 'Finance', p. 39.
57. Wade, 'Financial Regime Change?', p. 12.
58. Ibid. p. 6.
59. Žižek, *First as Tragedy*, pp. 10–11.
60. Badiou, 'Of Which Real is this Crisis the Spectacle?'.
61. Ibid.
62. Robin Blackburn, 'Value Theory', p. 129.
63. Mann, 'Colletti on the Credit Crunch', p. 125.
64. Badiou, *Being and Event*; Žižek, 'Repeating Lenin'; Hallward, 'The Will of the People'.
65. Coole, *Negativity and Politics*, p. 236. A similar difficulty bedevils John Holloway's re-politicisation of Adorno's negative dialectics in his essay 'Why Adorno?', which subsumes negativity under 'the power of human creativity' (p. 16) thereby rendering it as positive.
66. Virno, *Multitude*, p. 40.
67. Ibid. p. 190.
68. As is, ironically, Negri. In *Reflections on Empire* (2008), although not naming Virno, Negri argues that the grounding of the general intellect (the capacities of the multitude) in linguistic invariants is restrictive: '*Naturalism cannot satisfy the transformative dynamics the class struggle brings about*' (p. 102). See also Virno 'Natural-Historical Diagrams', and the sympathetic, but still critical, discussion of Virno's naturalism in Nina Power's review 'He's not Beyond Good and Evil'.
69. In Butler et al., *Contingency, Hegemony*, p. 224.
70. Deleuze, *Desert Islands*, p. 192.
71. Derrida, *Writing and Difference*, p. 308 note 4.
72. Negri, '*Kairòs*, Alma Venus, Multitudo', p. 250.

73. Deleuze, *Difference and Repetition*, p. 52.
74. Ibid. p. xviii.
75. See Badiou and Žižek, *Philosophy in the Present*, pp. 81–8 for this convergence.
76. See Simon Critchley, *Infinitely Demanding*.
77. Harvey, *Justice, Nature and the Geography of Difference*, p. 98.
78. Ibid. p. 106.
79. Anderson, *Arguments within English Marxism*, p. 18.
80. Ibid. pp. 23–4.

1. *On the Edge of Affirmation: Derrida*

It might well appear a strange decision to begin with the work of Jacques Derrida when one of the key features of contemporary affirmationism has been its tendency to claim to have surpassed or exceeded deconstruction. The persistent characterisation of Derrida's oeuvre in negative terms – infinite deferral, delay, marginality, anti-systemic fragmentation and, at worst, theoretical and political paralysis – has often been the starting point for the articulation of new affirmative alternatives. To take one instance, Alain Badiou, in relation to artistic practice, argues that we must 'renounce the delights of the margin, of obliqueness, of *infinite deconstruction*, of the fragment, of the exhibition trembling with mortality, of finitude and of the body'.[1] Regarding these forms as complicit with the ideological dynamics of contemporary capitalism Badiou opposes to them the need for 'monumental *construction*, projects, the creative force of the weak, [and] the overthrow of established powers'.[2] In the transfer of this schema to the philosophical and theoretical, a polemical gain is made, whereby deconstruction is confined to the past at the expense of the new; in fact, deconstruction is presented as a perpetually prevaricating theoretical endeavour that can never lead to anything new. While this trope has become something of a self-serving leitmotif, it does indicate the unstable position of deconstruction on the threshold of affirmationism or, as I prefer to characterise it, as a 'weak affirmationism'. In reviewing Derrida's work we can identify the features of affirmationism that will later take on more solid, and florid, forms.

The charge that deconstruction is negative, in the bad sense, is remarkably persistent. Even a thinker as heavily indebted to deconstruction as Giorgio Agamben does not hesitate to make this claim, although in the form of an esoteric allegory. In his essay '*Pardes*: The Writing of Potentiality' Agamben takes up the Talmudic story of

23

'*Pardes*', a parable concerning access to supreme knowledge.[3] It tells of four Rabbis entering paradise: Ben Azzai casts a glance and dies, Ben Zoma looked and went mad, Aher cut the branches and Rabbi Akiba left unharmed. Agamben identifies Derrida with the heretical Rabbi Aher who, in cutting the branches, remains perpetually outside paradise. This act is glossed by Agamben, through the Talmudic tradition, as an act of separation; in this case the separation of the pure potentiality of language.[4] Agamben's denial that Derrida leaves us 'to an infinite wandering or interpretation'[5] hardly rings true considering the fate of Rabbi Aher. By positioning Derrida in this way, Agamben can identify with Rabbi Akiba, who leaves paradise unharmed, and so claim to have passed beyond Derrida towards 'the decisive event of matter'.[6] Reiterating the charge in a different form in *The Time That Remains* (2000), Agamben accuses Derrida of an 'infinite deferment' that remains too close to the Hegelian *Aufhebung*, and which only leads to 'a thwarted messianism, a suspension of the messianic.' [7]

Derrida is quite open about his own engagement with negativity. In his early essay 'Cogito and the History of Madness' (1964), he invokes 'a negativity so negative that it could not even be called such any longer'.[8] Against what Derrida regards as the 'restricted economy' of Hegel he seeks a new 'general economy' in which negativity would be re-inscribed in terms of *différance*.[9] In the manifesto text of the same name, Derrida notes how this strategy can lead to the assimilation of his thought to a negative thinking, especially negative theology: 'the detours, locutions, and syntax in which I will often have to take recourse will resemble those of negative theology, occasionally even to the point of being indistinguishable from negative theology'.[10] In the same gesture, however, he already distances himself from what he regarded as an illegitimate confusion with that discourse. Whereas negative theology operates to disengage 'a superessentiality beyond the finite categories of essence and existence', *différance* is 'the very opening of the space in which ontotheology – philosophy – produces its system and its history . . . inscribing it and exceeding it without return'.[11] The paradox of negative theology for Derrida is that it is not negative enough, because it depends on positing a 'superessentiality', but also too negative, because it never reaches this point of excess. Derrida aims to avoid this impasse by the invocation of an ultra-negativity that does not reside in some 'superessential' instance, but functions as a productive excess opening the space of philosophy. This exacerbated negativity, which cannot be captured by dialectical contradiction or synthesis, is placed under the sign of affirmation.

I wish to problematise Derrida's construction of an ultra-negativity of radicalised excess that coincides with a superior form of affirmation. Unlike Deleuze, Foucault and Negri, Derrida does not embrace a full-blown 'anti-dialectical' affirmationism. Instead, his departure from Hegelian and Marxist theorisations of negativity is more fraught and complex. Hence Agamben's contention that Derrida is too close to Hegel is something Derrida himself would agree with, but only as a necessary mimicry to produce an effect of rupture.[12] At the same time, predominantly through a remarkably uncritical and undeconstructive deployment of Nietzsche, Derrida constantly appeals to affirmation as the decisive mechanism to save deconstruction from charges of perpetual delay and prevarication that might be thought to result from its non-dialectical model of difference. My aim here is not to rescue Derrida for a thinking of negativity, although that is perfectly possible.[13] Instead, in traversing Derrida's 'weak affirmationism' I aim to provide an initial delimitation of the problematic of affirmationism, particularly in political terms.

UNCONDITIONAL AFFIRMATION

At the core of high affirmationism lie a number of common features: the insistence that philosophy begins from affirmation, the systematic construction of ontology, the downgrading of critique and an anti-capitalist political ethos. Derrida exemplifies all these features, although in a qualified fashion. First, he insists that deconstruction is fundamentally affirmative.[14] Derrida formalises this by arguing that deconstruction always begins from a double affirmation, from the 'yes, yes', which he derives in the first instance from the fiction of Joyce. Contrary to the usual perception that openings and incompletion are the result of negativity fracturing what exists, Derrida argues that this 'yes, yes' structure re-codes such openings as fundamentally affirmative. In the beginning is the 'minimal, primary *yes*', and while '[n] egatives may ensue, but even if they completely take over, this *yes* can no longer be erased'.[15] The 'yes' becomes the primary opening, while negatives are made subsidiary as what can only secondarily then *deny* this opening. This, however, seems to leave affirmation only affirming what is. Therefore, in typically deconstructive fashion, Derrida argues that the first 'yes' always requires an answering second 'yes' to confirm it, and so the 'first' yes 'is never therefore simply originary'.[16] This second 'yes' confirms the first 'yes' by exposing it to a constitutive alterity. Affirmation is never complete in and of itself, but requires this doubling or repetition to function. This second 'yes' is both 'the light, dancing *yes* of affirmation, the open affirmation of the gift' – the 'yes' that disarticulates all foundational structures – and the 'yes' of 'recapitulative control and reactive repetition' – the 'yes' that secures all structures.[17] Again Derrida allocates the usual qualities of negativity – opening, alterity and dislocation – to affirmation, in the form of the second 'yes'. In fact, affirmation is responsible for both the effect of opening and any fantasm of closure.

The privilege given to affirmation is even more clearly visible if we consult *Archive Fever* (1995). Ostensibly this text appears to be devoted to the necessary possibility of radical destruction that haunts any and every archive, which is to say radical negativity. The very title – in French *Mal d'Archive* – indexes evil and sickness afflicting the archive. And yet this appearance of constitutive negativity is a deceptive one. Derrida insists that this negativity is the *result* of an affirmative opening and that: 'if there is an affirmation shielded from all discussion (psycho-analytic or Talmudic), an unconditional affirmation, it is the affirmation of the future *to come* [*l'àvenir*]'.[18] The primacy of affirmation is explicitly shielded from any critical interrogation, and withdrawn from the discourses of suspicion. If everywhere destruction rages around and within the archive this is only possible through the unconditional 'yes' that opens the archive to this destruction. Certainly we could see this as Derrida's deconstruction of negativity by correlating it with affirmation, however, as I will go on to argue later in this chapter, this is in danger of simply subordinating negativity to affirmation and reifying negativity as some unmoored excess. In the name of excess Derrida offers a recapitulative and controlling economy of his own.

We can see why Derrida is an affirmationist in the first instance, but his stress on the fracturing and disseminative form of affirmative opening would seem to preclude any possibility of a systematic philosophy or constructive ontology – the second hallmark of affirmative theory. Derrida's description of this opening, in the form of the gift or event, as 'preontological'[19] makes any ontology secondary and subsidiary. This resistance to the usual philosophical demand licenses the anti-systemic and post-metaphysical reading of Derrida, perhaps best exemplified by Richard Rorty's argument that, post-Derrida, philosophy is merely another kind of writing, with no means to secure any particular privileged status.[20] Despite widely-held variants on this claim appearances are deceptive. First, in terms of system, Derrida has argued that:

> If by 'system' is meant – and this is the minimal sense of the word – a sort of consequence, coherence and insistence – a certain gathering together – there is an injunction to the system that I have never renounced and never wished to.[21]

How can this statement be squared with the usual cliché of Derrida's movement from the more systematic and formal organisation of his early texts, such as *Of Grammatology* (1967), to a burgeoning taste for the fragmentary and experimental, as seen in *Glas* (1974) or *The Postcard* (1980)?

Despite this appearance of inconsistency the continual presentation of the strategic traces of *différance* implies systematic consistency. Remaining at the level of formal appearance and either berating or celebrating Derrida for his supposedly 'fragmentary' and 'playful' style has nearly always been the sign of a failure to read his construction of new forms of systematic argument.[22] In fact, we can find the systematic consistency of Derrida's texts precisely in their affirmationism: in the constant variations they play on the inscription of an affirmative opening to alterity, which can be traced back to his earliest works.[23] System, for Derrida, lies in his systematic fidelity to the necessity for inventive inscriptions of this affirmation. Of course, as Edward Said acerbically notes, the repetitive nature of the exercise can strike the reader as highly uninventive: '[deconstruction] is as insistent, as monotonous, and as inadvertently systematizing as logocentrism itself'.[24]

While we might accept that the repetitive tracing of this opening by Derrida is systematic, how can it be ontological? In a little-noted remark,[25] Derrida replied to Negri's plea for a post-deconstructive ontology by stating that he was prepared to accept ontology as a 'password . . . which only pretends to mean what the word "ontology" has always meant'.[26] Accepting a pretence or a mimicry of ontology, I would argue that Derrida's much-derided 'quasi-concept' of hauntology is exactly such a 'password' that 'only pretends to mean what the word "ontology" has always meant'. Hauntology literally inscribes ontology within itself, and exceeds or delimits it, by gesturing towards what 'ontology' might look like after the deconstruction of presence – that is against any ontology that would inscribe being in terms of self-presence or self-consistency. Hauntology does so by being the paradoxical 'ontology' of the '*non-contemporaneity with itself of the living present*'[27] – paradoxical because it cannot establish what usually goes by the name 'ontology'. For Derrida 'ontology' can only be a password that opens the door to the necessarily divided and fractured form of 'being'. Hauntology then rests in the oddly meta-ontological position of that which pre-emptively ruins the security and primacy of ontology by forcing it to open to the event.[28] Negativity appears to be in play again, as the means for breaking up the existent order of being determined by its self-presence, but once again this negativity is re-inscribed as affirmative. We could argue that this re-inscription amounts to a deconstruction of the usual binary of affirmation and negation, but this is a highly asymmetrical deconstruction. In contrast to Derrida's usual strategy of deconstructing a binary through a third term (*supplément*, *pharmakon*, *hymen*, etc.) here negativity is subordinated to the 'irreducibility of affirmation'.[29]

The affirmative strategies we have traced so far should have already suggested that Derrida does not assimilate deconstruction to critique. Derrida insists on this point in his 'Letter to a Japanese Friend' when he remarks: 'No more is [deconstruction] a critique, in a general sense or in a Kantian sense'.[30] The reason Derrida gives for this is that deconstruction takes critique as one of its themes, but we can suggest a stronger, more Nietzschean reason: the primacy of affirmation dictates that critique is a position of impurity, bad faith and *ressentiment*, which relies on a negative and external relation rather than departing from the necessity of affirmation. The critical element of deconstruction is articulated *through* affirmation, once again using the double affirmation that allows us 'to *reaffirm by choosing*'.[31] If the first yes indicates a primary acceptance or opening, its doubling by the second yes practices a selection. Of course, this is a highly constrained form of critique, which seems to only allow us to make a selection among what exists. For Derrida, however, it is only our routing of thought through the shielded affirmative promise of the 'to come' that allows us to 'produce events, [and] new effective forms of action, practice, organization, and so forth'.[32] It is this linking of the promise to questions of 'action, practice, [and] organization' which can lead us to the vexed question of Derrida's politics – the final and key differend that seems to divide Derrida from affirmationism.

To take some initial and minimal indices we should note that Derrida identified himself as belonging on the left,[33] and that his political texts engage with a number of liberal-left discourses – for example anti-apartheid politics or the politics of dissidence. The last phase of his work also involved a qualified endorsement of 'alter-globalisation' politics, which Derrida, in a 2004 interview, linked to his own Benjaminian invocations of the 'weak spirit' of messianism.[34] In a number of texts from this period Derrida devoted time to deconstructing the emergence of the new discourse of the 'war on terror', and to endorsing its contestation.[35] Too often this political contestation of neo-liberalism is regarded as a side-effect of Derrida's 'political turn', announced by *Specters of Marx* (1993), and flowing into his deconstructions of hospitality, immigration, national and linguistic identity, and the politics of religion. Contrary to this reading I would again insist, as does Derrida, on the strong political continuity in his oeuvre.[36] The supposed 'political turn' is, in fact, the making more explicit of the political elements of deconstruction, and the insistence on the necessity of its own flexible capacities to adapt to new and unpropitious circumstances.

This continuity, however, has always been the sign of a certain anxiety. As early as the 1971 interview 'Positions', conducted by two members of the *Tel Quel* group, Derrida stressed the irreducibility of deconstruction to a fixed political position, insisting on the disseminative capacity of the '*s*'.[37] This may have signalled an understandable resistance to dogmatism, especially of the *haut*-Maoist type just about to be embraced by *Tel Quel*. The obvious difficulty is that this irreducibly disseminative moment seems to wreck any possibility of a political project – which rests minimally on taking a position, or on what Lenin described as partisanship.[38] The rejoinder to Derrida's dissemination of position, not long in coming, was that the refusal to embrace a position is itself a position of a liberal sort: one of 'clean hands' that refuses to really engage with any actual politics. Derrida always resisted this interpretation, arguing for the (political) necessity of a tempo of thought and analysis that would not concede to immediate demands to take sides, but rather develop new forms of responsibility and new forms of urgency.[39] It is true, however, that these new forms of political practice could seem to indulge a taste for prevarication and delay, never being quite urgent enough in the face of the (relative) certainties of the militant.

Part of the impulse of affirmationist theory is, as we have seen, a politically-inspired rupture with this 'non-positional' stance. It tends to stress the urgency of political intervention through generic universality against the equivocations of difference, regarding Derrida as never quite affirmative enough, especially when it comes to political matters. Affirmationist theory makes a number of linked criticisms of deconstruction: first, that the dallying of deconstruction with the negative – in the form of suspense, delay and deferral – puts off the necessary moment of political decision;[40] second, that deconstruction's logic of de-totalisation is complicit with, or even identical to, the contemporary logic of capital;[41] third, that the micro-politics of deconstruction can never pass to a constructive stage of building or creating radical alternatives ('another world is possible'). These are certainly signs of political difficulty for deconstruction, although I obviously don't regard affirmationism as having solved them either. Instead, I see these difficulties as a result of the effects of real abstraction. In the case of deconstruction, on the one hand hauntology seems the perfect means for grasping exactly the quasi-ontological level of these abstractions. On the other hand, as we noted above, the very perfection of this fit seems to leave deconstruction as merely replicating real abstraction. This is especially true as Derrida severely qualifies those critical elements of Marx that would allow the conjuring away of the ghostly effects of real abstraction.[42] In resisting the ontologisation of Marx, Derrida is in danger of hauntologising, and therefore universalising, capitalism. I will return to these charges, but only after a lengthy detour through a closer assessment of Derrida's relation to negativity and the means by which he re-establishes his own weak affirmationism.

'NOT NECESSARILY NEGATIVE'

We have characterised Derrida as a 'weak affirmationist', and the relative weakness of his affirmationism lies in his consistent attempt to develop an excessive form of negativity. Of course I am not about to chide Derrida for his failure to be consistently affirmationist, but, on the other hand, I also find his engagement with negativity problematic. To analyse this second issue I want to focus on Derrida's *Aporias* (1993), which is particularly appropriate because affirmationist critiques of deconstruction constantly recur to the trope of aporia as the sign that deconstruction is unable to break through to a constructive orientation; even Derrida admits that '*aporia*, this tired word of philosophy and of logic, has often imposed itself upon me'.[43] What Derrida proposes is a new disseminative reading of aporia, pluralising it into 'aporias', which 'is not necessarily negative',[44] but instead thought in an 'affirmative fashion'.[45] This is typical of Derrida's weak affirmationism, but he has to explicate why he has chosen to make this affirmation in a '*negative form (aporia)*'.[46] In a fashion similar to *Archive Fever* it appears that affirmation finds its testing ground on the site of a radicalised and quasi-absolute negativity.

For Derrida the pluralisation of aporia is a means to maintain the perpetual opening to an experience of the event. In this context Derrida juxtaposes two forms of negativity: a 'bad' 'sterile negativity of the impasse',[47] and a 'good' formal negativity that strategically allows the opening to remain open. The first is the usual reading of negativity and aporia: a failure or paralysis that cannot accede to the creation of anything new. Of course, as Derrida is no doubt aware, this is also the common image of deconstruction. To displace this sense of negativity Derrida invokes a necessary negativity that refuses to stabilise or set the conditions for the event to arrive. The obvious difficulty is keeping these two forms of negativity separate, not least considering the usual commitment of deconstruction to re-inscribing such binaries, and to thinking whatever troubles or contaminates purity and gestures of purification.[48] The attempt to restrict the role of negativity to the merely formal seems unlikely at best. What is even odder is the implicit binary between bad 'sterile' negativity and good 'vital' affirmation. This would seem to link Derrida to thematics of vitality, production and life, to which he elsewhere displays a great deal of reservation or suspicion,[49] and which is foreign to the usual procedures of deconstruction.

Derrida makes negativity explicitly subordinate to the primacy of affirmation, and regards it as having a merely strategic and formal role in preserving the opening to the event. It is the fixation of readers on this secondary and subordinate role of negativity that accounts, from Derrida's point of view, for the usual image of deconstruction as obsessed with failure, delay and the inability to accede to the new. In contradiction to this view Derrida stresses that formal negativity is exactly what holds open the passage for the event without ontological, political or any other guarantees. What interests me, perversely, is the sterile negativity of the impasse that does not simply hold open the passage of affirmation. Instead of being a false lure, or subordinate moment, I regard it as the sign of a negativity that threatens Derrida's affirmationism. Derrida flirts with the necessity of the negative, all the while trying to constrain and restrain it to a disposable external form, a mere shell. I will argue, however, that this admission of negativity does not remain within the bounds Derrida sets, except at the cost of dogmatism. Again a parallel can be made with *Archive Fever*, which devotes page after page to the irreducible infinite destruction at work on and in the archive, only then to unconvincingly insist that it is only ever what makes the archive open to affirmation. The opening to the event is conditioned by negativity, but that conditioning remains within a restricted economy through the meta-condition of affirmation.

Similar difficulties operate on the side of the arrival of the event. According to Derrida, the event arrives as what must be affirmed. This arrival is what dictates the turn to the thinking of hospitality in this text, and more generally in the later Derrida.[50] Something or someone arrives without me expecting it or them, as a surprise. I must be open to this possibility of arrival through an 'expectation without expectation', which 'is hospitality itself, hospitality toward the event'.[51] For the arrival to be a new arrival it must be unexpected, or else it would already be programmed by our expectation – hence my expectation is the pre-emptive affirmation of a minimal and undetermined expectation of arrival itself. For this event of arrival to take on its full scope, as the arrival of the 'absolute *arrivant*', we must have a surprise that is:

enough to call into question, to the point of annihilating or rendering inde-
terminate, all the distinctive signs of a prior identity, beginning with the very
border that delineated a legitimate home and assured lineage, names and
language, nations, families and genealogies.[52]

The arrival of the *arrivant* dictates the possibility, although not the
necessity, of a complete destruction of all the signs and limits of identity
for both the host and for what arrives – the arrival of radical negativity.
But this arrival can only come second, pre-empted and controlled by the
initial and minimal affirmation.

On the side of the coming of the event there is the 'sterile' negativity
that holds open the unforeseen and unpredictable possibility of arrival.
On the side of the actual arrival of the event, there is an extreme negativity that threatens to consume and destroy the opening. In both cases
affirmation is deployed as a mechanism of control: to restrict sterile
negativity to a minimal function of formal opening, and to maintain
'absolute' negativity as pure possibility, in which the very extremity
of the conception guards against admittance of any significant role
for negativity. These are symmetrical reifications of negativity into
ideologically familiar forms of the negative: delay and failure, or radicalised and absolute destruction. While Derrida is trying to signal the
necessary binding of affirmation to negativity, this negativity is only
allowed to enter in these restricted and constricted forms. In particular,
the possibility of any immanent and politicised form of negativity is left
distanced or unthinkable.

We are left with a number of questions: why does Derrida insist
that the initial pre-ontological space of opening take the form of
affirmation? Is there any reason why, except by diktat, that Derrida
can impose this reading? If this is the space (or time, or space-time)
before ontology, transcendentality, philosophy and, we can hazard,
positivity, why is it grounded *in* the positive? I want to argue that this
dogmatic decision for affirmationism, itself circulated through the
medium of negativity, is finally undergirded by Derrida's uncritical
and undeconstructive appropriation of Nietzsche. Although Derrida
initially elaborated the 'yes, yes' through Joyce, and elsewhere claimed
the affirmative opening as common to Heidegger and Benjamin,[53] this
hardly rings true if we consider the role of Nietzsche. When asked in
an interview why he had never devoted an extensive deconstructive
reading to Nietzsche, Derrida replied that he had found it impossible
to stabilise a Nietzschean corpus.[54] But the difficulty in dealing with
Nietzsche's 'irreducible and singular multiplicity'[55] did not prevent
Derrida from isolating the philosopheme of affirmation in Nietzsche,
and then deploying it as the crucial anchoring point for his own texts.

In fact, Derrida casts Nietzsche himself as the symbol of excessive affirmation, of 'yea-saying' multiplicity. This is not only true for Derrida, but also for many other affirmationist theorists who rely on an avowed or implicit reference to Nietzsche. To adapt Marx's critique of Stirner in *The German Ideology* (Marx and Engels 1845), we could say that Nietzsche is the patron saint of affirmationism.

SAINT NIETZSCHE

Michel Haar points out that in Derrida's work Nietzsche is accorded 'a certain position of inviolability'.[56] Whereas everywhere else Derrida insisted on deconstruction as the deconstruction of authority,[57] when it came to Nietzsche '[i]n the face of this *authority* alone the ruthless and omnivocal cutting edge of deconstruction turns away'.[58] Derrida takes from Nietzsche the conditioning of philosophy by the undeconstructible double affirmation, and in doing so he affirms Nietzsche as an undeconstructible resource for deconstruction. The result is not so much an instance of a deepening hermeneutic circle of reading, but a vicious circle of auto-self-confirming authority. Derrida is usually condemned by affirmationist theory for the slowness of his work, but with Nietzsche we witness a remarkable instance of acceleration. This is not simply the result of a deliberate mimesis, as Derrida apes Nietzsche's call 'to dance with the *pen*',[59] but also the result of his use of Nietzsche to authorise a new tempo of writing that cancels the necessity for any substantial interrogation of Nietzsche.

This exemption of Nietzsche is predicated on casting his texts as radically unstable and lacking the usual forms of philosophical or metaphysical authority. Of course, this questioning of authority is confined to Nietzsche's disputing of the authority of philosophy and ignores, as we will see, his own highly authoritarian political stance. Derrida insists that it is the absolute mobility of the Nietzschean corpus, problematically indexed to Nietzsche's madness, which authorises a lack of hermeneutic authority. We are forbidden from 'forc[ing] his name into the straight jacket of an interpretation that is too strong to be able to account for him'.[60] While Nietzsche's own text incarnates an irreducible affirmative mobility, we are then subject to a surplus injunction to never reduce this mobility. In fact, Derrida defers or outsources his interpretation of Nietzsche to Gilles Deleuze. Writing after Deleuze's death Derrida noted the closeness between many of their themes, crucially including that of 'difference in the joyfully repeated affirmation ("yes, yes")'.[61] It is Deleuze's *Nietzsche and Philosophy* (1962) that is a key implicit text for Derrida, and one which allows him to conflate

Nietzsche with Deleuze's interpretation to establish Nietzsche as a purified thinker of affirmation *qua* difference. Also, as in the case of Nietzsche, this Deleuzian interpretation is not subject to any rigorous deconstruction by Derrida – with Deleuze remaining a largely mute presence in Derrida's texts.

The rapid deployment of Nietzsche by Derrida, and considering Nietzsche's own love of martial language the military metaphor might be appropriate, is not uncommon in affirmationism. While certainly there are few unequivocal or open embraces of Nietzsche, his thematics of strength, power, affirmation and excess, along with his relentless condemnation of weakness and *ressentiment*, shape the general mood or tone of affirmationism. The emblematic text here is Nietzsche's parable concerning the bird of prey and the lambs in *On the Genealogy of Morals* (1887).[62] From the lambs' point of view the bird of prey is 'evil' for carrying them off, and whatever is opposite, the lambs of course, is therefore 'good'. This is a *reactive* characterisation, responding to the bird of prey by demanding that strength 'should *not* express itself as strength'.[63] In contrast, the bird of prey merely hunts the lambs, and it is this active strength – indifferent to reactive evaluation – that the lambs try to make accountable. To use a relevant contemporary phrase they try to drag the bird of prey down to their level. While tending to avoid Nietzsche's dubious metaphorics, affirmationism often adopts this posture of lauding of self-affirming and deliberately unreflective strength or power against signs of critical *ressentiment*. Instead of passing over Nietzsche's texts, all the better to adopt them uncritically, I want to return to them with a critical eye – not so much as a bird of prey but as a lamb. What we will find is another fraught negotiation with negativity, similar to Derrida's, but expressed in more explicit and extreme forms. The very stridency of Nietzsche's affirmationism, I will argue, is a sign of his failure to establish a philosophy of affirmation.

Ecce Homo (1888), Nietzsche's last book, is the one that, as Walter Kaufmann puts it, offers: 'Nietzsche's own interpretation of his development, his works, and his significance'.[64] This certainly does not give it an unequivocal authority over the interpretation of Nietzsche, but it does indicate that invocations of textual mobility and multiplicity do not mean we have to pass over problematic elements of this mobile ensemble. In *Ecce Homo*, although we find the usual affirmation of 'a Yes-saying without reservation',[65] we also find that this affirmation appears indistinguishable from negation: 'I know the pleasure in destroying to a degree that accords with my powers to destroy – in both respects I obey my Dionysian nature which does not know how to separate doing No from saying Yes'.[66] Here affirmation and negation become indistinguishable, in the same way that Derrida links ultra-negativity to a new form of irreducible affirmation. Of course, like Derrida, this could be read as the sign of the subordination and interiorisation of negativity within affirmation. However, it also indicates a more general problem for Nietzsche: that of distinguishing between active and reactive forces, especially as his genealogical tracing of events constantly throws up profound reversals, shifts and moments of transformation: the weak overcome the strong; decadence must be welcomed as the recognition of the necessity of waste and decay to the growth of life; health and sickness are indistinguishable; pessimism is both a sign of strength and a sign of decline, as is nihilism. Nietzsche's radical monism of forces seems to preclude the critical distinctions that would be necessary to establish a hierarchy of differences. We are thrown back onto the authority of his nose for 'smelling out' such differences.[67]

This is hardly adequate, but then we also have the key operator for Nietzsche that is supposed to ground and produce this moment of selection between forces: the thought of the eternal recurrence. In one of his late notebooks Nietzsche wrote: 'The idea of recurrence as a *selective* principle, in the service of strength (and barbarism!!)'.[68] While it might seem that the eternal recurrence would imply the return of everything, Nietzsche hints that in recurrence we find the possibility of selection, and so affirmation. Not everything returns, but only the strong and affirmative. As Nietzsche puts it, in his late notebooks, 'I teach the No to all that makes weak – that exhausts. I teach the Yes to all that strengthens, that stores up strength, that justifies the feeling of strength.' [69] Nietzsche's superior 'No' is, precisely, a refusal of negativity, which leads to a superior 'Yes'.

It is this hint that Deleuze develops in a creative fashion in *Nietzsche and Philosophy*. He does so by insisting on the double affirmation of the eternal recurrence: the first, physical, affirmation of the being of becoming, and the second affirmation as the moment of a 'selective ontology'.[70] First we affirm the dispersed becomings that operate everywhere and then affirm those particular becomings that add strength. Of course this is precisely the model that Derrida adopts with the 'yes, yes', shorn of the reference to ontology. For Deleuze the doubling of affirmation as a mechanism of difference distinguishes the Nietzschean operation from any thinking of negation or negativity, which is tied to opposition. Negativity, for reasons that are not fully clear, does not survive the test of the eternal recurrence. Instead, in the second selection only affirmation survives, as the affirmation of difference and of multiplicity, and so: 'The lesson of the eternal return is that there is no return of the negative'.[71] This means that 'negation is only one face of the will to power',[72] a false aspect that is eliminated by selection in the eternal recurrence. For Deleuze the will to power 'both transforms the negative and reproduces affirmation'.[73]

Certainly this is true to Nietzsche's own self-characterisation. In *Twilight of the Idols* (1889), Nietzsche expresses the need '[t]o be true to my nature, which is *affirmative* and has dealing with contradiction and criticism only indirectly and when compelled'.[74] The difficulty is that the eternal recurrence does not seem to be able to transform the negative and (only) reproduce affirmation. Pierre Klossowski points out that the eternal recurrence does not constitute a principle of differential selection, but is rather the parody of a doctrine.[75] Contrary to Nietzsche's intentions it cannot select out forces, but merely produces a generalised and neutral 'becoming'. Making a similar point Brassier argues that the eternal return is 'at once the apex of affirmativeness . . . and the nadir of negativity'.[76] The eternal return is the absolute inscription of affirmation, but it is also the absolute inscription of negativity – rendering these two terms indistinguishable. This confirms Klossowski's insight that it is the parody of a doctrine: it provides no principle of identification or determination. If the world is thought according to the eternal return then, as Nietzsche admits, it 'has no goal, no final state, and is incapable of being'.[77] A similar problem of establishing affirmation also afflicts Deleuze's re-reading of Nietzsche; as pointed out long ago by Vincent Descombes, Deleuze's careful reconstruction of Nietzsche's thought also grinds to a halt in trying to definitively split affirmation from negativity.[78]

Affirmationism runs aground at this point. We can see why Derrida did not pursue an inquiry in Nietzsche's texts, but preferred to play the double game of treating them as the inviolable source of affirmation and insisting on their irreducible mobility. That mobility is crucial in licensing Derrida's extraction of affirmation from Nietzsche via Deleuze, and protecting it from any critique. If, as we have done here, we resort to Nietzsche's text to delimit affirmationist theory then it is always possible to insist that its mobility has escaped us. We have imposed a singular interpretation, while the affirmationist revels in textual multiplicity. The bad faith of this argument is self-evident. What it dogmatically excludes is the failure to create an affirmative philosophy that can truly select, rather than merely reproduce things as they are. This, however, is not merely a philosophical matter.

Nietzsche's solution, made more explicitly than in Derrida, is to impose affirmation by fiat. The thought of the eternal return is accompanied by the birth of the one who 'breaks the history of the world in two'.[79] It is the subject, in the form of the over-man (*übermensch*), who is required as the extra element to force affirmative difference into existence, and to resist its disappearance within eternal recurrence. Of course there is no reason why the arbitrary establishment of a new super-subject as the operator of affirmation should not come to grief on the neutral monism of Nietzsche's physics of forces. What it does indicate is a dubious political overdetermination of Nietzsche's thinking. This is not the identification of the over-man with the usual Nazi or fascist suspects, but a tendency present in Nietzsche to a reactionary consolidation of social hierarchies in the name of affirmative difference.

UNEMPLOYED NIETZSCHE

Nietzsche invokes the over-man as the figure that can break with the world as it exists and affirm a new world. This breaking of the world in two, however, is more of a reactionary re-ordering of the world; again, the selective affirmation of particular hierarchised 'forces' rather than others – better a bird of prey than a lamb. The selective power of the over-man is contrasted with another figure: the dialectician. Against the aristocratic power of the affirmative over-man dialectics is the weapon of the weak: 'Dialectics can be only a *last-ditch weapon* in the hands of those who have no other weapon left'.[80] The dialectic is the weapon of the rabble, a form of revenge that allows the weak to 'play the tyrant'.[81] The Nietzschean distinction between the affirmative over-man and the dialectical rabble is made possible through a vitalist thematics of life. Whereas the rabble, including the anarchists and socialists, are 'weak' and 'decadent', the over-man is the aristocratic man of power, filled with the over-spilling forces of life. Life for Nietzsche is growth, contrasted with the socialist negation of life. In contrast, the over-man glories in the growth of life, combining Dionysian 'ecstatic affirmation of the total character of life' with Apollonian self-sufficiency.[82] The structural oppositions are remarkably simple, and politically dubious.

This 'ecstatic affirmation' of life is figured within the field of the living subject *qua* over-man, but it is always an expanding field of vital powers. A sense of this expansion of given by Deleuze's later argument, in the appendix to his *Foucault* (1986), that we must think the over-man or super-man as the ability to 'super-fold' new powers that lie outside the constraint of the usual anthropological forms of the human.[83] Deleuze analyses this expansion particularly along two axes of life: 'the foldings proper to the chains of the genetic code, and the potential of silicon in third-generation machines'.[84] The powers of life overflow the human, both 'internally' into the coding of DNA, and 'externally' towards the new powers of computers. But at the same time these powers are integrated, or folded, as new forces of man: 'the formal compound of the forces within man and these new forces'.[85] What is left unproblematised is the nature and form of these affirmative expansions. In a prescient remark, directed against Foucault's 'molecular' and 'microphysical' concept of power, Baudrillard noted in 1977 that the borrowing of the DNA model leads to 'the kind of generative inscription of the code that one expects – an immanent, ineluctable, and always positive inscription that yields only infinitesimal mutations.'[86] This 'wallowing in the molecular' results in the rediscovery of an apparatus (*dispositif*) of desire in 'what the cyberneticists have described as a matrix of code and control.'[87] The embrace by Deleuze of DNA, as another source of power for the over-man, actually worsens matters by leaving us with only the slight powers of mutation and submitted to code and control in the name of the ecstatic affirmation of the powers of life.

Deleuze's expansion of the over-man towards the 'inorganic matter (the domain of silicon)'[88] produces similar problems. This theoretical movement towards the over-man as cybernetic post-human, later spurred on by new technological developments in home computing and such cyberpunk fictions as William Gibson's *Neuromancer* (1984), would become highly influential. Leaving aside the question of whether this post-human future is merely another kind of super-humanism, in which humans integrate and increase their own powers as 'prosthetic gods', the affirmation of the overflowing of human limits leaves us unable to answer political questions concerning the integration of the digital into the human. In the same fashion as the integration of DNA, this affirmative orientation risks an uncritical acceptance of any form of augmentation or integration as the source of new powers and liberation – with the usual proviso 'if sufficiently radicalised': 'Humans, one more effort, if you would be post-human!', to paraphrase de Sade. Deleuze's cashing out of Nietzschean affirmationism in the terms of new developments in biology and computing, although for radical political ends, demonstrates the flaw that it requires accepting that nearly anything that adds to our powers is good. This affirmationist and accelerationist model of increasing and developing powers, whatever the costs, debars critical assessment except in terms of higher or stronger powers versus lower or weaker powers. In this case we lose any significant capacity to critique the 'domain of silicon'.[89]

We can see here the dangers of a certain kind of vitalism: the affirmation of what is in the name of the creative powers of life, at the expense of any substantial means of critical assessment. Certainly Derrida is by no means as wild in his political thinking, and his refusal to engage with any modified version of vitalism, or a metaphysics of power, can be regarded as a sign of political good sense. This, however, does not solve the problem of politics. Derrida surreptitiously relies on the power of Nietzschean affirmationism and vitalism to underwrite his own circumscription of negativity. Re-inscribing negativity as a general economy of excess, at the expense of any 'sterile' negativity, leads to a failure by Derrida to engage with Nietzsche's deeply ambiguous politics of life. In contrast Deleuze actually offers a more direct engagement, and therefore tries to rescue Nietzsche from a merely reactionary aristocratism by insisting on an aristocracy of affirmation available, potentially, to all. I would say, despite all the differences, that affirmationist theory has been driven by a horror of *ressentiment* into a deeply problematic rejection of negativity and critique as 'life denying'.

Nietzsche's deliberately flamboyant identification of the powers of the over-man with power hierarchies, especially in some quasi-imaginary new feudalism of the 'aristocracy of the future',[90] should give us pause. The over-abundant life-enhancing powers of the over-man are not so easily detached from existing and future reactionary distributions of actual power. If dialectics is the 'weapon of the weak' we can see that a Nietzschean energetics of excess is the weapon of the strong. The reason Nietzsche has for rejecting dialectics is precisely because it is a thinking of opposition, and particularly opposition to social and metaphysical hierarchies: 'Opposites replace natural degrees and ranks. Hatred against the order of rank. Opposites suit a plebian age because easier to comprehend'.[91] We might wonder what is so wrong with 'hatred against the order of rank', and also consider the merits of living in a 'plebian age'. Of course, Nietzsche's insistence on the futurity of his writing and its 'untimely' nature would seem to dictate that it cannot correspond to existing power arrangements. That said, his lauding of strength, power and aristocracy is always posed against any radical levelling contestation of power arrangements – from democracy to socialism or anarchism:

> The lower species ('herd,' 'mass,' 'society') unlearns modesty and blows up its needs into cosmic and metaphysical values. In this way the whole of existence is vulgarized: in so far as the mass is dominant it bullies the exceptions, so they lose faith in themselves and become nihilists.[92]

To take the dangerous step of reversing Nietzsche, I would argue that this 'unlearning of modesty', this 'vulgarisation' and this 'bull[ying] [of] the exceptions' might make a good programme for plebian or proletarian education. The 'vulgarisation of existence' would then be the necessary negation of the 'exceptions' that would generate its own counter-metaphysics.

Certainly there is a radical left tradition of reading Nietzsche as the means for re-thinking socialism, communism and anarchism, but, especially since the 'New Nietzsche' of contemporary theory, little attention has been paid to Nietzsche's condemnatory dynamic directed at socialism and communism.[93] One exception has been Malcolm Bull's suggestion that for the left it might well be essential to re-read Nietzsche from the position of the losers in Nietzsche's hierarchies.[94] What if, instead of praising the strength of the subject who can 'break the world in two', we follow those subjects who cannot tolerate this supposed rupture? Perhaps (to use a favourite Nietzschean word) it is the losers, the dialecticians, who have more sense of the effects of the negative? This would not simply involve a return to the position of *ressentiment* or the reactive position. We could step back from the uncritical celebration of Nietzsche's Zarathustra, as the new prophet of secularised radicalism, to ask what might it mean to identify with the plebian, with hatred of the order of rank, with vulgarisation; a politics of the *untermensch*, not the *übermensch*. Such a counter-image has been suggested by Marcuse:

> [M]an intelligent enough and healthy enough to dispense with all heroes and heroic virtues, man without the impulse to live dangerously, to meet the challenge; man with the good conscience to make life an end-in-itself, to live in joy without fear.[95]

This is a subject who does not aspire to the 'glory' of prodigal excess, or to the transcendence of the merely animal or human.

In this reversal of Nietzsche we already see the emergence and fleshing out of the possibility of a new post-Nietzschean politics of negativity. Such a politics would require a detachment from the heroic politics of pure creation, novelty and the over-powering event associated with Nietzsche, and often adopted by affirmationism, although Derrida is usually, but not always, more prudent on this score. The obvious difficulty is that such a rejection of heroism could lead to defeatism, either political or metaphysical or both. To embrace the non-heroic would seem to lead us down the path of weak thought and the embrace of things as they are in the guise of the deconstruction of subjectivity.[96] Negativity would then be divided between the aesthete's unemployment (as in Jean-Luc Nancy), or the saint's weakness (as in Agamben). I want to suggest that this problematisation of heroism, made via Marcuse, does not entail a (pseudo-) libertarian embrace of dispersion, fragmentation or weakness. This leaves us detached from the world, or resigned to it, with no possibility of critical purchase on the world. Instead we could see the refusal of a (class-loaded) concept of heroism as the means to encourage other virtues: tenacity, the refusal to 'live dangerously', and what Badiou calls courage – a virtue of 'endurance in the impossible', contrasted with heroism as a 'posture'.[97]

The subject of courage is not a subject transfixed with breaking the world in two, but one who practices, in Badiou's words, a virtue that takes time as its 'raw material' and that involves 'holding on, in a different duration from that imposed by the law of the world'.[98] Affirmationism, in contrast, can only reinforce or radicalise an exisistent duration due to its dependance on the quasi-Nietzschean thematics of increasing power, strength and accumulation. This politics of prodigality, of the over-man as 'overladen with energy',[99] is intoxicating. For this reason it must be resisted, because, according to Nietzsche: 'The essence of intoxication is the feeling of plenitude and increased energy'.[100] Contra to an affirmation of the increase in energy, the expansive endorsement of what is, I am arguing for a politics of negativity that disrupts this accumulation – not least because this model of accumulation, even if enlisted in a supposed left politics, repeats the gesture of capitalist productivity and deterritorialisation.[101]

SPECTRAL SUBJECTS

Nietzsche's affirmationism succeeds because of the necessary supplement of a dubious vitalist politics. Derrida, in his reliance on Nietzsche as the figure to found an affirmative thinking, finds his work exposed, at one remove, to this politics. Of course, the traces of this politics are scattered and minor in Derrida, and at many points contested and refused. The difficulty that remains, however, is that in detaching deconstruction from a vitalist politics of power vectored through the super-subjectivity of the over-man, Derrida risks detaching deconstruction from *any* form of agency, and political agency in particular. Even a critic as sympathetic to deconstruction as Geoffrey Bennington recognises the difficulty:

> [I]t's very hard to ascribe an agent to an event of deconstruction. Derrida in his early work occasionally suggested an analogy with the middle voice in Ancient Greek; so, neither a passive voice nor an active voice but some middle voice which is neither passive nor active in any simple sense.[102]

This analogy is not properly fleshed out, however, and often the accent or emphasis in the later work of Derrida seems to fall on the passivity of the subject, which is seized by an event that 'comes upon me from on high' – the theological overtones being overwhelming.[103]

Once again we can return to the suspicion hanging over Derrida's work that it is politically incapacitating, a suspicion particularly and persistently focused on Derrida's deconstruction of the subject and the suggestion of a resulting passivity or dispersion. Of course it is not true that Derrida made no connection between deconstruction and political agency, but these connections remain highly attenuated and unstable. In his more directly political writings often agency remains localised in particular singular figures: Chris Hani, Nelson Mandela and Vaclav Havel, for example; although of course these figures were always linked by Derrida metonymically to mass movements. Derrida's explicit engagement with the alter-globalisation movement is a more promising case, but his over-hasty assimilation of the movement to his own 'weak messianism' leaves political agency unclear – although it does, ironically, reflect the actual political weaknesses of the 'movement of movements'. The choice appears to be between a Derridean political astuteness, bought at the cost of the lack of any substantial intervention, and a post-Nietzschean vitalism, in which we get all the agency we want, and more, but in problematic, or even fantasmatic, political terms. These are not the only options of course, but certainly the demand to decide between the prevarications of deconstruction and the decisiveness of some alternative affirmative orientation characterises the recent moment of contemporary theory.

The problem of the Derridean attenuation of agency reached its apogee, at least for Derrida's Marxist critics, with the proposal for a 'New International' invoked in *Specters of Marx*.[104] Terry Eagleton offered one of the most scathing criticisms, denouncing it as:

> [T]he ultimate poststructuralist fantasy: an opposition without anything as distastefully systemic or drably 'orthodox' as an opposition, a dissent beyond all formulable discourse, a promise which would betray itself in the act of fulfilment, a perpetual excited opening to the Messiah who had better not let us down by doing anything as determinate as coming.[105]

In his reply to his critics Derrida insisted, with some justification considering the emergence of the alter-globalisation movement, that the 'New International' 'is already a reality'.[106] That 'reality' has, however, entered a state of routinisation and seeming decline, which again raises the question of Derrida's tendency to futural invocations of agency.

Instead of simply settling this question by a decision 'for or against Derrida' I want again to return to the question of the current conjuncture. The seeming attenuation or absence of agency in Derrida could easily be linked to the political situation of the 1980s and 1990s, when actual political agency on the left receded radically, or was crushed out of existence, as with the 1984 miners' strike in Britain. This is the substance of Antonio Negri's comment, referring in part to *Specters of Marx*, but also to Derrida's *Politics of Friendship* (1994), that: 'There's something that's exhausted in these pages, like the shadow of that melancholic libertinism when, at the end of another counter-revolutionary age, men who were still free testified in refusal of the Counter-Reformation and awaited the martyrdom of the Inquisition'.[107] We have another poetic allegory of the failure of deconstruction to be quite affirmative enough, and the implication that with the end of this counter-revolutionary age a new joyous thinking is possible (coincidentally, perhaps something like Negri's?). In a more combative tone Eagleton accused Derrida's deconstruction of Marxism for its failure 'to engage with [Marxism's] positivity',[108] and repeated the usual tropes that deconstruction cannot accede to such positivity because it is obsessed with 'slippage, failure, aporia, incoherence, [and] not-quiteness'.[109] The implication in both cases is the same: deconstruction must become 'positive', or give way to a more positive theoretical orientation.

We have the irony of affirmationist critics constantly chiding Derrida for being negative, while ignoring Derrida's own weak affirmationism; affirmation, production, construction, (positive) resistance, are all supposed to fill the (theoretical and practical) gap created by deconstruction, while deconstruction invokes the same values to perform the same role. Rather than a dispute between contrasting orientations then, we have a more internal dispute over the grounds of the *degree* of affirmation and positivity. What I want to suggest goes missing in this debate is a more rigorous engagement with the *forms* of capital. For example, Eagleton's polemical contrast between a supposedly lightweight deconstruction and the tough materiality of Marxism completely ignores Marx's own deconstruction of the usual opposition between the abstract and the concrete through the category of real abstraction.[110] Not only that, but Eagleton's invocation of Marxist 'positivity' is actually even more abstract, and more spectral (in the bad sense), than Derrida's New International, because it rests on supposing organisational forms that either no longer exist, or are in extreme crisis. The final irony is that Derrida's thinking of hauntology more closely approaches the concept of real abstraction, and so is more faithful to Marx, than Eagleton's own markedly abstract invocations of 'materiality'.[111]

Derridean hauntology seems almost perfectly configured for the reign of what Jameson called 'finance-capital spectralities'.[112] The difficulty is the degree to which hauntology permits us to come to grips with and rupture these real abstractions, rather than merely reflecting them in thought. Here we could remark on a certain deliberate temporal and spatial wavering by Derrida. On the one hand, hauntology is the most general re-inscription of the ontological commitments to presence that Derrida repeatedly traces in Western metaphysics. Hauntology is 'always-already' inscribed in any concept of the living present as its necessary division, which opens it to alterity. On the other hand, this macroscopic traction is also linked by Derrida to the more specific conditions brought about by the changing forms of capital – hauntology is revealed by capital, and in a sense capital itself is deconstructive; as Badiou has noted the de-sacralising dynamic of capital has virtue of 'denounc[ing] every effect of the One as a simple, precarious configuration'.[113] The difficulty is not that deconstruction is dependent on capital to reveal what was always there, although perhaps more careful consideration by Derrida of the risk of writing relations specific to capital back into the past might have been advisable.[114] The problem is that Derrida's lack of specificity in analysing the relation between hauntology and capitalism results in the tendency of hauntology to slip back into a more general description that occludes the precise forms taken by real abstractions.

In casting hauntology at the most general level, as an interruptive effect essential to all thought and by implication all social formations, the nature of capitalism as a social formation starts to become blurred and we 'smudge over all historical differences' (Marx).[115] For example, in Derrida's deconstructive account of Marx's commodity fetishism we find Derrida implying that the 'spectral' nature of the commodity is irreducible and general, that is, not confined to capitalism.[116] While if we take fetishism at this high level of generality we certainly can identify its effects before capitalism and, as Derrida notes,[117] possibly after capitalism, this level of generality blunts any real grasping of the exact form of commodity fetishism under capitalism. Derrida's deconstruction of Marx also downplays the deconstructive 'spirit' of Marx's analysis of real abstraction in the *Grundrisse* and *Capital*, and instead prefers the usual cliché that Marx tries to hold on to a critical grounding in some impossible point of (ontologised) presence (use-value / the concrete / labour) to exorcise the capitalist ghost. I will not pursue an exercise in filial Marxology here; instead I am more concerned with Derrida's occlusion of the 'reality' of real abstraction by his generalising and 'smudging' of its effects. No doubt Derrida is wary of the kind of grand temporal schemas of the rise of simulation and spectrality due to mutations in capitalism to be found in Jameson or Baudrillard; but his wariness risks instantiating and even grander temporal framing: 'Western metaphysics'. Derrida is insistent that his deconstruction of Marx does not efface differences and should permit 'a more refined and more rigourous restructuration.' [118] However, his failure to register such resources in Marx, and the lack of the promised fine-grain analysis, leave us, finally, at the mercy of real abstraction.

Hauntology is, of course, a Janus-faced concept: turned not only towards the description of what is, in terms of the necessity of deriving ontology from the fracture of the 'living present', but also to what can be, the evental disruption and opening of the living present to a future 'to come'. Hauntology inscribes the imminent necessity of events that will disrupt the capitalist 'hell of the same'.[119] Žižek notes that the matrix of Derrida's reading is that Marx and Marxism fail to respect spectral alterity as an irreducible event 'to come', and so tend to ontologise spectrality into a positive project.[120] This seems to remain within the terms of Negri and Eagleton's criticisms – that Derrida cannot grasp the positivity of Marxism. The twist is that Žižek argues that Derrida positivises the 'negative' moment of spectrality, and it is this failure to traverse towards negativity that actually leaves capitalism intact while we await the grand and shattering arrival of the spectral event 'to come', which never truly materialises as such. Negri and Eagleton are right, but for the wrong reasons. They are right that Derrida does not really provide a meaningful moment of political agency; they are wrong because this is not the result of deconstruction being a prevaricating 'negative thought' that cannot accede to the positive moment of acting or organisation. Rather it is because deconstruction fills out spectrality as such, as a reified 'positive' and irreducible moment that 'comes from on high'. This also means that Negri and Eagleton are wrong when they draw the conclusion that a *greater* ontologisation or positivity is required to resist the 'weightless' spectrality of capital. Such an ontologisation or positivisation only mimics capital, or becomes merely gestural or spectral in turn.

Derrida stands at the threshold of affirmationism proper. While his de-reifying of negativity from a stultifying synthetic dialectic is promising, his 'weak affirmationism' rebinds ultra-negativity to a newly reified and positivised irreducible but unspecified alterity ('from high'). Of course, in response affirmationists demand a return to new positivities, against dialectics and Derridean 'ultra-negativity', to surpass deconstructive melancholy in a new joyful politics. This leaves us with a false choice between weaker or stronger forms of affirmation. Instead, a more precise and politicised form of negativity is possible. We have already seen some of the rudiments of this politics, in terms of our critique of Nietzschean heroic voluntarism. This kind of subjectivism, which promises a world-historical rupture in the name of affirming a new world, avoids any engagement in the patient work of disrupting this world in which we live. Contrary to Nietzsche it is the 'plebian' immersion within the forms of labour and commodification that gives access to a potential contestation of the continual genesis of real abstraction in the labour process and commodification, especially in terms of the negation of the capitalist synchronisation of time to value-production.[121] To develop this thinking requires us first to traverse the various major forms of full-blown affirmationism.

NOTES

1. Badiou, *Polemics*, p. 133; my emphasis.
2. Ibid. p. 133; my emphasis.
3. Agamben, *Potentialities*, pp. 205–19; further discussion of the significance of the four Rabbis in the Jewish tradition, which casts interesting light on Agamben's identifications, can be found in M. A. Sweeney's essay 'Pardes Revisited Once Again'.
4. This identification of Derrida with Rabbi Aher gains a further political edge when we read it alongside Agamben's previous use of the same story in the article 'Marginal Notes on *Commentaries on the Society of the Spectacle*' (1990), collected in *Means without End* (2000), pp. 73–89. There he identifies Rabbi Aher's act of separation with the evil of the capitalist separation and nullification of language (p. 84). Reading prospectively, then, we could argue that Derrida figures the capitalist idling of language, *qua* separation, which would then require Agambenian redemption.
5. Agamben, *Potentialities*, p. 209.
6. Agamben, *Potentialities*, p. 219.
7. Agamben, *The Time That Remains*, p. 103; in an interview with Lorenzo Fabbri, Jean-Luc Nancy offers critical comments on Agamben's hostile attitude to Derrida, including its personal aspects ('Philosophy as Chance', p. 435).
8. Derrida, *Writing and Difference*, p. 308 note 4.
9. Derrida, 'From Restricted to General Economy', in *Writing and Difference*, pp. 251–77.
10. Derrida, *Margins of Philosophy*, p. 6.
11. Ibid. p. 6.
12. Derrida, *Positions*, p. 44.
13. See Hägglund, *Radical Atheism*.
14. Derrida, *Spurs*, p. 37.
15. Derrida, 'Ulysses', p. 298.
16. Ibid. p. 304.
17. Ibid. p. 308.
18. Derrida, *Archive Fever*, p. 68.
19. Derrida, 'Ulysses', p. 302.
20. See Rorty, 'Philosophy as a Kind of Writing'; Derrida remarks 'I am, in

fact, not at all, truly not at all in agreement with Rorty, especially where he takes his inspiration from my work' ('Marx and Sons', p. 247).

21. Derrida and Ferraris, *A Taste for the Secret*, p. 3.
22. Marion Hobson's *Jacques Derrida* (1998) is the most sophisticated attempt to trace these various 'systematic' infrastructures in Derrida's texts.
23. Derrida, *Writing and Difference*, p. 293.
24. Said, 'Opponents, Audiences', p. 9.
25. Cesare Casarino is an exception in noting this remark ('Philopoesis', p. 85), but he then proceeds to locate it firmly within Antonio Negri's form of affirmative theory.
26. Derrida, 'Marx and Sons', p. 261.
27. Derrida, *Specters of Marx*, p. xix.
28. It is this double feature that places the deconstruction of ontology in close proximity to Alain Badiou's metaontological project in *Being and Event* (2005 [1988]); see Badiou's comment on this proximity in *Logics of Worlds* (p. 545).
29. Derrida, *Specters of Marx*, p. 90.
30. Derrida, 'Letter', p. 273.
31. Derrida, *Specters of Marx*, p. 16.
32. Ibid. p. 89.
33. See Jason Smith, 'Jacques Derrida, "Crypto-Communist?"', for a suggestive account of how much is still to be done in excavating Derrida's relation to Marx and Marxism.
34. Derrida, 'For a Justice to Come', p. 6.
35. See, in particular, Derrida, *Rogues*.
36. Derrida, *Rogues*, p. 39.
37. Derrida, *Positions*, p. 92.
38. See Toscano, 'Partisan Thought'.
39. In *Rogues* Derrida insists on 'the urgency and imminence of an *à-venir*, a to-come' (p. 108).
40. Hallward, 'The Politics of Prescription', p. 778.
41. Nealon, 'Post-Deconstructive?', p. 77.
42. In *Specters of Marx* Derrida argues that: 'Marx continues to want to ground his critique or his exorcism of the spectral simulacrum in an ontology. It is a – critical but pre-deconstructive – ontology of presence as actual reality and as objectivity' (p. 170).
43. Derrida, *Aporias*, p. 12.
44. Ibid. p. 19.
45. Ibid. p. 19.
46. Ibid. p. 19.
47. Ibid. p. 32.
48. Derrida, *Monolingualism of the Other*, p. 46.
49. For example, see *Rogues* p. 54, p. 109.
50. See Derrida, *Of Hospitality* (2000), and *On Cosmopolitanism* (2001).

51. Derrida, *Aporias*, p. 33.
52. Ibid. p. 34.
53. Derrida, *Negotiations*, p. 219.
54. Ibid. p. 216.
55. Ibid. p. 216.
56. Haar, 'The Play of Nietzsche', p. 53.
57. See Derrida, 'Force of Law'.
58. Haar, 'Play of Nietzsche', p. 53.
59. Nietzsche, *Twilight*, p. 66.
60. Derrida, *Negotiations*, p. 217.
61. Derrida, 'I'm Going', p. 193.
62. Nietzsche, *On the Genealogy of Morals / Ecce Homo*, pp. 44–6.
63. Ibid. p. 45.
64. Kaufmann, in Nietzsche, *On the Genealogy of Morals / Ecce Homo*, p. 272.
65. Nietzsche, *On the Genealogy of Morals / Ecce Homo*, p. 272.
66. Ibid. p. 327.
67. Ibid. p. 233.
68. Nietzsche, *The Will to Power*, p. 545.
69. Ibid. p. 33.
70. Deleuze, *Nietzsche*, p. 72.
71. Ibid. p. 189.
72. Ibid. p. 198.
73. Ibid. p. 198.
74. Nietzsche, *Twilight*, pp. 64–5.
75. Klossowski, 'Nietzsche, Polytheism, and Parody', in *Such a Deathly Desire*, pp. 99–122.
76. Brassier, *Nihil Unbound*, p. 208.
77. Nietzsche, *The Will to Power*, p. 546.
78. Descombes, *Modern French Philosophy*, pp. 159–67.
79. Nietzsche, *On the Genealogy of Morals / Ecce Homo*, p. 333; Alain Badiou argues that the Nietzschean affirmation that 'breaks the world in two' is an archi-political and anti-philosophical act that leads to madness because it can only think the creation of a new world as the act of (individual) will ('Who is Nietzsche?', p. 9).
80. Nietzsche, *Twilight*, p. 27.
81. Ibid. p. 167.
82. Nietzsche, *The Will to Power*, p. 539.
83. Deleuze, *Foucault*, p. 131.
84. Ibid. p. 131.
85. Ibid. p. 131.
86. Baudrillard, *Forget Foucault*, p. 34.
87. Ibid. p. 34.
88. Deleuze, *Foucault*, p. 132.
89. See Alexander R. Galloway's *Protocol* (2004), and his work with Eugene

Thacker, *The Exploit* (2007), which draws attention to how effects and operations of power are built in to the very architecture of computing and other networks, however, ironically, they promote an acceleration-ist position of 'pushing through' and de-stabilising these protocols from within.

90. Nietzsche, *The Will to Power*, p. 464.
91. Ibid. p. 24.
92. Ibid. p. 19.
93. An important exception is Waite, *Nietzsche's Corps/e*.
94. Bull, 'Where is the Anti-Nietzsche?'.
95. Marcuse, *Eros and Civilization*, p. 13.
96. This, it seems to me, is the effect of Simon Critchley's anti-heroic politics of finitude, as set out in *Infinitely Demanding* (2007).
97. Badiou, *The Meaning of Sarkozy*, p. 72; this can be compared to Walter Benjamin's argument, in 'Theses on the Philosophy of History', that in the class struggle 'refined and spiritual things' makes their presence felt 'as courage, humour, cunning and fortitude' which 'have retroactive force and will constantly call in question every victory, past and present, of the rulers' (*Illuminations*, p. 255).
98. Badiou, *The Meaning of Sarkozy*, p. 73.
99. Nietzsche, *Twilight*, p. 72.
100. Ibid. p. 72.
101. Chrissus and Odotheus, *Barbarians*, p. 68.
102. Bennington, *Deconstruction*, p. 249.
103. Derrida, *Rogues*, p. 84.
104. Derrida, *Specters of Marx*, pp. 85–6.
105. Eagleton, 'Marxism', p. 87; see also Ahmad, 'Reconciling Derrida', pp. 104–6.
106. Derrida, 'Marx and Sons', p. 239.
107. Negri, 'The Specter's Smile', p. 10.
108. Eagleton, 'Marxism', p. 86.
109. Ibid. p. 86.
110. Marx, *Grundrisse*, p. 100–1.
111. In his other works Eagleton has tended to correlate 'materiality' with suf-fering and the finite body, which is then to be redeemed in spiritual terms; for example, see *Sweet Violence*.
112. Jameson, *The Cultural Turn*, p. 188.
113. Badiou, *Manifesto for Philosophy*, p. 56.
114. In the *Grundrisse* Marx specifies the retroactive temporality of capital which, through its deployment of real abstraction and subsumption of previous forms of production, provides the key to those past forms, but stresses we must not then subsume those historical differences under capital (p. 105).
115. Marx, *Grundrisse*, p. 105. On the historical specificity of the commodity-form, see also Lukács, *History and Class Consciousness*, pp. 84–6.

116. Derrida, *Specters of Marx*, p. 160.
117. Ibid. p. 160.
118. Ibid. p. 163.
119. Baudrillard, *The Transparency of Evil*, pp. 113–23.
120. Žižek, 'The Spectre of Ideology', pp. 26–7.
121. Lukács, *History and Class Consciousness*, pp. 168–9; for a historical account of the genesis of capitalist time, see E. P. Thompson, 'Time, Work-Discipline, and Industrial Capitalism'.

2. Adieu to Negativity: Deleuze

Gilles Deleuze is the affirmative philosopher *par excellence*; as he writes in *Nietzsche and Philosophy* (1962): 'Affirmation itself is being, being is solely affirmation in all its power'.[1] The striking consistency of Deleuze's affirmationism throughout his life and thought is often, however, deliberately fractured when he is assimilated into the contemporary affirmationist bloc. This insertion is usually achieved by severing his thinking from his equally affirmative co-written work with Félix Guattari (most especially *Anti-Oedipus* (1972) and *A Thousand Plateaus* (1980)). In this fashion Deleuze is (re-) constructed through his own self-identification as a 'pure metaphysician',[2] but what is lost, as Éric Alliez notes,[3] is the political Deleuze who, with Guattari, articulated lines of flight as the liberation of capital's flows towards a new absolute deterritorialisation. We have here an almost perfect example of the kind of 'deferred' temporality we identified in our introduction – Deleuze happens 'twice'. In the first instance Deleuze is the ecstatic libertarian philosopher of lines of flight, which become mired in their congruence with capital's deterritorialised flows, and this then dictates the necessity of the second instance of Deleuze reborn as 'pure metaphysician', depoliticised but a useful ally in the re-foundation of grand philosophy. In fact, in contemporary affirmationism we have the uneasy co-existence and oscillation between both these figures of Deleuze: militant *and* metaphysician.

The construction of the 'New Deleuze' as pure philosopher is most clearly visible in Badiou's *Deleuze: The Clamor of Being* (1997). While Badiou is deeply critical of Deleuze as a vitalist thinker of the One, he is also willing to accept Deleuze as an antagonistic ally in the renewal of metaphysics. This unlikely alliance comes at the cost of an unequivocal severing of Deleuze from his image as an 'anarcho-desirer', popular, according to Badiou, among 'the bearded militants of 1968, bearing the standard of their gross desire'.[4] Badiou's pungent outburst, interrupting the austere clarity of his reconstruction and restoration of Deleuze to philosophy, returns, in an occulted fashion, to an old polemic between Badiou and Deleuze in the 1970s. Writing in 1976 Badiou had violently rejected Deleuze and Guattari's neo-libertarian thinking as secretly fixated on an unnuanced image of 'Power'.[5] In a text written under the pseudonym Georges Peyrol, Badiou reiterated his charge, labelling Deleuze and Guattari's rhizomatic conception of ontology as an instance of 'potato-fascism' (*'fascisme du pomme du terre'*).[6] For Badiou, Deleuze and Guattari were not just misguided in their quasi-anarchist hostility to political organisation, but danger-ously complicit with an aestheticised fascism of desire. When it comes to his later recovery of Deleuze as fellow member of the affirmationist bloc Badiou settles this old political debate in philosophical terms – re-interpreting Deleuze as an austere and aristocratic figure led astray by a better-forgotten political engagement.

The contemporary return of Deleuze as an affirmationist tends to simply ignore the past political moment in his work, which is then sidelined, tactfully ignored or blamed on Félix Guattari. My aim here is not to take sides in this dispute. I neither chide Deleuze for being insufficiently constructive or affirmative in his politics,[7] nor do I defend or recover the neo-libertarian Deleuze.[8] Instead I want to trace how Deleuze originally constructed himself as an affirmative thinker in his work of the 1950s and 1960s. In particular I want to single out Deleuze's interpretation of structuralism as the site in which he nego-tiates most closely with the persistence of the negative, and so also indicate his somewhat eccentric status *vis-à-vis* what is usually named poststructuralism. Although I have already identified Nietzsche as the crucial figure for Deleuze's affirmationism, and we could also nominate Spinoza, I want to suggest the role of Bergson as truly influential. As we will see it is Bergson's critique of the negative that underpins the con-sistency of Deleuze's affirmationism, which later acquires Nietzschean or Spinozan accents. The third section of this chapter will consider Deleuze's own brief reflections on politics, and more particularly Marx, in *Difference and Repetition* (1968). This suggests a more compli-cated image of Deleuze's political trajectory, intractable to the image of Deleuze as neo-libertarian, but also to the image of Deleuze as an 'unpolitical' philosopher. I trace this heterogeneous political moment in Deleuze via the question of revolutionary subjectivity, and especially in the little-noted analysis Deleuze makes in his *Foucault* (1986). Despite the usual image of poststructuralism as involving the death or disper-sion of the subject, reinforced in Deleuze's case by his and Guattari's invocations of the 'Body without Organs' (BwO), we find that Deleuze, problematically, tries to develop a thinking of political subjectivation.

By returning to this lost political Deleuze, before the full-blown moment of his political conjunction with Guattari post-May '68, we can more clearly reveal the importance of politics to Deleuze and his consistency in refusing negativity. If we read 'Deleuze before Guattari' then this will allow us to problematise the current Deleuze revival that rehabilitates Deleuze as affirmationist against 'Deleuze and Guattari'. Another Deleuze emerges from this reconstruction: one far more directly engaged with questions of political subjectivation and with Marxist theories of revolutionary subjectivity than is usually recognised. Again, this is not simply a work of textual archaeology, but a critical reconstruction attentive to the traces and effects of a disavowed negativity especially as they operate in the re-thinking of political subjectivity. Despite all their differences we will see emerging a set of parallels with the thought of Derrida; the signal contrast is Deleuze's frontal engagement with politics, and the re-invention of the political category of the subject. It is this direct engagement that will also allow me to further flesh out a thinking of negativity as the condition of thinking agency.

THE POSITIVISATION OF DIFFERENCE

Deleuze always intervenes against negation and negativity; it is a constant refrain in his work. One of those interventions is particularly telling – his reading of structuralism. Contrary to what one might expect considering the usual *doxa*, Deleuze's 1967 essay 'How Do We Recognize Structuralism?' presents a surprisingly sympathetic account.[9] He carefully reconstructs structuralism's essential element – the development of a new order of the symbolic that functions as a 'transcendental topology' of sites and positions. This involves the construction of a field of elements that specify each other relationally, deploying Saussure's well-known description of language (or to be more precise, the system of *langue*) as a series of 'differences, *without positive terms*'.[10] In fact, Deleuze is quite strictly structuralist in his insistence that: 'language is the only thing that can properly be said to have structure'.[11] Within this structure, traceable by a transcendental topology, one element is crucial: a paradoxical element both lacking from the structure and in excess of it, through which the structure gains its mobility. This 'empty square', or void point, can take multiple forms: the 'dummy hand' in Bridge, the blind spot, *mana*, the letter in Poe's 'The Purloined Letter', the handkerchief in *Othello*, and so on. It is:

the only place that cannot and must not be filled, were it even by a symbolic element. It must retain the perfection of its emptiness in order to be displaced in relation to itself, and in order to circulate throughout the elements and the variety of relations.[12]

In this way Deleuze appears to accept the inscription of a particular form of negativity, as an instance of 'lack' that opens a point of intervention. It is the empty square that opens structure to the intervention of the subject, to 'new values or variations, and the singularities capable of new distributions, constitutive of another structure'.[13]

Of course this 'lack' is non-dialectical, one not open to inscription in terms of either opposition or contradiction. Instead this mobile lack, equally inscribable as excess, gets the structure moving without having a 'place' of its own. It is also the point that overturns the usual image of structuralism as an ideology of a static or cybernetic capitalism – a 'system which was never created and which will never come to an end', in Guy Debord's words.[14] On the contrary, Deleuze argues for the possibility of a structuralist 'hero' composed of 'non-personal individuations and pre-individual singularities',[15] who can break up structure. The intervention of this subject – as an 'ideal event' – takes place via the 'mutation point [that] precisely defines a praxis, or rather the very site where praxis must take hold'.[16] We might say that with Deleuze we see that 'structuralism' is not fully 'structuralist' but rather, already, *post-structuralist*. It is the void point – the site of intervention and the event – that opens the structure to mobility and change, rather than leaving it as an eternal static form.

Deleuze defines this poststructuralist reading of structuralism in terms of a new conception of mobile subjectivity:

> Structuralism is not at all a form of thought that suppresses the subject, but one that breaks it up and distributes it systematically, that contests the identity of the subject, that dissipates it and makes it shift from place to place, an always nomad subject, made of individuations, but impersonal ones, or of singularities, but pre-individual ones.[17]

Unlike Derrida's analysis, which stresses the de-centring of structuralism as the internal effect of a structure seemingly without a subject,[18] Deleuze correlates the empty square with the surging forth of the subject. The empty square retains its function as making the structure 'open to new values or variations', but this requires the structuralist 'hero' (or heroine).

What already emerges here is a political ontology of intervention that answers in advance the May '68 slogan 'Structures do not march in the street'. Slavoj Žižek has argued that Deleuze simply discards this earlier structuralist moment for the false solution of affirming productive becoming. He argues that there are two ontologies at work in Deleuze: the 'good' structuralist ontology of the sterile immaterial effect, associated particularly with Deleuze's *The Logic of Sense* (1969), and the 'bad' expressivist ontology of productive power, associated with Deleuze's work with Guattari.[19] The illegitimate elimination of the first ontology results, according to Žižek, in fatal philosophical and political consequences – the valorisation of production leads to the over-coding of the distinction virtual / actual with the opposition between production and representation.[20] This simplification results in a political model that opposes molecular political productivity, correlated with a libertarian self-organisation, to a molar, totalising power. In fact, this can help explain why today we have two contemporary affirmative images of Deleuze running side by side: Deleuze as a 'pure metaphysician' recovered from his political 'illness', and the quasi-anarchist political Deleuze of affirmative libertarian becomings. In both cases the subterranean link is the constriction of Deleuze to this second expressive ontology of production posed against political and philosophical representation.

While I am certainly suggesting a similar line of attack to Žižek, I would also note the limits of his critical schema. First, Žižek neglects the political ontology of intervention set out in Deleuze's article on structuralism, arguing instead for a return to the Deleuze of *The Logic of Sense* as the starting point to develop a new political ontology more adequate than that of pure production. He also neglects the later scattered hints in Deleuze concerning a thinking of revolutionary subjectivity, which I will return to at the end of this chapter. Žižek obscures the discontinuity in Deleuze's political thinking, which is not always bound to an expressivist productivism. Second, Žižek presents an oversimplified view of the political impasse in which Deleuze finds himself. For Žižek it is the difficulty of drawing out an adequate politics from the thinking of the sterile event that leads Deleuze to the false solution of the jump into alliance with Guattari, and his endorsement of a neo-libertarian productivism (what I have labelled 'accelerationism'). I want to suggest that Deleuze already had the rudiments of a different political ontology, but that he chose a different path for his own internal reasons – not least the necessity, in terms of his own thinking, to downgrade the negative. In this sense Žižek is right, but for the wrong reasons.

This shift, or tension, in political ontologies is already built in to Deleuze's work from the beginning. We do not confront a suddenly emerging impasse requiring a solution, but the image of Deleuze as internally fissured along the axis of negativity. We do not have a simple temporal shift from a 'good' to a 'bad' Deleuze, but rather a continuing struggle within Deleuze's work with these effects of negativity. How, at this point, does Deleuze eliminate the potential opening of non-dialectical negativity incarnated in the 'empty square' as site of the formation of revolutionary subjectivity? Simply by re-conceiving the void point: 'This void is, however, not a non-being; or at least this non-being is not the being of the negative, but rather the positive being of the "problematic," the objective being of a problem and of a question'.[21] Deleuze translates the negative void into the positive 'problematic' almost by fiat. As we will see, however, there is a reason behind this seemingly magical transformation.

THE PROBLEM OF THE NEGATIVE

In *Bergsonism* (1966) Deleuze begins from Bergson's re-definition of philosophy as a matter of stating problems rather than solutions. It is only through the statement and creation of true problems that solutions may emerge. In addition, the ability to state true problems has a political correlate: 'True freedom lies in a power to decide, to constitute problems themselves'.[22] This power of decision, which Deleuze links to Marx,[23] makes philosophy a political matter. What is crucial, and this explains Deleuze's re-inscription of difference as the 'positive being' of the problematic, is that: 'The negative is . . . the false problem *par excellence*'.[24] The difficulty with the negative is that it requires and posits the idea of 'Being', to which it opposes the abstract and loose category of 'non-Being'. In positing this idea of non-being the drive towards the negative is dependent on, and secondary to, the positive idea of being. It then has to *add* to this positive idea the (ironically) positive operator of negation and, in another addition, the positive psychological motive for negation – desire for a 'missing' object, or regret that reality does not provide us with what we want.[25] For Deleuze and Bergson the negative is a false problem because it cannot admit the primacy of the positive, and in trying to deny this it merely adds new layers of positivity in the pretence of negating.

In addition the abstractness of the generalised operation of negation, which poses 'Being' against 'non-Being', cannot grasp the true articulations of the real. Of course this generalised model of abstract negation does not fit so well with Deleuze's sympathetic description of structuralism, which is, precisely, a matter of grasping how the real is articulated through a transcendental topology of difference and non-dialectical negativity. This means we have to follow more closely not only this general dismissal of negativity as a false problem, but also the more specific way in which Deleuze transforms this non-dialectical negativity into a positive problem. This seeming *deus ex machina* becomes explicable if we place Deleuze's texts back in sequence and re-read his 1956 article 'Bergson's Conception of Difference', which might with justice be re-titled 'Deleuze's Conception of Difference'.[26] This essay provides a graph of the transformation of negativity into a positive problem through its presentation of a constellation of new forms of the concept of difference; these forms overlap and reinforce each other in resistance to any theory of difference that would 'imply the presence and the power of the negative'.[27] My presentation of this article will, unfortunately but necessarily, involve a somewhat arbitrary and teleological movement through the different concepts of difference Deleuze proposes: internal difference, vital difference, virtual difference and ontological difference. It is important to remember these are not so much separate concepts of difference as different *aspects* of difference, which overlap and reinforce each other. Although seemingly arbitrary, this presentation does allow us to explore Deleuze's own positivisation of the concept of difference.

Deleuze begins his article with a dual structure: Bergson's theory of difference operates at both a methodological level and an ontological level. In fact it is the methodological level – the determining of differences of nature between things in order to return to things themselves – that leads to the ontological level of specifying that difference itself is something. Through the method of intuition we move from differences of nature, 'carving nature at the joints' in Bergson's deployment of Plato's metaphor, to finding the nature of difference. It is this that specifies the task of philosophy:

> If philosophy has a positive and direct relation to things, it is only insofar as philosophy claims to grasp the thing itself, according to what it is, in its difference from everything it is not, in other words, in its *internal* difference.[28]

How does intuition achieve this deepening of difference? First it traces the articulation of the real through this process of dissection or cutting, but then it recomposes the factual lines or tendencies that underpin these differences (the well-known Bergsonian 'dualisms': matter and memory, intelligence and instinct, space and time, etc.).[29]

Bergsonian analysis recovers difference: 'It is not things, nor the states of things, nor is it characteristics, that differ in nature; it is *tendencies*'.[30] This recovery of difference in the tendencies is an operation remarkably similar to Kant's, however, whereas Kant recovers the transcendental conditions of experience, Bergson works on the conditions of real experience.[31] Also, although these conditions are composed of dualist tendencies, this dualism is re-composed with the privileging and dominance of *one* of the tendencies: duration or, in Bergson's *Creative Evolution* (1911), the *élan vital*. As Deleuze puts it: 'Dualism is therefore only a moment, which must lead to the re-formation of a monism'.[32] How can such a monism have anything to do with difference? This is a monism of difference, as 'duration is *what differs from itself*'.[33] Bergson's method allows us to find the ontological fact of difference – a self-generating difference. We have converged on internal difference.

Truly internal difference is the differentiation of the thing itself, not its specification in a mapping of degrees of difference. For this reason Deleuze asserts that: 'Internal difference will have to distinguish itself from *contradiction, alterity,* and *negation*'.[34] From the Bergsonian position these three forms of the negative create an abstract, baggy and external or relational form of difference. So contradiction, associated with Hegel, tends to set up an abstract opposition between Being and non-Being, 'instead of grasping the different realities that are indefinitely substituted for one another'.[35] The void is simply one object in place of another, rather than the absence of an object. Alterity, associated with the Platonic model, requires that differentiation is guided by an external end point; ultimately, in Plato, the 'good beyond being'. This is ruled out by Bergson's specification of the articulations of the real, which means that an internal difference does not require any such externality. Such articulations are not determined from the outside, and are not relational, instead they are the effect of difference differing in itself. Difference is *immediate*, not mediated, and so does not go as far as contradiction, alterity or negation. In a slightly confusing mixture of metaphors Deleuze argues that internal difference is at once beneath these mediated forms of difference, in the sense of being closer to the actual reality of the articulations of difference, and above them, since it composes the material for a 'superior empiricism'.[36]

How, though, does internal difference really distinguish itself? To render the real immediacy of difference in Bergsonian terms requires a concept of difference irreducible to external or abstract degrees of difference. Deleuze argues that 'such a difference *is* vital, even if the concept itself is not biological'.[37] It is 'life' that provides us with the concept of difference as irreducible self-differentiation. This strange vitalism, which, according to Deleuze, is not 'biological', is conceptualised by thinking of life as 'the process of difference'.[38] This process is one of internal differentiation as the result of an explosive internal force carried by life, or, as Deleuze would specify in his final text, 'a life'.[39] 'Life' or 'a life' plays the role of just such a Bergsonian real transcendental, of a condition of real experience that is itself a field of pure singularities. This conception of life also links to the necessity of stating correct problems: 'Life is essentially determined in the act of avoiding obstacles, stating and solving a problem. The construction of the organism is both the stating of a problem and a solution'.[40] When Deleuze later re-codes the structuralist void as a positive problem he is therefore rejecting the usual image of aridity associated with structuralism (in Derrida's metaphor, structuralism presents 'the architecture of an uninhabited or deserted city, reduced to its skeleton by some catastrophe').[41] Reading between these two texts we can see that Deleuze restores structures to the 'richness' of a life.[42]

This transcendental function of life as force (of difference) is correlated with the virtual, which then replaces contradiction and negation. What the virtual provides is a 'place' in which the tendencies converge. While we might be tempted to see in Bergson's dualisms the re-introduction of degrees of difference, and so an external, relational negative, in fact: 'The opposition of two terms is only the actualization of a virtuality that contained them both: this is tantamount to saying that difference is more profound than negation or contradiction'.[43] The result is that opposition is strictly secondary, and so any dialectical or contradictory model of opposition is merely the misreading of this positive actualisation. The virtual composes a pure concept of difference as the co-existence of degrees or nuances of difference. For this reason the 'empty square' cannot be read as an instance of transcendental absence, but is rather the sign of the virtual which 'defines an *absolutely positive* mode of existence'.[44] Once again we can see how Deleuze had already prepared his later positivisation of structuralism.

In *Bergsonism* Deleuze indicates that the virtual has a reality, a positive reality, which consists of the fluxions of difference. The virtual is not posited as some kind of standing-reserve of positive difference, which would have to pass through the constricting effect of the negative to 'enter' into reality. In actualisation, 'the virtual cannot proceed by elimination or limitation, but must *create* its own lines of actualization in positive acts'.[45] This, then, is the answer to any attempt to re-inscribe the negative in Bergson (and Deleuze): lines of differentiation are always creative, inventive and positive. The appearance of opposition or the negative is merely that, an appearance. By re-composing difference as the virtual the negative becomes simply an obstacle, at best. This elimination of the negative then undergoes its final twist by Deleuze's inscription of difference as ontological. Of course this has been implicit (and even explicit) in all the conceptions of difference we have traced so far. Deleuze's starting point was that an intuitive method would proceed from real differences to revealing the reality of difference, and here we have completed the circle: 'Being in fact is on the side of difference, neither singular nor multiple'.[46]

The final consequences of this position, and the reconnection of this Bergsonian vitalism to Nietzsche, are best spelt out in *Difference and Repetition*. Deleuze asserts that:

> Negation results from affirmation: this means that negation arises in the wake of affirmation or beside it, but only as the shadow of the more profound genetic element – of that power or 'will' which engenders the affirmation and the difference in the affirmation. Those who bear the negative know not what they do: they take the shadow for the reality, they encourage phantoms, they uncouple consequences from premises and they give epiphenomena the value of phenomena and essences.[47]

This clearly states the complete subordination or even elimination of negativity by the reconnection of Bergsonian vitalism to a more Nietzschean thematic of power and will, closing the circle of affirmationism.

The difficulty with Deleuze's radical subordination of negativity is that, in Bergson's phrase, it leaves us 'immersed in realities and [we] cannot pass out of them'.[48] This 'stuffed' conception of the virtual, and of difference, seems to allow little space or freedom for truly new actualisations or realities. When we cannot pass out of realities then the possibility of change would appear to be completely foreclosed. Ernst Bloch had already pointed out this difficulty in Bergson's conception of time; as Fredric Jameson summarises:

> For insofar as he defined the latter as process or change, it is always in another sense the same at any moment; Bergson never managed to think his way through the fundamental conceptual category which presides over the experience of the future and which is precisely the *novum*, the utterly and unexpectedly new, the new which astonishes by its absolute and intrinsic unpredictability.[49]

Badiou essentially makes exactly the same point against Deleuze: in taking over Bergson's ontology in the name of change, Deleuze repeats the error of positing a perpetual change that never reaches beyond an abstract re-shuffling of existent realities.[50]

This is precisely the difficulty with Deleuze's re-coding of the structuralist 'empty square' – which permitted the actualisation of non-dialectical negativity as the rupturing of the structure – as positive problematic. Of course internal difference is supposed to sponsor the proliferating birth of the new. But the actualisation of the new along tendencies or lines of differentiation only permits an active creativity that plays with the re-arrangement of existent realities.[51] We can already see how Deleuze's 'Bergsonism' is an incipient accelerationism, later to be actualised with Guattari in *Anti-Oedipus* (1972). It is only through the radicalisation of existent plural realities that the new can be produced, an accelerated deterritorialisation, because there is no possibility of rupture with existent realities. While we are not denying Deleuze's, and Marx's, insight into the necessity to trace and act upon the tendencies of capitalism, we are suggesting that the elimination of negativity leaves us fully exposed to these tendencies without the means for intervention or resistance, except the supposition of a 'higher' power of positivity that can overflow the 'negative' effect of capital.

There is, however, evidence that Deleuze does recognise the necessity of negativity. In his discussion of Deleuze's model of artistic creativity Toscano points out Deleuze's concession to a 'negativism beyond all negation' as the necessary mechanism for any truly new creation,[52] which recalls Derrida's ultra-negativity. Deleuze understands such forms of creation not simply in terms of affirmation, but also as requiring a patient work of extirpation, a creative work of destruction inflicted on all that mires us in the present order (on what Sartre calls the 'practico-inert').[53] This appearance of a 'negative' Deleuze is, however, deceptive or momentary, because, as Toscano goes on to state, '[t]he exoteric mechanisms of negativism are the preludes to an esoteric, ontological moment'.[54] Slavoj Žižek reinforces this point when he argues that Deleuze seems loath to admit 'a negativity that is *not* just a detour on the path of One's self-mediation'.[55] Negativity can only ever be fleetingly admitted, and yet the concession to the negative as essential to creating the truly new suggests that Deleuze's self-mediation of negativity within the affirmative 'One' is not as happy as it would appear. Now I want to explore how this relentless subsumption of the negative within a 'higher' power of affirmation impacts on Deleuze's thinking of politics and political subjectivity.

THE GRANDEUR OF MARX

Deleuze's last, and now semi-mythical, text was to have been titled *La Grandeur de Marx*. Marx, of course, was not an absent figure from Deleuze's oeuvre, especially in the two volumes co-produced with Guattari. Here, however, I wish to return to Deleuze's pre-Guattari writing on Marx in *Difference and Repetition* (1968). Antonio Negri proclaims, in a grandiose and slightly bizarre fashion, that: 'Deleuze's *Difference and Repetition* was a truly explosive event. And this was a philosophical event that corresponded exactly to what was taking place politically in Italy at the time'.[56] This reading of *Difference and Repetition* as a philosophical event with a political correlate runs against its usual presentation as the first work of Deleuze's philosophical maturity, as endorsed by Deleuze: '[this] was the first book in which I tried to "do philosophy"'.[57] In fact, we can make more direct political links, rather than an analogical reading, by re-tracing the brief but telling discussion of Marx and Marxism in the text. We already saw in our discussion of Deleuze's Bergsonian re-interpretation of structuralist difference his deployment of terms like 'tendencies' and 'problematics' – key terms for Marx and Marxism.[58] This lexical link prepares the ground for the strange 'alchemical marriage' Deleuze brokers between Marx and a virtual and non-biological vitalism.[59]

To achieve this Deleuze passes through Althusser's structural Marxism and, in exactly the same way he did with structuralism, he re-interprets it in a vitalist fashion.[60] Deleuze begins, promisingly, from abstraction thought as a differential series of relations and the 'economic instance' as 'a social multiplicity'.[61] This 'structure', and here Deleuze follows Althusser, is constituted as a diverse field that incarnates that diversity in different societies – this simultaneity means that the 'economic' is a 'differential *virtuality*'.[62] Already, then, we can see how the language of Bergson is introduced to account for the transcendental status of the 'structural'. Deleuze continues this line of thought by considering the economic as 'the totalising of the problems posed to a given society, or the synthetic and problematising field of that society'.[63] 'Synthetic' is, of course, hardly an Althusserian concept; in fact Althusser's reading of the dialectic precisely resists any synthetic moment.[64] Deleuze, in contrast, makes the shift from a differential structuralism (dis-) organised through the void-point of intervention, to structure re-interpreted as virtuality and actualisations, or as the field of problems to be correctly stated and overcome.

This 'structure' of the economic as a synthetic field of problems can rest for its justification on Marx's comment, in his preface to 'A Contribution to the Critique of Political Economy' (1859), that:

> Mankind thus inevitably sets itself only such tasks as it is able to solve, since closer examination will always show that the problem itself arises only when the material conditions for its solution are already present or at least in the course of formation.[65]

Deleuze refines this to argue that the economic is best treated as a 'social Idea', a heterogeneous series of differential relations between differential elements that composes the general field of the various problems or tasks posed. The social Idea is determined by its actualisation in a specific differenciation – the actual economic problem we face in a particular situation. Deleuze insists that: 'the negative appears neither in the process of differen*t*iation nor in the process of differen*c*iation'.[66] Once again, as we saw with the Bergsonian virtual, Deleuze proclaims that the Idea is a 'pure positivity' that 'knows nothing of negation'.[67] The idea is a problem, a formation of differential places and thresholds, that constitutes the 'genetic or productive elements of affirmation'.[68] This actualisation involves no introduction of the negative or negativity, but rather further 'finite engendered affirmations'.[69] While Deleuze concedes that the negative can appear in actual terms and real relations, this is only so once they are cut off from the convergence within the virtual, and so the negative is always and ever only secondary, 'never original or present'.[70]

To perform this excision of negativity Deleuze turns to Marx, by arguing that Marx's break with Hegel is a break with Hegelian conceptions of contradiction and alienation driven by the motor of negativity. In an implicitly Althusserian fashion, considering Althusser's hostility to the teleological and expressive elements of Hegelian thought, Deleuze argues Marx founds a new positive form of the social multiplicity. An interesting moment occurs, however, when Deleuze seems to recognise the risk being run in simply evacuating these effects of the negative: 'the philosophy of difference must be wary of turning into the discourse of beautiful souls: differences, nothing but differences, in a peaceful coexistence in the Idea of social places and functions'.[71] It is exactly this anxiety that concerns us: to simply *produce* difference as positive is to produce a stabilisation, in the form of a multiplicity that has no structure of antagonism. For Deleuze the solution to this possible neutralisation of positive difference in a non-antagonistic play is to (again) invoke Marx. It will be Marx's reading of the antagonism of the economic that will take us away from a contemplative projection of difference on to the world.

Deleuze notes that the economic problem is actualised as a false problem: 'the solution is generally perverted by an inseparable falsity'.[72] In the case of the economic the false problem is the fetishism of the commodity conceived as 'an objective or transcendental illusion born out of the conditions of social consciousness in the course of its actualisation'.[73] This fetishism produces effects which both enable some to live and others to suffer – the false problem makes history 'the locus of non-sense and stupidity'.[74] We have a situation in which the nonsense of alienation and exploitation is rendered as ideological commonsense, precisely through the inscription of this nonsense in social consciousness. Commodity fetishism is both real and false. For this reason we cannot appeal to consciousness as the site of a solution; it appears that Deleuze implicitly rejects the Lukácsian solution of 'class consciousness' to the riddle of commodity fetishism.[75] Instead his analysis prefigures Althusser's argument that the imaginary conditions of ideology create an effect by which consciousness is by necessity 'false'.[76] How does Deleuze resist the danger of functionalism Althusser courts, in which the depth of ideological structuring appears to prevent any rupture with such a system? Deleuze argues that to perform this rupture requires the power to raise the false existent sociability to the level of a 'transcendent exercise' that can break this regime of commonsense. This 'transcendental object' is revolution as 'the social power of difference, the paradox of society, the particular wrath of the social idea'.[77]

Although sketched with startling rapidity the conclusion appears to be that to prevent the stabilisation of affirmative differences in happy co-existence – 'the counterfeit forms of affirmation'[78] – it is necessary to return to the virtual to re-actualise the true problem that will break with this necessary illusion of individual consciousness and sociability. What is left unclear at this point is the *agency* that will perform this 'transcendent exercise' and so resolve the problem, or raise it to a higher level. The question of revolutionary subjectivity is implied but not resolved. In a lecture course on Bergson given in 1960 Deleuze points out that: 'The living is essentially a being that has problems and resolves them at each instant'.[79] In relation to the question of history Deleuze clarifies this by arguing that there is an added peculiarity: humanity pursues a path as far as it can possibly go but should it encounter an insurmountable problem then: 'it effects a true qualitative leap and takes another path that leads further than the previous one'.[80] Prefiguring the later analysis of the line of flight, and Deleuze and Guattari's accelerationism, this suggests that if the economy should pose the insurmountable problem of necessary falsity then humanity will be forced into a qualitative leap to re-pose the problem – or, in the language of politics, a revolution. Although this may not make the question of agency particular clear, it does specify more the nature of the transcendent exercise of the 'particular wrath of the social idea': to create an exit door, or way out, along a new affirmative path. The re-posing of the problem of the economic requires a return to the virtual / transcendental to re-actualise new possibilities and new problems.

Here we return to the negative as false problem *par excellence*, because it is the negative that shadows the problem and creates the field of the false problem. In a manner that is difficult to grasp negativity seems to shape the falsely oppositional and differential field that creates the alienation of fetishism. Deleuze identifies negativity with the stalled dialectical position of the 'beautiful soul', contrary to its actual role as what propels the dialectic forward through such stages.[81] This then allows Deleuze to argue that revolution, as affirmative force, is the means to break this stalled negativity:

> [Revolution] never proceeds by way of the negative but by way of difference and its power of affirmation, and the war of the righteous for the conquest of the highest power, that of deciding problems by restoring them to their truth, by evaluating that truth beyond the representations of consciousness and the forms of the negative, and by acceding at last to the imperatives on which they depend.[82]

In an act of legerdemain, reminiscent of Derrida's, the usual qualities of negativity are passed over into affirmation. Now it is revolution which is identified with the virtual in all its power (and once again we have a relay here to Nietzsche, as well as to Bergson), and made the means to make a true qualitative leap – reversing Lenin's materialist reading of Hegel as the philosopher of qualitative 'Leaps! Leaps! Leaps!'[83]

The undoubted power of Deleuze's thinking of Marxism, recognised by Žižek,[84] lies in its articulation of the 'economic' as virtual 'positivity'. This allows Deleuze to give full ontological weight to the problem of real abstraction, and he will later formalise this in his work with Guattari in their description of capitalism as an 'axiomatic' machine of de- and re- territorialisation. The difficulty is that this positivisation of the economy gives capitalism a 'full' reality. First, this neglects capitalism's own 'labour of the negative' in the action of accumulation. Although the couplet de- / re- territorialisation provides perhaps one of the most powerful means for grasping the new articulation of capitalism, the conception of such a 'structure' as positive neglects the 'creative destruction' of capital, which operates by a 'negation of negation' that captures and integrates elements into new positivities of accumulation. The 'use' of Hurricane Katrina to re-organise and ethnically cleanse the urban space of New Orleans to create a new tourist city by the state and corporations is merely one spectacular instance of such processes.[85] Second, the couplet de- / re- territorialisation also fails to provide the interventional space of negativity to disrupt the capitalist re-composition of such positivities. Instead we are called, already, to an accelerationism that would exceed capitalist deterritorialisation in an 'absolute deterritorialisation'.[86] This philosophy of the absolute, conceived of course as absolute difference, risks the absolutisation of capitalism as 'untranscendable horizon' in the very act of trying to transcend it.

Such a formulation gained political purchase by its formulation in relation to a real movement of opposition – this is Negri's point in relation to *Difference and Repetition*, and was confirmed by *Anti-Oedipus* as the book of the libertarian tendencies post-May '68. The problems intrinsic to the theory became more self-evident in the light of the dissipation of that movement, which occurred precisely along the lines of deterritorialisation. The fading of the movements that could accelerate and fulfill the tendency of deterritorialisation left us simply with the 'positive' reality of those tendencies. This is not, of course, to suggest an unnuanced image of the triumph of capitalism as in certain moments in Baudrillard.[87] The difficulty, however, is that the Baudrillardian image of an auto-consumptive self-destabilising capitalism comes to be the truth of Deleuze (and Guattari's) position once they lose any figure of actual agency. The crisis is therefore a crisis of agency. This, however, is not merely a local crisis, resulting from a particular political failure. Instead, the subordination or virtual elimination of negativity, especially as the 'lever' of agential intervention, poses a fundamental theoretical question to any attempt to articulate political agency in terms of vital positivity.

REVOLUTIONARY SUBJECTIVITY

Deleuze's *Foucault* (1986) is one of his supreme ventriloquist performances. Its final chapter is dedicated to addressing the problem that Foucault's affirmationist conception of power as a multiplicity of productive points seems to leave the subject as a mere *product* of power.[88] In fact, this can be seen as a displacement and answering of the problem that also afflicts Deleuze's affirmationism: how do we actualise a disruptive subjectivity in the face of capitalism's subsumption of those lines of flight on which liberation was supposed to be produced? For this reason I would dispute Slavoj Žižek's claim that '[i]t is crucial to note that *not a single one* of Deleuze's own texts is in any way directly political'.[89] This *is* a 'directly' political text, as Deleuze argues that this problem of agency is not generated through a faulty theory, but by the actuality of new forms of post-Fordist power. According to Deleuze, Foucault 'found the impasse to be where power itself places us, in both our lives and our thoughts, as we run up against it in our smallest truths.'[90] The totalisation and productivity of power, dispersed through a multiplicity of relations, is an effect of the crisis of state-centred Fordism. In *Cinema 2* Deleuze suggested that Italian neo-realism emerged not purely as a result of internal formal shifts in cinema, but was also the result of 'the proliferation of empty, disconnected, abandoned spaces' in the wake of the Second World War.[91] In similar fashion we can say that reality intrudes into theory in the 1970s with the proliferation of new forms of power, themselves responses to the forms of liberation resulting from the struggles of the 1960s and early 1970s.

In this situation, Deleuze asks: 'what happens . . . if the transversal relations of resistance continue to become restratified, and to encounter or even construct knots of power?' [92] He links this problem imme- diately to the political failure of the prison movement – the *Groupe d'Information sur les Prisons* (GIP) – with which he and Foucault had been involved, and to other political failures of the period. Political failure dictates an admittedly delayed thinking of ways to avoid the re-stratification of resistance, or what is more usually referred to as the problem of recuperation: capitalism's ability to absorb and re-channel dissent. This problem became particularly acute for a number of New Left thinkers in this period, as revolutionary hopes waned. It is not a reason for cynicism, or for conceding defeat, but of the necessity of asking another, supplementary, question: how are we to 'release trans- versal lines of resistance and not integral lines of power'?[93] For Deleuze, writing retrospectively, we must first concede that capital was not simply a 'molar' power bloc, but also had considerable capacities for 'molecular' penetration and, in light of this, we must develop new strat- egies and forms of resistance. Contrary to the model of the subject as mere subject of power, Deleuze argues we can find in Foucault a think- ing of the possibilities of 'subjectivation': the capacity of the subject to detach themselves from the historically sedimented determinations of power.

To draw this out Deleuze pursues his previous formalisation of three sets of relations in Foucault: the relations between strata (Knowledge), the relations between forces found in the diagram (Power), and the absolute relation to the outside (Thought). In tracing these relations can we find an 'interior' capacity for resistance and freedom, or is the 'internal' space of the subject fully determined by 'exterior' operations of power? On the face of it Foucault implies that the 'inside' of the subject is 'an operation of the outside',[94] a folding or interiorisation of the outside that forms the surface of the inside – something like a pocket. Of course, if we simply interiorise the outside, or are formed by it immediately, then we have no real freedom and are completely at the mercy of power – a common enough image of Foucault's work. Deleuze traces the way out of this impasse by specifying the exact forms in which the operation of folding takes place, something considered by Foucault in his volumes of *The History of Sexuality* on Greek and Christian self-knowledge.[95] Freedom from power comes *through* the folding of power, in which 'the *relation to oneself* assumes an inde- pendent status.'[96] It is our ability to 'ben[d] the outside',[97] to mould and shape the exterior forces that constitute and act upon us, which opens the space of subjectivation, and so of freedom. In this way we can form 'a dimension of subjectivity derived from power and knowledge without being dependent on them'.[98]

This is a remarkably fragile form of 'freedom', dependent on a mysterious capacity to bend or fold existent exterior forces – a kind of subdued accelerationism. If Foucault always traces such 'foldings' in particular historical configurations then Deleuze, contrary to the more modest and positivist spirit of Foucault's analyses, *ontologises* this capacity for resistance: 'There will always be a relation to oneself which resists codes and powers'.[99] In this way the seeming fragility of the capacity for resistance is given an ontological, and vitalist, substantiality. The result is a rather uncomfortable coordination between the historical variability of the formation of the subject, in the tectonic shifts of Foucault's *epistemes* or in his more 'local' analyses of the production of subjects in the asylum, clinic, prison, etc., and the Deleuzian supplement of an intrinsic ability to disrupt and re-work these conditions. Deleuze suggests that although we are '[r]ecuperated by power-relations and relations of knowledge, the relation to oneself is continually re-born, elsewhere and otherwise'.[100] Inverting Foucauldian pessimism, with its always interlocked spirals of power and resistance, leads to an ontological optimism that grounds resistance, but in an intrinsic fashion that seems to leave very little specification of *how* the continual re-birth of resistance will actually take place in particular historical conditions.

Deleuze endeavours, despite the seeming antinomy between objective structures and subjective resistance, to articulate ontological resistance with history. First, more than Foucault, Deleuze stresses the malleability and variability of the historical conditions of subjectivation.[101] Our awareness of these conditions is, as the end of *The Order of Things* (1966) implied, often a result of their crisis. Foucault suggested the eclipse of the figure of 'man' was the result of an epistemological crisis, caused particularly by the mutations of anthropology and psychoanalysis.[102] Deleuze adds that this was also the result of a *political* crisis, caused by the emergence of new contestatory subjectivities of May '68. Using Foucault's Kantian terminology Deleuze states that: 'The events which led up to 1968 were like the "rehearsal" of these three questions [What can I do? What do I know? What am I?]'.[103] The implication is that May '68 will involve the subjective activation of these questions, leading to the rupture of the *episteme*. Second, Deleuze also argues that the folding of the outside by the subject interacts with the past condensed inside us.[104] This means that the crisis of an *episteme*, of our relation to the usual regime of knowledge, frees us from the determinations of the present by activating these internal 'virtual' pasts. In this way our 'interior' is not hollow, but a series of heterogeneous 'pasts' awaiting historical actualisation and realisation. The result is a to-and-fro process of 'calling up and producing new modes of subjectivation'.[105]

There is also a more surprising moment of consideration of the historical possibilities of political subjectivation, which is left in a long footnote in the Foucault book, and which has attracted little critical attention. I will take the liberty of quoting this footnote at length not only because it is germane to my analysis, and because it overturns the contemporary depoliticised image of Deleuze, but also simply as a *reminder* of what happened in May '68. Guy Debord remarked that: 'Nothing in the last twenty years has been so thoroughly coated in obedient lies as the history of May 1968'.[106] For Deleuze May '68 is not simply the invention of a few intellectuals, but the result of a striking convergence:

> On the level of world events we can briefly quote the experiment with self-management in Yugoslavia, the Czech Spring and its subsequent repression, the Vietnam War, the Algerian War and the question of networks, but we can also point to the signs of a 'new class' (the new working class), the emergence of farmers' or students' unions, the so-called institutional psychiatric and educational centres, and so on. On the level of currents of thought we must no doubt go back to Lukács, whose *History and Class Consciousness* was already raising questions to do with a new subjectivity; then the Frankfurt school, Italian Marxism and the first signs of 'autonomy' (Tronti); the reflection that revolved around Sartre on the question of the new working class (Gorz); the groups such as 'Socialism or Barbarism', 'Situationism', 'the Communist Way' (especially Félix Guattari and the 'micropolitics of desire').[107]

May '68 is therefore the moment of the intersection and intensification of these two sequences – of events and of thought – which produced a new world-historical power of subjectivation, and new forms of mass political struggle.

To unpack this highly condensed analysis we should first note that Deleuze refuses any reactionary erasure of the event of 1968. The historical irony, pointed out by Jacques Rancière,[108] is that it has been left-wing thinkers (or ex-left-wing thinkers) who have done most to popularise the critique that May '68 was simply an effect of the cunning of capitalist reason. This position puts a perverse twist on the concept of recuperation: capitalism does not recuperate radical struggles, it has already moulded them in advance – hence capitalism is the only game in town. Christopher Leigh Connery describes this as the position of 'always-already cooptation'.[109] In fact the US-based *Telos* group came close to this position in the late 1970s. They argued that many, if not all, of the protest movements of the 1960s embodied an 'artificial negativity' that was actually incited by capitalism to create a certain amount of friction that would improve its functioning.[110] It is exactly this kind of cynicism dressed up as tough-minded political realism that Deleuze rejects by his fidelity to May '68.

In contrast to the usual iconoclastic image of Deleuze, his recovery of revolutionary subjectivity is reconstructed in impeccable lineage with critical Marxism. The struggle-subjectivity nexus passes through vectors of contestation and through vectors of thought, and through perhaps the most surprising 'monstrous-coupling' of all: Deleuze-Lukács. Deleuze's micro-history of the 'production' of subjectivity suggests a more ecumenical attitude than one might assume from the partisan of Bergsonian affirmationism. Instead of taking a doctrinaire political line Deleuze is willing to engage with thinkers of negativity and with Marxism in its most Hegelian forms: the Frankfurt School and the Situationists. Implicit is a negotiation with negativity as a capacity or form of the subject, and the suggestion is that this might be crucial to what Deleuze formulates as 'subjectivation'. Of course, as we have noted previously, Deleuze is happy enough to take note of negativity, but only as then mediated by, and finally subordinated to, affirmation. This seems to be the case here, with the previous articulations of subjectivity in terms of negativity leading to the teleological conclusion of the work of Félix Guattari, that is, back to the affirmation of desire. We also find a similar re-coding when we return to the body of the text, where Deleuze's own model of a form of subjectivity capable of resisting the new micro-political capitalist penetrations is still couched within a Bergsonian language of the positive: 'The struggle for subjectivity presents itself, therefore, as *the right to difference, variation and metamorphosis.*'[111] The 'right to difference' is relayed into the usual forms of mutation, production and positive variation.

The strategic possibilities of Deleuze's thinking, which could perhaps have been enriched by the encounter with Marxism and negativity, finally give way to the usual dubious affirmation of ontological power.[112] The various foldings of subjectivity find their 'fundamental' referent in being, or, to be more precise, in the *univocity* of being. In tracing the political consequences of this thinking of the fold, Alain Badiou argues that, first, it involves a conservation of what already exists – folding is the folding of virtual-past, and second, this folding leads to an equation of thought with the One, under the aegis of philosophy.[113] Badiou indicates the fundamental conservatism of this kind of thinking, as the fold merely folds what is, or re-folds it, without allowing any rupture of the ontological that would allow the emergence of the new. The political problem of the terms 'difference, variation and metamorphosis' is that they imply dependent adaptation of what is – more of the same, or mere 'modification' in Badiou's terminology – which is particularly vulnerable to the endless metamorphoses of capitalism. We can recall Baudrillard's criticism that such models of mutational and molecular power are mirrors of capitalism.[114] In the end, why proclaim the need for a right to difference, variation, and metamorphosis, if capitalism will supply them in far more radical, a-subjective, and inhuman forms than any mutated subject?

The irony is that Deleuze's 1990 text 'Postscript on the Societies of Control' is one of the best statements of the problems that mire such models of resistance as mutation and modulation.[115] Deleuze periodises a shift, which is implicitly dated to the mid-1970s, between the older 'disciplinary societies', condensed in the figure of the Fordist factory and its labour discipline, and the new 'societies of control', condensed in the figure of the new corporate business models of flexibility and 'precarious' labour. Deleuze points to the ambiguity which would seem to strike at the heart of his own formulations: the crisis of the older forms of enclosure (the hospital, prison, school, factory, etc.) 'could at first express new freedom, but they could participate as well in mechanisms of control that are equal to the harshest of confinements.'[116] Although not accepting such equivocal liberations as the signs of the cunning of capitalist reason, Deleuze recognises that they have helped to form a new regime of power / knowledge. Instead of being faced by the 'moulding' power of the disciplinary forms of power, we now face new powers of control that operate by a continuous process of 'modulation'.[117] The result is that we are no longer individuals, but '*dividuals*', constituted through constant sampling, assessment and training.[118] What is fascinating is that Deleuze does not really reflect on how this dynamic of modulation, flows and coding tends to coincide with his own previous models of liberation. The powers of 'variation and metamorphosis' that Deleuze had proffered as a solution to the impasse of articulating a left-libertarian critique of capital are vitiated by a capitalism that operates through the continual 'modulation' of the 'dividual' – blocking any ability to form or fold new powers by exposing the individual to the constant demand to change and adapt.

Deleuze ends his short text with a declaration of faith in the young to develop new forms of resistance to these new forms of molecular power,[119] however he does not seem to undertake any significant strategic re-orientation of his own thinking. The result of leaving subjectivation dependent on the ability to ontologically fold existent forces of power is that despair can set in when capital everywhere seems to dominate and control through such ontologically positive mechanisms of power. This is exemplified by the Italian post-autonomist thinker Franco 'Bifo' Berardi. He makes the Deleuze-style argument that, as we can no longer detect any cycle of the production of new (revolutionary) subjectivities, we will soon be confronted by a 'wave of suicides'.[120] Certainly such a proposition has the merit of being empirically testable. . . While not holding Deleuze responsible for this outburst of pessimistic hyperbole, the problem it points to is real. If we do not have the production of subjectivities in struggle then we are free to draw the conclusion that no such subjectivities *can be* produced. The very inscription of struggle in terms of productivity and accumulation not only mimics the forms of capital, but also leaves us at the mercy of the lineaments of current realities – conceived of as an unnuanced 'plane of immanence'.

To avoid the kind of pessimism that Berardi indulges in, which can easily flip over into an equally facile optimism when conditions change (as we witness in his recent text lauding the election of Barack Obama as the sign of the victory of the 'cognitariat'[121]), requires a re-orientation of our thinking to a negativity that refuses to sanction things as they are. What Deleuze's footnote opens, and his main text then closes, is the possibility of a more *strategic* thinking of subjectivation, and one that would take into account negativity. His own earlier thinking of structuralism, although cast in overly transcendental and ontologised forms, also indicated the strategic possibility of interventional 'void-points' as sites of subjectivation. In shutting down this option resistance is left as a perpetual possibility, but one only ever tied to some 'positive' existence. What are lost are more occult forms of negation and resistance within and against the unfolding of the new modulated powers of capitalism.

To reiterate, this is not to offer a magical theoretical solution to the very real problems and impasses of agency we face in the current conjuncture – problems that Deleuze had the prescience to notate and grasp in their emergence. Gregory Elliott points out that in the wake of the collapse of historic communism: 'The cruces of an alternative – agency, organisation, strategy, goal – that could command the loyalties and energies of the requisite untold millions await anything approaching resolution'.[122] While we certainly should not expect theory to solve this problem, it can *à la* Deleuze, pose the problem in a better fashion. In particular, this involves resisting the inscription of a passive form of agency dependent on its mimicry and exceeding of capital's own forces of production as our saviour. The constant focus on the *production* of the subject or subjectivation, coupled to some irrepressible ontological power, reproduces the nature of the capitalist value-form, in which value production rests on the positing of labour-power as inexhaustible source of value. Instead, I am arguing that negativity can better figure the necessary disruption and rupture of the value-form, in ways which are immanent to it, but not simply dependent on it. This is, of course, a large enough claim in itself. It comes with the added irony that the recourse to negativity, too often viewed as pessimistic and reactive, is actually the means to set the conditions for the invention of new forms of non-commodified living; whereas affirmationism, which exalts creativity and novelty, is really at risk of reproducing the capitalist 'hell of the same' (Baudrillard) in the guise of novelty.

This strategic possibility of negativity does flicker intermittently in the interstices of Deleuze's work. We noted its appearance in his derivation of non-dialectical negativity in structuralism. It is also visible in Deleuze's deployment of Foucault's 'thought of the outside' (derived originally from Blanchot), which Foucault presents as a hyper- or ultra-non-dialectical negativity that has always haunted Western reason.[123] Deleuze argues that in folding this 'Outside' we can find an undetermined point of freedom for the subject. In Deleuze's re-coding this becomes the 'savage exteriority', which is the 'final' point of non-specification and de-stratification from which existent positivities 'emerge': 'savage particular features, not yet linked up, on the line of the outside itself, which form a teeming mass especially just above the fissure. This is a terrible line that shuffles all the diagrams, above the very raging storms.'[124] Of course Deleuze folds this thinking back into a mediated moment on the transition to affirmative ontological folding, but this subordination could always be read in reverse: as the sign that Deleuze's thinking remains inextricably bound to, or entangled with, negativity.[125]

The difficulty, of course, is the form in which this negativity is cast by both Foucault and Deleuze. In Foucault it takes the form of an unmediated and transhistorical 'Outside', which nudges it back towards the thematics of the *tout Autre*. While Deleuze takes more seriously the political integration of this line, the difficulty is that it still remains unspecified and indeterminant – 'a teeming mass'. Also, Deleuze's affirmationist insistence that such a 'raging' negativity 'shuffles all the diagrams' leaves us back within a Bergsonian suggestion that we can only exchange the realities we are immersed in, rather than truly alter them. The irony is that the very place in which the 'de-stratification' of the subject could and should operate, and which is blocked by the re-stratification of capital under the sign of the 'dividual', is left hanging, only underwritten by a quasi-mystical 'pure' formless negativity.

Instead I want to suggest that these 'savage *particular* features' *could* offer a stronger political valence if we were to link them to the possibility Deleuze invoked in relation to structuralism: a 'mutation point [that] precisely defines a praxis, or rather the very site where praxis must take hold'.[126] Negativity would be 'employed' in the linkage of a 'mutation point' with a praxis, precisely in refusing to leave that point as mere 'mutation'. Rather the question is of a precise, or determinate, negation, which would refuse to simply take off into further accelerated mutations, but instead re-work and fissure such a 'point'. Also, such a 'point' would not simply have to be the grand ontological operator of transcendental revolution, instead the fissuring effect of negativity suggests the multiplicity of such points, distributed along the chains of capitalist 'modulation' – the very proliferation of sites of capture, of real subsumption and real abstraction, proliferating points of negation and resistance. Of course this is very close to Deleuze's formulations, even right up against them. The crucial difference is, however, the refusal to cast this work of intervention in terms of a 'shuffling', modulation, mutation or play, with the existent positive forces of 'reality' or 'virtuality', effects which are finally anchored in the ontological invocation of some supreme and abstract power of life that always provides resistance. It would also avoid the symmetrical valorisation of a 'pure' negativity that would incarnate some free-floating power of the 'teeming mass' or absolute 'Void'. Instead, in the margins of Deleuze another possibility emerges of a more fine-grained tracking of these mutational points, these voids, as sites of praxis. In the next two chapters I will trace the occlusion of this possibility by the attempts of Bruno Latour and Antonio Negri to positivise and ontologise relations. It will be after this detour that we can return to the work of Alain Badiou as the site of starting to bring together the threads of a praxis of negativity.

NOTES

1. Deleuze, *Nietzsche and Philosophy*, p. 186.
2. Deleuze, 'Responses'; see also Villani, '"I Feel I am"'.
3. Alliez, 'Badiou'.
4. Badiou, *Deleuze*, p. 12.
5. Badiou, 'The flux'.
6. Quoted in Power and Toscano, 'The Philosophy of Restoration', p. 38.
7. See Hallward, *Out of this World* (2006) and Žižek, *Organs Without Bodies* (2004).
8. See Alliez, 'Badiou' and '*Anti-Oedipus*'.
9. In Deleuze, *Desert Islands*, pp. 170–92.

10. Saussure, *Course*, p. 118; trans. mod.
11. Deleuze, *Desert Islands*, p. 170.
12. Ibid. p. 189.
13. Ibid. p. 191.
14. Debord, *Society*, #201.
15. Deleuze, *Desert Islands*, p. 191.
16. Ibid. p. 191.
17. Ibid. p. 190.
18. Derrida, 'Structure, Sign and Play', in *Writing and Difference*, pp. 278–93.
19. Žižek, *In Defense*, p. 365.
20. Ibid. p. 366.
21. Deleuze, *Desert Islands*, pp. 189–90.
22. Deleuze, *Bergsonism*, p. 15.
23. Ibid. p. 16.
24. Deleuze, *Difference*, p. 208.
25. Deleuze, *Bergsonism*, p. 17; Bergson, *Creative Evolution*, p. 283.
26. In Deleuze, *Desert Islands*, pp. 32–51. In what follows I will not be directly engaging in the question of whether Deleuze's reading of Bergson is an accurate one; as Deleuze's remarks in *Difference and Repetition*: 'a commentary should act as a veritable double and bear the maximal modification appropriate to a double' (p. xxi).
27. Deleuze, *Desert Islands*, p. 38.
28. Ibid. p. 32.
29. Deleuze, *Bergsonism*, p. 21.
30. Deleuze, *Desert Islands*, p. 34.
31. Ibid. p. 36.
32. Deleuze, *Bergsonism*, p. 29.
33. Deleuze, *Desert Islands*, p. 37.
34. Ibid. p. 38.
35. Deleuze, *Bergsonism*, p. 20.
36. Ibid. p. 30.
37. Deleuze, *Desert Islands*, p. 39.
38. Ibid. p. 39.
39. Deleuze, *Pure Immanence*, pp. 25–33.
40. Deleuze, *Bergsonism*, p. 16.
41. Derrida, *Writing and Difference*, p. 5.
42. It is important to note that this privileging of life does not simply correlate with human life. Grasping the articulations of the real: 'open[s] us up to the inhuman and the superhuman (durations which are inferior or superior to our own), [allowing us] to go beyond the human condition' (Deleuze, *Bergsonism*, p. 28). That said, Deleuze does follow Bergson in giving a certain privilege to the human as the site that permits this opening to multiple durations.
43. Deleuze, *Desert Islands*, p. 43.

44. Ibid. p. 44; my emphasis.
45. Deleuze, *Bergsonism*, p. 97.
46. Deleuze, *Desert Islands*, p. 25.
47. Deleuze, *Difference and Repetition*, p. 55.
48. Bergson, *Creative Evolution*, p. 276.
49. Jameson, *Marxism and Form*, p. 126.
50. Badiou, *Logics of Worlds*, p. 384; see also Garo, 'Deleuze, Marx and Revolution', p. 611.
51. Peter Hallward, in *Out of this World* (2006), has provided the most exhaustive analysis of the recurrence of the thematic of creativity in Deleuze's thought. Hallward argues that creativity plays a fundamentally theophanic role for Deleuze – redeeming a fallen world from its various 'failed' creations. This makes, he contends, Deleuze's philosophy unworldly – finally indifferent to actual worldly relations and experiences in the name of a 'higher' virtual creativity. Ironically, my argument is that Deleuze's positivity and creativity make his philosophy too worldly, by making it too dependent on existing lines of flight, and on compromising with existent forms of capitalist creativity.
52. Toscano, 'In Praise of Negativism'.
53. Deleuze wrote admiringly of Sartre in the article 'He was my Teacher' (1964) (in *Desert Islands*, pp. 77–80).
54. Toscano, 'In Praise of Negativism', p. 64.
55. Žižek, *Organs without Bodies*, p. 52.
56. Negri, in Casarino and Negri, 'It's a Powerful Life', p. 154.
57. Deleuze, *Difference and Repetition*, p. xv.
58. It is Negri who has done most to draw out the concept of the tendency as central to Marxism, especially in his 1971 work *Crisis of the Planner-State: Communism and Revolutionary Organization* (in Negri, *Books for Burning*, pp. 1–50). On the 'problematic' the crucial work is, obviously, Althusser's – see especially *For Marx* (1966).
59. On the 'mystic' Deleuze see the excellent archaeology of *Difference and Repetition* carried out by Christian Kerslake in *Deleuze and the Unconscious* (2007).
60. Kerslake, 'Becoming Against History', p. 18.
61. Deleuze, *Difference and Repetition*, p. 186.
62. Ibid. p. 186; my emphasis.
63. Ibid. p. 186.
64. Christian Kerslake points out, in 'Becoming Against History', that this 'challenge and response' model of history is derived from Arnold Toynbee: 'One of Deleuze's specialities was in producing "monstrous couplings" between contemporary and half-forgotten, unfashionable thinkers; Deleuze's conjunction of Althusserian structuralism with Toynbee's rather grizzly brand of "universal history" is a nice example' (p. 18).
65. Marx, *Early Writings*, p. 426.

66. Deleuze, *Difference and Repetition*, p. 207.
67. Ibid. p. 207.
68. Ibid. p. 207.
69. Ibid. p. 207.
70. Ibid. p. 207.
71. Ibid. p. 207; this provides a precise characterisation, *avant la lettre*, of the thinking of Bruno Latour (see Chapter 3).
72. Ibid. pp. 207–8.
73. Ibid. p. 208; it would certainly be possible to link this presentation of commodity fetishism as 'transcendental illusion' anchored as the shadow of social reality to Slavoj Žižek's argument that commodity fetishism is incarnated into social reality in the form of materialised beliefs (*The Sublime Object*, pp. 31–7).
74. Ibid. p. 208.
75. See Lukács, *History and Class Consciousness*, especially 'Class Consciousness', pp. 46–82.
76. See Althusser, 'Ideology and Ideological State Apparatuses', in *Lenin and Philosophy*, pp. 121–73.
77. Deleuze, *Difference and Repetition*, p. 208.
78. Ibid. p. 208.
79. Deleuze, 'Lecture Course', p. 74.
80. Ibid. p. 75; see also the diagram on p. 74.
81. Bruce Baugh's *The French Hegel* (2003) offers a useful account of the dominance of the theme of the 'beautiful soul' in the reaction to Hegel in France. His solution, however, is to endorse Deleuze and Foucault's affirmationism as the means to break with this paradigm.
82. Deleuze, *Difference and Repetition*, p. 208.
83. See Bensaïd, '"Leaps Leaps! Leaps!"'.
84. Žižek, *In Defense*, p. 288.
85. See Seymour, 'Drowning by Numbers'.
86. Deleuze and Guattari, *A Thousand Plateaus*, p. 88, p. 90.
87. For example, this discussion of money in Baudrillard's 1989 text 'Anorexic Ruins' at once figures and reinforces the ideological reality of finance capital and real abstraction:

    Look at money. Inflation, that is the crisis, agreed. But something else is far more disturbing or, better, more astounding: the mass of floating money globally encircling the earth. It is the only really artificial satellite. Money has become a pure artefact, an artefact of a celestial movement, of a momentary exchangeability. Money has finally found its proper place, one far more unusual than in the stock exchange: the earth['s] orbit, in which it rises and falls like an artificial sun. (pp. 32–3)

88. See Foucault, *The History of Sexuality vol. 1*.
89. Žižek, *Organs without Bodies*, p. 200.

90. Deleuze, *Foucault*, p. 96.
91. Deleuze, *Cinema 2*, p. 272; it is for this reason that Žižek argues that Deleuze's thought is fundamentally materialist, while also pointing out the excess of an event over its conditions:

> One can, of course, explain neorealism by a set of historical circumstances (the trauma of World War II, etc.). However, there is an excess in the emergence of the New: neorealism is an Event that cannot simply be reduced to its material/historical causes, and the 'quasi cause' is the cause of this excess, the cause of that which makes an Event (an emergence of the New) irreducible to its historical circumstances. (*Organs without Bodies*, p. 27)

92. Deleuze, *Foucault*, p. 94.
93. Ibid. p. 95.
94. Ibid. p. 97.
95. See Foucault, *The Use of Pleasure* and *The Care of the Self*.
96. Deleuze, *Foucault*, p. 100.
97. Ibid. p. 100.
98. Ibid. p. 101.
99. Ibid. p. 103.
100. Ibid. p. 104.
101. Ibid. p. 114.
102. Foucault, *The Order of Things*, pp. 373–87.
103. Deleuze, *Foucault*, p. 115.
104. Ibid. p.119.
105. Ibid. p. 120.
106. Debord, *Comments*, p. 14.
107. Deleuze, *Foucault*, p. 150 n. 45.
108. Rancière, in May et al., 'Democracy, anarchism and radical politics today', p. 178; Alberto Toscano's review article 'Beginnings and Ends' provides further contextualisation of the recuperation of May '68.
109. Connery, 'The World Sixties', p. 87.
110. See Piccone, 'The Changing Function of Critical Theory', p. 34.
111. Deleuze, *Foucault*, p. 106; my emphasis.
112. Ibid. p. 114.
113. Badiou, *Deleuze*, p. 91.
114. Baudrillard, *Forget Foucault*, p. 34.
115. Deleuze, 'Postscript on the Societies of Control', pp. 3–7.
116. Ibid. p. 4.
117. Ibid. p. 4.
118. Ibid. p. 5.
119. Ibid. p. 7.
120. Berardi, *Precarious Rhapsody*, p. 129.
121. Berardi, 'Communism is Back'.
122. Elliott, *Ends in Sight*, p. 111.

123. Foucault, 'Maurice Blanchot', p. 16.

124. Deleuze, *Foucault*, p. 122.

125. Reza Negarestani has done most to explore this possibility of an intrinsic binding of being and the subject to an essential negativity, see *Cyclonopedia* (2008) and 'The Corpse Bride: Thinking with Nigredo' (2008). In both cases Negarestani figures this binding through an epidemic affirmationism, in which we find an almost ironic, considering my thesis, affirmation of the essential infiltration of the negative.

126. Deleuze, *Desert Islands*, p. 191.

3. The Density and Fragility of the World: Latour

Nothing that is can be subtracted, nothing is dispensable.

Friedrich Nietzsche[1]

Bruno Latour is an anomaly. On the one hand he appears to be a radical exception to the usual forms of affirmationist theory I am delineating. His work is not rooted in the anti-hegemonic struggles of the 1970s and, in fact, he evinces considerable political scepticism with regard to the Marxist or revolutionary tradition: Latour endorses the revisionism of François Furet in regard to the French revolution, pours scorn on the historic attempts of revolutionaries to 'change man', and the flavour of his ironic and provocative political stance is indicated by the title of a 2007 interview: 'We are all reactionaries today'.[2] Also, unlike in the case of the rehabilitation of Deleuze as 'pure metaphysician', Latour does not regard himself as a professional philosopher and professes his discomfort with doing metaphysics.[3] On the other hand, Latour might be regarded as a quite quintessential example of the wider mood or tone of the affirmationist consensus. His very refusal to engage in political activity or theory (at least from the 'Left' as usually identified), his self-identification as a patient anthropological or sociological tracker of networks, conceived of as material assemblages that include the human and nonhuman in 'equal' or democratic terms, and his dismissal of the modernist problematic of critique, make him emblematic.

It is this second element of Latour's thinking that in fact defines the first: being a patient tracker of networks entails, for Latour, the rejection of any radical or revolutionary model of change. To affirm the world as it is, a world in which nothing may be subtracted and nothing is dispensable, dictates a new political gradualism that can respect the contours of the world as we find it. Latour makes explicit the implicitly conservative political effects of affirmationism, especially in its more generic and 'low' forms. Rather than simply rejecting this position out of hand, a gesture that finds itself disarmed by Latour's concomitant rejection of the reductionism of critique, I want to trace the singular articulation Latour gives to affirmationism in all its scope as a rejection of any radical politics. It is the passage through Latour's work that will give us opportunity to further sharpen the political stakes of our thinking of negativity.

Latour himself has refined and re-defined his own position, within certain continuities. What stands at the core of his thought is a new constructivism that can account for, and dissolve, the distinction between social and natural. Latour has reached this position by tracing networks of hybrid objects assembled together at a level that does not privilege the social over the natural, or the human over the nonhuman, in the process of the construction of facts. In particular it has been his work as a sociologist or anthropologist of science that has defined this stance, with the defiant material success of science resisting reduction to one particular privileged form of explanation. Latour's project has been described by Caspar Jensen as the collapsing of epistemology into ontology, in which the focus is on the reconfiguration of realities, rather than the replacement of naturalist explanations of science with social ones.[4] It is this practice of reconfiguration that I take as key: a practice of tracing and sustaining connections, holding together 'objects', and attending to the materiality and density of what exists. While treating Latour's work on its own terms I want to suggest, in a deliberately provocative fashion, that his manner of proceeding can also be used to characterise the wider currents of affirmationism in the humanities and other disciplines.

In particular what also makes Latour key is how he deploys this effect of reconfiguration against the concept of critique. He offers one of the firmest linkings between affirmationism and the rejection of critique by assimilating it to a principle of division that constantly tries to establish a pure point of sure knowledge against a sea of myth, ideology or false consciousness. The classic example is the Cartesian cogito, although more vital, in terms of influence, is Kant's transcendental subject. For Latour modern thought has simply performed a series of substitutions for that subject, replacing it by the unconscious, society, economy, language, episteme, etc., while preserving its function of legislation.[5] The real target I suspect, with good reason as we will see, is Marxism, which Latour tends to assimilate to ideology-critique linked, 'in the last instance', to a reified conception of the economic as Prime Mover.[6] In whatever form, critique is taken as functioning as a kind of theoretical imperialism, extending its domain out from its chosen central point and subsuming all around it. Latour therefore offers a triple challenge:

undermining the usual resources of left politics, undermining the distinction between the human and the nonhuman, and disengaging from a critical thinking that, he claims, would firmly police these distinctions.

DISPUTING THE MODERN

Latour's thought operates under the sign of crisis, but this crisis is given none of the pathos of defeat that it holds for the affirmationists of the left. His is the pathos of victory – 1989 signifies for him not the crisis of state socialism and capitalist triumphalism, but a happy crisis that allows us to say goodbye to the dreams of critique, of modernity and of total revolution. In *We Have Never Been Modern* (1991) Latour identifies 1989 as the year of the 'perfect symmetry' between the end of socialism and the end of the dream of a limitless nature, correlating the collapse of the modern project with what he regards as its most pernicious form – a state socialism that had the pretence to control both the social and the natural.[7] For Latour the modern project has been overwhelmed by what confronts us every time we open our daily newspaper – the constant appearance of new hybrid 'objects' that defy the neat and tidy divisions of social and natural: '[a]ll of culture and all of nature . . . churned up again every day.'[8] The hole in the ozone layer, for example, is an 'object' that is at once natural, social and political. It is the overwhelming effect of these 'objects' that have led to the crisis of the modern, and the opportunity to begin again.

Crisis is not the crisis of capitalism, but the crisis of the modern project – or, as Latour prefers, the modern constitution. This constitution is the result of the surreptitious coordination of two practices: purification and translation. It is translation which 'creates mixtures between entirely new types of beings, hybrids of nature and culture'.[9] Instead of conceding the primacy of translation the modern constitution imposed on it the practice of purification that generates two ontologically distinct zones: the human and the nonhuman. The irony is that it was this denial, repression and parcelling-off of hybrids which permitted their massive production. Whereas attention to translation might have led to control over hybrids, their banishment into the general zone of the nonhuman kept them at safe distance while 'render[ing] the work of mediation that assembles hybrids invisible, unthinkable, unrepresentable'.[10] Philosophy, Latour contends, merely ratified this distinction, with a few noble exceptions – notably Whitehead and Serres. It too maintained the distinction between the human and the nonhuman, and condemned itself to the perpetual and pointless task of trying to invent devices to bridge these supposedly distinct domains.[11] Today, just like the modern constitution, philosophy finds its own purifying practices overwhelmed by the hybrid constructions of translation.

This situation is not to be greeted with regret. Instead the breakdown of the modern compact permits an unparalleled opportunity to discard the exhausted intellectual options of the present. The proliferation of hybrids, Latour contends, disrupts any anti-modern project that hopes to end man's domination of nature through the return to some fantasmatic prelapsarian state of concord between man and nature.[12] It also brings to an end a postmodern melancholia, which, despite all its claims to constituting a 'gay science', remains in a suspended scepticism still mired within the coordinates set by the modern compact. Finally, we cannot continue to try to be modern, which for Latour is simply an outmoded option. Oddly, considering their diametrically opposed positions, Latour is in agreement with Badiou in giving 1989 as the end – Badiou prefers the term saturation – of a particular sequence. Whereas Badiou takes this as the opportunity to re-invent the modern project in a fidelity to the twentieth-century's passion for the real,[13] Latour sees it as well buried. Latour's contention, as the title of his book suggests, is that we fortunately never achieved the 'modern'. We can now see that purification never really triumphed over translation and begin again by conceding the primacy of translation. This is to take what Latour calls an 'amodern' position: the happy acceptance of the production of hybrids, coupled to an engagement with their multiplicity and proliferation.

It is the network that is the privileged figure for this tracing of the various translations that constitute any hybrid 'object'. In Latour's formulation this does not necessarily simply refer to *actual* networks, although obviously new networks like the Internet have given a boost to network thinking. Instead, Latour prefers to speak of actor-network theory as the means for tracing points of connection, and disconnection, that flow into 'objects', while remaining agnostic on whether these connections are social, political or natural.[14] Such concepts are the *result* of translation, and not its origin. The network is '[m]ore supple than the notion of system, more historical than the notion of structure, more empirical than the notion of complexity, [and] the idea of network is the Ariadne's thread of these interwoven stories'.[15] The investigator is a Theseus who does not aim to kill the Minotaur – for that would be vulgarly modern – but rather perpetually traces the thread to support and reconfigure 'uncanny, unthinkable, [and] unseemly' hybrid constructions.[16]

The positive philosophical complement of Latour's network-thinking is an equalitarian or 'flat' ontology,[17] exemplified by Latour's claim, in

'Irreductions' (1984), that 'nothing is more complex, multiple, real, palpable, or interesting than anything else'.[18] Graham Harman, in his sympathetic philosophical reconstruction of Latour's work, summarises this as a baseline argument for 'absolute concreteness'.[19] This recourse to a flat and concrete ontology is the means by which Latour hopes to cure materialism of its idealistic tendency to posit one particular form of matter as superior to any other. Instead we have a plurality of equally real constructions or hybrids, which philosophy treats as equal matters of concern. This equal treatment, however, turns out to be more selective than we might imagine; Latour's supposed metaphysical neutrality is not allowed to get the better of his anti-left politics.

While all entities should be equally real some are less real than others, and these just happen to be entities associated with a critical left politics; no irreduction allowed for the supposed reductionists. As usual Latour does not shrink from putting his case in the most provocative of forms:

> It has often been said that 'capitalism' was a radical novelty, an unheard-of rupture, a 'deterritorialization' pushed to the ultimate extreme. As always, the Difference is mystification. *Like God, capitalism does not exist.* There are no equivalents; these have to be made, and they are expensive, do not lead far, and do not last for very long. We can, at best, make extended networks. Capitalism is still marginal even today. Soon people will realize that it is universal only in the imagination of its enemies and advocates.[20]

There is much to criticise here, and much to invite sarcasm. Pending a consideration of how Latour disarms criticism, however, let us take this claim from the inside. In Latour's terms the argument is that capitalism as macro-explanation, as category of division, has only gained reality through an alliance of proponents and critics. What this alliance has ignored is that capitalism itself is, at best, 'local' in its effects and does not ever achieve grand entity status.

Writing with Michel Callon, Latour turns the screw further by using Marxism against Marxism, claiming that it runs the risk of reifying capitalism whereas there are only ever 'capitalisms'.[21] This radicalised nominalism allows Callon and Latour to radically restrict the status of capitalism, while also allowing them to insist that we recognise that capitalism is 'the ongoing, unflagging, violent effort to define, format, gather together, and extend "market economy" as an autonomous sphere'.[22] In a slightly uncomfortable fashion, considering Latour's earlier blanket dismissal, capitalism now re-appears as a 'formatting regime' – the constitution and performance of economic categories that are oriented to profit. This particular effect of the commercial mode is to produce inequality as an externality, to leave this effect outside of the zone of the 'economic'. For Latour and Callon capitalism is an eminently vulnerable regime, always subject to being generated by local effects and so capable of disruption. In this way Latour has his cake and eats it: outflanking Marxism by accusing it of reification and inattention to the detail of capital, and retaining an attenuated critique of capital that has a disavowed reliance on Marxism.

In contrast, for Latour, this 'de-reification' and pluralisation of capitalism opens it to a 'micropolitics',[23] which engages with what he refers to as the 'pixelisation of politics' – what is more commonly referred to as its fragmentation. Instead of taking this fragmentation as negative Latour argues that 'pixelisation' offers us the opportunity to attend to the autonomy of each pixel, refusing any 'grand' politics that might take a larger frame as, in Bergsonian style, loose and baggy. In particular this 'deconstruction' of abstractions allows us to refuse the reification of the 'economy' into a new nature – a place of immutable, or at least very difficult to resist, 'laws'. By attending to the concrete we find that: 'in practice, of course, the economy is pixels. It consists of small aggregates, collections, new hybrid forms, etc.'.[24] This re-politicisation and de-naturalisation of the 'economy' leaves him in the unlikely company of Slavoj Žižek, although Žižek casts this necessary politicisation in more classical Marxist terms.[25] It might seem that the advantage of Latour's position over that kind of traditional left thinking is its deflation of 'capitalism' from an unchangeable monstrous world-dominant regime to a micro-generated network amenable to change. This shift, however, is brought at the cost of any meaningful politics and a questionable metaphysics. Latour's commitment to ontological equality, figured as the positivity of all objects, lacks the ability to grasp capitalism's ontology of real abstraction, and this is coupled, or even perhaps determined, by his own political critique. In an unlikely fashion Latour coquettes with Marxism, but he is only mouthing the phrases as, all the while, he undermines the possibilities of intervention he claims to be opening.

The concept of formatting approaches what we have discussed as real abstraction, but real abstractions are precisely what undermine the usual ontological distinction between the concrete and the abstract. Real abstraction indicates that capital constitutes itself as a totality, or, in Hegel-ese, posits its own presuppositions.[26] This 'totality' operates through the distribution of positive differences and the void of capitalism itself – its own lack of content. Latour's conception of a world of concrete differences and his voiding of the category of capitalism merely reproduces this ontology of real abstraction at one remove. He also falls into the naïveté of supposing that capital only exists as the imposition of formatting on a richer and more concrete world of differences. This leads him to reproduce a model of capitalism in terms of what Marx calls 'formal subsumption', in which capital 'takes over an *existing labour process*, developed by different and more archaic modes of production.' [27] This model of early capitalism supposes precapitalist forms, which are then taken over by capital, and in a similar fashion Latour continues to suppose a world outside capital subject to its formatting. What Latour cannot recognise is 'the development of a *specifically capitalist mode of production*', which Marx calls 'real subsumption, when capitalism '*revolutionizes* . . . the real nature of the labour process as a whole.' [28] The result is that Latour shoots too soon by supposing that we can reach concrete differences directly, without passing through the process of abstraction, and so occludes capitalism's ontological power to determine its own limits as the mechanism of accumulation.

Latour's stress on the fragility of capitalism apes a left denial of the capitalist mantra 'There is no Alternative' (TINA), but his presentation of this 'fragility' entirely misses its target. It seems like he give us more opportunities for agency, after all for Latour capitalism is mere external abstraction that never really exists as such and which certainly can never fully subsume reality. In fact, however, this is an over-inflation of the possibilities of action, because it neglects the function of real abstraction and real subsumption in shaping forms of agency. At the same time this neglect also results in the contradictory minimisation of agency, because Latour does not analyse how agency is formed within and against the ontological terrain of capital. What Latour cannot countenance is that being immanent to capital does not mean being completely determined by it, but instead dictates the need to struggle on that terrain if one should want to overturn it – what is classically called 'class struggle'. Neglecting the fact that capitalism is a *contradictory* totality results in a peculiar sort of reformist voluntarism: we have all the will associated with voluntarism, after all 'capitalism' never really exists to constrain us, but we are always compelled to a reformism that only ever makes micro-changes, why change what doesn't really exist? Latour's political formulations, such as '[o]ne makes a difference only in a world made of differences',[29] court fatuity – a world of differences is precisely what *prevents* us making a difference. Unfortunately, it is no coincidence that Latour's micro-politics of intervention plays the rules of the (capitalist) game: local, modest, democratic and treating capitalism as no real problem at all. Such a politics is no politics at all.

This treatment of capitalism as a fantasy of total domination at work in the heads of its critics and supporters is achieved by posing a ridiculously high standard for what would constitute capitalism. Latour himself abstracts or reifies capitalism by arguing that it can only exist if it were to fulfil its own internal obligation: 'that an *absolute* equivalence has been achieved'.[30] In this way he ignores the actual definition of capitalism by Marx as the formal operation of accumulation, structured through real abstractions, that would confront 'absolute equivalence' as its own limit – and that is therefore riven by contradiction. In particular, and Latour's recourse to financial metaphor is telling ('There are no equivalents; these have to be made, and *they are expensive*, do not lead far, and do not last for very long'), it is money that is the form of general equivalence. To lapse into a Latour-style example, when I go and get a haircut I have to pay (£10 in fact). This mediates this exchange and abstracts it at a general level, and obviously does not exhaust it. The price does not, necessarily, guarantee the quality of the haircut, the ambience of the salon, the conversation between me and the hairdresser, or whether he or she will respect my desire not to have a conversation, and so on. It provides, however, the form of the exchange, mediates the labour of the hairdresser, and mediates the labour I undertook to earn the money.

Latour's conclusion is that if capitalism doesn't reach its own standard it simply doesn't exist. He therefore misses the way in which capitalism certainly does constantly make and re-make itself through real abstraction and real subsumption. Latour's vision of a world in which 'nothing is dispensable' and therefore 'nothing can be subtracted' reproduces capital's own fantasy of a world constantly available and amenable to abstraction and subsumption. As we have seen this can only disable agency by inflating it, leaving it cast in terms of the ability of actors, whether human or nonhuman, to handle what he identifies as 'political issues' – a re-designation designed to avoid the 'grand' abstractions of modern politics.[31] The result is that we are only left able to handle such issues on the terms set by capital itself, which is the usual limit of any reformism. This is not to simply deny the value of reforms, or how they might educate us in the neuralgic points of capital's contradictions. What I am suggesting is that Latour's merely verbal dissolution of capitalism leaves us all the more vulnerable to capitalism.

It might appear that the problem of agency I have traced is imposed from without onto Latour, forcing him into a Marxist schema obviously antithetical to his own work. Graham Harman, however, has detected an internal problem of agency for Latour that chimes with my concerns. This is the fact that Latour's model of 'objects' as persisting and operating through their actualisation in networks leaves us with a difficulty in explaining change. To change requires disengaging from the actuality of the current situation, but this cannot be done if the actant is taken only as the sum of actualised alliances – which constrain the existent situation. While we can certainly change alliances, we must be *able* to change alliances: 'things must be partially separated from their mutual articulations'.[32] Without this possibility of separation 'we would have a purely holistic cosmos',[33] and so Latour would create his own fantasmatic totalisation of the world. What is absent is an immanent conception of negativity, which has been replaced by the flat world of ontological positivity and affirmation. To be even more precise I would argue that, despite Latour's claims to remove an abstract capitalism and replace it with a world of rich concrete actualities, his evacuation of negativity actually reproduces the vision of an entirely seamless capitalism that he claims to contest.

Before returning to this question of negativity I want to return to Latour's disabling of critique. Obviously these two manoeuvres go together, and we have already seen with Derrida and Deleuze how the affirmationist attempt to delimit negativity is linked to the rejection of any 'negative' critique. In the case of Latour he makes this dual process perfectly explicit, and draws out its political consequences. If nothing can or should be reduced – '[n]othing is, by itself, either reducible or irreducible to anything else'[34] – then critique is impossible, as, I would add, is any meaningful social or political change.

ACRITICAL

Latour discovered the necessity of abandoning critique through his encounter with the work of Michel Serres. We might say that Latour wears Serres's philosophy like a mask, in a fashion similar to Deleuze's free-indirect method of reading philosophers. This assimilation of Serres's thought to Latour's own project is not without tensions, which are evident in the series of interviews with Serres conducted by Latour.[35] These interviews trace a fascinating game of cat-and-mouse, in which Latour constantly tries to make-over Serres into a purely affirmative thinker while resisting Serres's own 'purificatory' tendencies – his Catharist side, as Latour puts it.[36] In this way Latour stages his own exit from critique by removing any trace of critique from Serres. Of course, this is largely true to Serres's own thinking, who argues: 'Criticism is never fertile, and evaluation of the sciences is not even possible, since they fluctuate so rapidly. Although it is valued in academia, criticism is easy, temporary, fugitive, quickly out of style.' [37] That said, as we will see, important traces of tension and anxiety remain.

The case is first stated in Latour's introduction to Serres's philosophy in his article 'The Enlightenment without the Critique: A Word on Michel Serres' philosophy' (1987). The crucial element for Latour is Serres's rejection of revolutions – any kind of putatively absolute break or rupture, whether that be scientific, political or within the field of academic micro-politics. Once again the reader attuned to politics, especially from the left, is right to be immediately suspicious. Latour, with his usual keen eye for any sign of implicit Jacobinism, which he regards as the French disease *par excellence*, wants to break from the revolutionary model. What Latour takes from Serres is a double point against 'revolution': first, that such declarations hide, repress or disguise certain effects of violence and decision that are made to appear self-evident; second, that 'revolutions' never really establish themselves, and so never really take place. Revolution, it seems for Latour, is like capitalism: both are perversely violent abstractions, which are fundamentally futile because ineffective, at the same time.[38]

Latour proceeds through a series of contrasts, trying to draw out and delineate a new 'acritical' thinking in place of critique. The fundamental operation of critique is the 'reduction of the world into two packs, a little one that is sure and certain, [and] the immense rest which is simply believed and in dire need of being criticized, founded, re-educated, straightened up'.[39] To clarify the difference in procedure Latour focuses his contrasts around the question of literary interpretation. The critique-form of interpretation is founded on three assumptions: first, the critic offers a meta-language that subsumes and re-codes the language of the text being commented on. Second, the critic's language is far more impoverished than the text being commented on, so a theoretical term like the Oedipus complex explains a large number of texts or features of texts. Third, the critic has precedence and dominance over the text; the critic knows better than the text what it really means. Serres, in Latour's account, rejects all these assumptions. He does not stand over the text with his own critical language that would reduce the text to a series of 'true' features, rather 'the text under scrutiny is always more rigorous, more lively, more modern, than the commentator and always provides a richer repertoire'.[40] In this way Serres rejects meta-language, the impoverishment of theoretical commentary and a position of critical dominance. In place of the subtractive operation of critique we have a new operation of affirmation, addition and description. Any reader of Latour will be familiar with his faithfulness to this programme, especially with his taste for description.

Of course this presentation of critique is a caricature, but one thing that any reader of Latour also quickly becomes used to is his setting up of simplified models, often with diagrams, to dismiss large swathes of existing critical practice. It is almost too tempting to point out how this kind of reductionism, carried out in the name of 'irreduction', seems to reproduce the very error he is criticising. Rather than remaining at the level of *tu quoque* argument I want to unpack further the implications of Latour's position. At its heart lies the fundamental distinction between an additive and enriching acritical position and a subtractive, desiccating, negative position. This chain of identification is extended by identifying the negative and dialectics with war and violence. In this model historical change is only thought in terms of destruction. Here we might recall the reported lapidary assessment of May '68 by Alexandre Kojève – the arch-prophet of a quasi-Hegelian and quasi-Stalinist philosophy of history as dialectical violence – that as there was no bloodshed nothing happened.[41] In effect Latour relies on the implicit correlation of all forms of critique with state-communist violence. In a manoeuvre that may have surprised Lenin, critique becomes both the philosophy of imperialism and the philosophy of communist revolution. Against this unlikely amalgam Serres / Latour proffer a thinking in which '[t]he world is innocent as well as positive and new'.[42] In case we should suspect any taint of Nietzschean heroism Latour insists that this gay science requires no overcoming of *ressentiment*, but simply *is*.[43]

The difficulty for Latour's construction of Serres is that Serres is hardly entirely enraptured with the 'positive and new'. On the contrary, Serres's rejection of critique is the result of a suspicion of the destructive powers of technoscience, condensed, for him, in the dropping of the atomic bomb; as he states: 'Hiroshima remains the sole object of my philosophy'.[44] Matters are not as happy as Latour's own assumption of the passage into the acceptance that 'we have never been modern' would seem to suppose. While Serres may be acritical in terms of his analysis of the violence by which effects of division are produced he is also critical of the fact that: 'Violence is not mopped up by science but fantastically increased'.[45] In the conversations between Serres and Latour this becomes a repeated point of tension for Latour's desire to move into a happy and innocent anthropology of science, versus Serres's more critical insistence that we remain aware of and think of the massive increase in the scale of violence offered by science.

The solution that Latour offers in the name of Serres is a principle of selection that would allow us to assess science without being critical: when sciences add variety to the world they are to be used, when they subtract variety they are to be rejected.[46] This baroque axiomatic is reiterated by Latour in a later essay: 'Is it really possible to transform the critical urge in[to] the ethos of someone who *adds* reality to matters of fact and not *subtract* reality?'[47] In this he follows Serres, who writes: 'I have always preferred to construct, or put together, rather than destroy'.[48] Taking this to the ontological level means that Latour practices a principle that is the reverse of Ockham's razor – ontological addition rather than subtraction. The problem is that this principle hardly seems adequate when confronted by actual disputes about science (or politics, or anything else for that matter). Virtually every scientific discovery, virtually every new hybrid, is *ipso facto* an addition to the variety of the world. The dropping of the atomic bomb on Hiroshima has often been defended as the lesser evil in terms of comparative casualities that would have resulted from the ground invasion of mainland Japan. Similar defences have been made of the Cold War stand-off of 'mutually assured destruction'. In this kind of quasi-Leibnizian theodicy any present violence or subtraction can be traded off against some future gain or addition.

Failing on its own terms, this ethics of affirmative addition also disavows its own violence in the incitement for us to choose the greater addition as (always) the lesser evil. This is reproduced at the level of Latour's style, which in rejecting critique aims at, as Jensen notes, a new style of writing characterised by 'a lightness and vividness capable of seizing the reader and holding firm his or her interest'.[49] Adopting the pragmatic desire to convince as the standard again reproduces the equation of what is successful with what is right. In his qualified defence of sophistry Latour denies this involves the equation of might with right, but instead argues that it permits an opening of democratic debate through a questioning of the authority of knowledge.[50] The difficulty is that in Latour's case this does not appear to be the result. Instead of 'lightness and vividness', we find a stylistic smugness which feels free to violently dismiss whole realms of thought and practice while claiming the virtues of non-violence. Latour's style is determined by violence, but by a violence that is constantly displaced onto others. As we have already seen this is visible in how Latour's own flat ontology requires the elimination of particular 'objects' or 'actants' that would compromise its own functioning, notably 'capitalism' and 'revolution', in the name of opposing violence. Driven by the desire for preservation, Latour endorses a pragmatics which celebrates effects of force, with the proviso that these effects are exercised in the expansive and generous form of a soft Nietzscheanism that makes new alliances, expands our conception of the concrete 'richness' of the world, and weaves together 'the heavens, industry, texts, souls, and moral law'.[51]

If this concept of effective force dictates Latour's metaphysics and style, what happens to (supposedly) ineffective objects? If there is no means to deal with the shifting from the 'ineffective' to the effective then nothing new can take place and all we have, as with Bergson, is the shuffling of existent effective possibilities. As Harman puts it, Latour 'seem[s] unwilling to concede any reality outside articulation via alliance'.[52] Latour's solution, as Harman notes, is the concept of 'plasma', briefly sketched in *Reassembling the Social* (2005). What 'plasma' offers is something like a 'reserve' or potentiality of objects or actants as a domain of 'unformatted' phenomena: what has not yet been measured, networked, formatted or socialised.[53] Latour, in a figure he had already used in discussing the work of Serres, conceives of reality as: 'a vast ocean of uncertainties [i.e. 'plasma'] speckled by a few islands of calibrated and stabilized forms'.[54] He at first seems to conceive this reserve as a field of positive possibilities, which would be something like the Deleuzian virtual or plane of immanence. When Latour comes to define it, however, he admits a need for negativity, in the reified form of absence: '*Emptiness* is the key in following the rare conduits in which the social circulates'.[55] Latour leaves negativity in a safe and ideological space, as the inexplicable fractures, faults and fissures that somehow make possible the necessary room for change. We have a disavowed reliance on negativity, which is left unquestioned and unintegrated.

ACTS OF VIOLENCE

Sande Cohen has argued that Latour's work 'lends itself to a suppression of social and intellectual violence'.[56] As we have seen it occludes both its own violence, not least in its characterisation of other positions, and its elimination by fiat of certain entities which embody critique. It also suppresses violence more generally by conceiving of reality as something always in need of preservation, and by diminishing the possibility or question of any systemic violence. In contrast to Serres's more explicit anxieties, Latour's suppression of violence aims at voiding the question of violence from technoscience or networks altogether. Despite being 'acritical' Serres buys into a minimal point of critique, even if it is disavowed. Latour (violently, I am implying) eliminates this minimal point of critique, in which Hiroshima and the capacities for technoscience to fantastically increase violence are quietly pushed off-stage. More than this Latour takes over Serres's rapid, and anti-Marxist, equation of the violence of the sciences with the 'intellectual terrorism' of Marxism in its Stalinist forms.[57] To parody Max Weber, we could say that for Latour it is not the state but Marxism that has a monopoly of violence. . .

Cohen's general point can be can be refined further. First, Latour's work operates a suppression of social and intellectual violence in terms of its own intervention to re-shape the intellectual field, and in the 'violence' necessary to its own segmentation and selection of networks. Second, the potential violence of networks is largely left to one side and we are encouraged, in an affirmationist vein, to simply *accept* the existence of networks whatever their violence. This is linked to the minimisation or dismissal of network forms of violence, as macro-networks such as capitalism or imperialism disappear into localisation. Third, the question of violence, in quite typical fashion, is displaced onto the political violence of 'communist' terror. Latour's triumphalist substitution of the crisis of 1989 for Serres's crisis of Hiroshima is a telling sign.

This is a result of the network model that supposes, or constructs, a world where change is only possible at a micro-scale. The very 'power' of the network model lies in it constructing a normative account of change that resists any macro-level events, while operating as a 'macro' explanation even if built from the local. It imposes a piecemeal reformism as the only true model of change, or at least the only effective model of change. I would argue that the anxiety concerning the effects of violence is not simply general, but turns on the problem of *revolutionary* violence. What revolutionary violence proposes is a macro-level change, violence directed against the limits of the microscale changes of networks in favour of the change of the 'network' itself (or, of course, the changing or violent disruption of particular points of the network). This anxiety concerning revolutionary violence cuts both ways: Latour uses it to condemn traditional 'left-wing' forms of such violence, and to ignore the 'revolutionary' violence of capitalism (in which, as Slavoj Žižek puts it, 'the predominant "normal" way of life . . . becomes "carnivalized," with constant self-revolutionizing, reversals, crises, and reinventions').[58]

Latour deploys a number of strategies to minimise and repress the question of revolutionary violence in the first sense, as the 'left-wing' overturning of capitalist relations. First, he claims that revolutionary violence does not, or cannot, truly destroy mediations. The material density of networks, or the ontological composition of things, prevents a destructive revolutionary violence ever truly having its effects. These grand changes are always blunted by the effects of the world. Second, therefore, this means that such violence is rendered irrelevant by the density of the world. Not only do they not effect the promised changes but they never could. The revolutionary is condemned to a furious impotence that can only feed an accelerating fantasy of violence. Third, if we should have acts of revolutionary violence, then in trying to destroy mediations they only ever produce new mediations. Even in trying to subtract and purify they merely add to reality. These positions irresistibly recall Freud's kettle-logic (I never borrowed a kettle from you, I returned it to you unbroken, the kettle was already broken when you lent it to me), or an impoverished version of Hegel's critique of the Terror – impoverished because for Hegel the Terror has its own necessity.[59] The 'logic' here, and it is not Latour's alone, appears to be 'revolutionary violence is impossible . . . *so don't do it!*'

To act the amateur psychoanalyst, the fear appears to be that the impossible *can be done*, which is precisely the definition of the revolutionary act according to both Slavoj Žižek and Alain Badiou. This fear is detectable because of this surplus forbidding – what is impossible must also be forbidden. It is reminiscent of the argument that Sir James Frazer made against the claim that the incest taboo was the result of an instinctive biological aversion: 'Why would a deep human instinct need to be reinforced by law? What nature forbids and punishes does not require law as well'.[60] It is pointless to chide Latour for a lack of revolutionary ardour, considering his avowed political position. Can we gain a better critical understanding of the reasons for this rejection of revolutionary violence? One vital point, made in a work that Latour himself lauds, is that of Luc Boltanski and Eve Chiapello:

> In fact, underlying the whole debate between 'reform' and 'revolution' is a problem that remains largely implicit today: the legitimacy of using violence. It remains implicit because those who, after two world wars and episodes of mass extermination in the fascist and communist countries, still advocate large-scale use of violence are fewer and farther between than in Sorel's time. But if support for violence on grounds of revolutionary necessity is rejected, how are reformist movements to be distinguished from revolutionary ones?[61]

The question they raise concerns the very definition of what it means to be revolutionary in the face of the lack of the divisive effect produced by violence, so crucial to thinkers such as Lenin, Fanon and Guevara.[62]

Traces of this same anxiety are detectable among the other, more politically radical variants, of affirmationist theory. Latour regards the 'disciples' of Antonio Negri (note the careful distancing manoeuvre) as holding a persistent false belief in the effectivity of total revolution.[63] This is a slightly ironic charge considering the often noted reformist (if not necessarily undesirable) programme for political change that concludes Hardt and Negri's *Empire* (2000).[64] Hardt and Negri, problematically as we will see, try to close the distinction between reformism and revolution. Once again Latour exaggerates a contrast for polemical effect, and ignores the ways in which the model of 'total revolution' dependent on the purificatory logic of violence has been questioned from the left. In fact affirmationist thinkers have been a part of this re-thinking, with the questioning of the logic of critique often accompanied by a questioning of the logic of revolutionary violence. Against Marx's Hegelian chiasmus that 'the weapon of criticism cannot replace criticism of weapons',[65] the 'weapon of criticism' has been equated with the 'criticism of weapons' to suspend both.

It is no doubt legitimate, and necessary, to re-think revolutionary violence in the context of the failures of the 'criticism of weapons' in the twentieth century. This re-consideration is in no way simply false, or the sign of falling back from some revolutionary virtue, but is rather a sign of a thinking of the failures and defeat of such forms of violence. The question then concerns whether we reject violence completely, or re-think violence and negation. It is Žižek who has posed this problem most acutely in his engagement with the Jacobin legacy and the question of the Terror. He notes that in 1990 the contemporary radical left itself became ashamed of the Jacobin legacy and sought to abandon the Jacobin paradigm (and Latour belongs to this moment). The reason he gives for this links precisely with our analysis of the affirmationist consensus:

> In our postmodern era of 'emergent properties,' chaotic integration of multiple subjectivities, of free interaction instead of centralized hierarchy, of a multitude of opinions instead of one Truth, the Jacobin dictatorship is fundamentally 'not to our taste' (the term 'taste' should be given all its historical weight, as a word capturing a basic ideological disposition).[66]

Žižek argues against this *doxa*, which paralyses any form of radical intervention, by claiming that the left needs to accept revolutionary terror as part of its inheritance and that the contemporary left needs to radicalise this legacy towards an 'inhuman terror'.

For all those quick to criticise Žižek for residual Stalinism such an invocation provides predictable evidence. What, however, does Žižek mean by 'inhuman terror'? In fact, it comes very close to what we have been arguing concerning the persistence of the negative. For Žižek the 'inhuman' is a position of absolute freedom, of radical detachment from 'human' ties, without guarantees (in the Lacanian formulation it is not covered by the Other, as it fully accepts 'there is no Other of the Other').[67] Contrary to the usual revolutionary model of the individual as the incarnation of an external revolutionary will, figured in the Party or the Leader, Žižek suggests that this inhumanity requires our own absolute subjection to the task of revolution. In particular what the revolutionary subject rejects are *habits*, which Žižek defines as the dense web of meta-rules which tell us how to apply the explicit norms of society.[68] These 'meta-rules' always involve *jouissance*, the adhesive enjoyment, or, to be more precise, the fantasy of enjoyment, that polices and incites our ideological conformity. For example, the school as an institution is not so much organised by the explicit rules imposed by teachers as much as by the particular way or style in which those rules are to be observed, which is often enforced by the children themselves. Hence bullying can function to 'police' the various hidden hierarchies that the overt ideology of access and opportunity occludes, but also depends on. When the revolutionary breaks the rules they do not so much break the explicit rules as their ideological underpinning, rupturing with those hidden rules that really do the ideological work.[69]

To refine our earlier point, Latour not only misses the level of real abstraction, he also misses this meta- 'network of networks' – the density of little bits of *jouissance* that attach us to these real abstractions. Latour's anxiety concerning revolutionary violence is in fact entirely true from his own position. It indicates the refusal to think of the actant unresponsive to alliances and networks, committed to undermining this web of meta-rules. For, as Žižek indicates, real terror is not simply the terror of mass execution – in Hegel's memorable formulation 'the coldest and meanest of all deaths, with no more significance than cutting off the head of a cabbage'[70] – but the concrete terror of changing everyday relations, such as the utopian attempts to re-invent the routines of everyday life after the Bolshevik revolution. Contra Latour, this was a violence that *added* complexity to social relations, especially in the vast number of 'utopian' experiments that tried to develop non-capitalist forms of life.[71] Therefore violence is not always 'violence', we could say; the violence we are talking of here is experienced as violence, particularly by those committed to defending the established order, but is not necessarily the classical mortal violence associated with revolution. It is 'violence' in the sense of the rupture of the usual coordinates of existence, a kind of unmooring posed precisely against the unbearable lightness of (capitalist) being.[72]

FORMS OF VIOLENCE

What might it mean to re-think such concrete forms of terror, then, in the contemporary context? We need strategies of negation and 'violence' that can disrupt and break up the meta-rules that bind us through ideological enjoyment, including those injunctions to create and invent which flatter our powers at the expense of any real change. While capitalism offers us continual 'cultural revolution', in the form of constant 'change', to impose real change requires a negativity that can track points of rupture – the points of ideological and material domination.

As a model for this disruptive negation of everyday ideological domination I want to propose another reference to Žižek's re-invented Leninism: the non-Leninist, anti-mediatory, libertarian communist thought of the Situationist International (SI) (1957–72). What particularly dictates the choice of the work of the SI, which retains a certain notoriety, and is by no means unproblematic, is that they chose to develop strategies to work on real abstractions (condensed in Debord's apt concept of the 'spectacle'). Also, they cast these forms of strategy in a libertarian form that at once involved the imposition of internal discipline with a refusal of the delay of gratification until after the revolution. For example, the Watts uprising of 1965 was taken by the SI as exceeding both the mediations imposed by the capitalist spectacle as well as the reaction of the international left, which 'deplored the irresponsibility, the disorder, the looting (especially the fact that *arms and alcohol* were the first targets for plunder)'.[73]

One of the most common criticisms of the work of Debord and the SI is that they remain within a highly abstract condemnation of the 'spectacle', which then commits them to an impossible position of revolutionary purity supposedly outside its domain. This is what T. J. Clark and Donald Nicholson-Smith call 'the burning-with-the-pure-flame-of-negativity thesis'.[74] Jean-Luc Nancy provides the most refined philosophical version of this criticism. He argues that the SI's attempt to designate a domain of non-appearance operates within a desire for presence that fails to learn the Nietzschean lesson – that the real world is a fable – and instead posits an 'authentic reality'.[75] Such a critique is impossible on its own terms, claims Nancy, and the SI's attack on mediation or representation results in a sterile paradox as 'the denunciation of mere appearance moves effortlessly within mere appearance'.[76] The playground version of this runs as follows: 'You critique the society of the spectacle, but do so you have recourse to language or images and so you simply add to the spectacle'.

This position on the SI repeats the strictures Latour imposes on critique and revolutionary violence. In the case of Debord and the SI their iconoclasm leaves them circulating in the paradox of trying to break the dominance of appearance through new modes of appearing – what they called 'constructed situations'.[77] These 'momentary ambiances of life' with a 'superior passional quality' are played off against the stifling regime of the spectacle. They find their origin in a vitalist metaphysics of desire and life as protean excess irreducible to representation. This vitalist metaphysics is most self-evident in the work of Raoul Vaneigem, such as when, in *The Book of Pleasures* (1979), he posits the force of 'real life' 'pushing through, under my very feet'.[78] Of course the difficulty is that this supposedly irreducible force has to re-enter the domain of representation, and so we turn constantly in a dialectic of recuperation – captured rather precisely by the designation of such situations as 'momentary'. This style of argument converges with the anti-mediatory expressivist currents within affirmationist theory, such as Deleuze and Negri. Against this neo-vitalist retention of a ground of reality as positivity I want to suggest that we take the negative further through a *traversal* of Debord and the SI.

First, we have to note that this dismissal of Debord and the SI rests on the treatment of politics, or anti-politics, as philosophy. A specific (political) assault on particular mediations (of the state and of capital) is treated as a (philosophical) attack on representation itself. This is what then supposedly leads this thought into bad metaphysics, as it can only naïvely posit some underlying 'true' alternative to the reign of representation. In aiming to destroy all mediations one has to posit some unmediated point from which to mount this critique. T. J. Clark and Donald Nicholson-Smith make the point that: 'We shall never begin to understand Debord's hostility to the concept "representation," for instance, unless we realize that for him the word always carried a Leninist aftertaste'.[79] Contra Nancy, it is not a matter of a violent attack on representation itself for the sake of some Rousseauist fantasy of dancing round the social may-pole, but a general assault on political mediation that threatens leftism as much as capital.

Matters are even more clear if we actually explore the strategies of this mode of thought and practice rather than simply confining it to some theoretically and politically superseded past, usually coded as the '60s' and condensed in the stereotypical images of May '68. If we actually examine the writings and practices of a group like the SI we find close attention to issues of representation, violence and memory, as well as the negation of capital and the state. What is at stake are the very memories of struggle the current consensus would rather not think about, except in yet another nostalgic documentary or exhibition on May '68, or when viewed through some post-Leninist or post-Maoist lens that can only see them as signs of another 'infantile disorder' requiring the imposition of the correct (Party) line. The strategy of negation pursued here is as much one of recovery as one of destruction; or, to be more precise, insisting on the necessity of 'destruction' or 'violence', in terms of the disruption of the spectacle, as what permits and facilitates the recovery of revolutionary memory. There is not simply opposition between representation and 'authentic reality', but a dialectical re-working of what fissures representation.

This attention to work on mediations and representations is most evident in the film work of Guy Debord. In fact it is the repression and forgetting of this work that has permitted the (false) construction of the usual image of the SI (Debord himself commented that: 'My very existence as a filmmaker remains a generally refuted hypothesis').[80] The fact that Debord could make films as weapons of critique suggests the vacuity of the criticism that his work involves a total iconoclasm. For Debord the cinema is 'not inherently mendacious',[81] but the images of cinema must be subject to *détournement*. The much abused, in both senses, strategy of *détournement* is defined as the 'reuse of preexisting artistic elements in a new ensemble'.[82] As the SI make clear in their critique of Godard this should not be mistaken for a 'method of *combining neutral* and indefinitely interchangeable elements';[83] the result then is only 'post-modern' *bricolage* and deliberate intertextuality. To quote the SI again: 'In all cases, detournement is dominated by the dialectical devaluing/revaluing of the element within the development of a unifying meaning'.[84] Crucial here is the work of negation, rather than the affirmation of power, or of some new ontology. This is a more or less patient work on existing elements, not simply as Latour would suppose through an act of purification, but through their arrangement in a new ensemble. What is not denied though is the necessary violence of this operation, both at the level of representations in the abstract, say elements from existing films, and also at the level of practice.

Consider Debord's final film, *In girum imus nocte et consumimur igni* (1978) (a Latin palindrome meaning 'We go round and round in the night and are consumed by fire'), which is structured as a dual reflection on the misery of (then) contemporary cinema, and the memory of those revolutionary moments that might have led to another cinema. The central image of the film is the charge of the light brigade, from Michael Curtiz's 1936 film of the name, which figures the adventure of the Situationists. This is not simply an image of heroic futility, but the image of the evanescent eruption of the Situationists into history. In his commentary Debord argues that the film is organised by two elemental themes: water, as the representation of the flowing of time, and fire, as the representation of momentary brilliance, in which water always drowns out this 'fire'.[85] While it would be quite possible to give this a quasi-mystical reading it is, in fact, deeply political. The flow of time, which exceeds and ruptures the imposed time of capitalist subsumption, or what Benjamin called 'homogeneous, empty time',[86] is both revealed and disrupted by the momentary emergence of negation. This is momentary because, as the film's soundtrack commentary announces: 'Avant-gardes have only one time; and the best thing that can happen to them is to have enlivened their time without *outliving* it'.[87] The 'momentary' is no longer a simple sign of failure, but of the recognition of the necessity that if avant-gardes are required to pass into time then it is essential that they do not make the pretence to stand outside it. The very momentary nature of the group is the condition of its openness to the *Augenblick*, the instant of intervention.

The negation of the image opens a thinking of time. Debord and Sanguinetti argued that 'the SI had been a vaster and more profound project than a simply political revolutionary movement'.[88] Its profundity lies not in some mystical cretinism, but in its thinking of time as 'made up of qualitative leaps, irreversible choices, and opportunities that will never return'.[89] It is the irreversibility of time that requires strategies to prevent the solidification and recuperation of the revolutionary moment. Of course this negotiation appears problematic when avant-gardes simply seem to disappear with no replacements, when time no longer appears to be flowing, but rather coagulated in the framings of capitalist abstractions. This was the pessimism courted by Debord's *Comments on the Society of the Spectacle* (1988), with its vision of the integrated spectacle that has extended its capillary domination into the recesses of everyday life and across the world. Instead of this pessimism, or the flip side of the uncritical valorisation of Debord and the SI, I am suggesting a kind of *détournement*, in turn, of their work. Instead of over-attention to Debord's conceptualisation of the spectacle, which has achieved the dubious status of cliché, I am more concerned with the strategic thinking of Debord and the SI, which offers means for thinking interventions into real abstractions and the necessity to use the memories of past struggles as resources for contemporary politics.

And yet matters are still more complex than simply the risk of falling into pessimism. In this conception of a residual but ever-present flow of time Debord and the SI recapitulate Bergson's vitalist philosophy of duration, simply re-casting time from pure productivity into pure negativity. Lucio Colletti has noted that Bergson's philosophy is the birthplace of the theory of reification, in which: 'the original élan and jubilation of Life is inverted and petrified into a mass of inert "objects" with well-defined features'.[90] It would not be difficult to extend Colletti's rebuke to Marxism for its flirtation with Bergsonian mysticism to Debord and the SI. To answer this criticism involves us refusing the model of time as pure and absolute flow, which even in the form of negativity implies an ever-changing flux that produces no real interruption or change. Instead, I would suggest, negativity can never be pure but must always be thought of as a relation of rupture, mixed in with and continually contesting positivity. Without this thinking negativity would simply return to the function of a transcendent outside, a pure wellspring of alterity.

Our conception of what Bhaskar calls 'deep negativity'[91] is resistant to just this assignation of the negative to what Foucault terms the 'thought from the outside'.[92] The error of Foucault is to re-code negativity on the model of absolute alterity, and to regard any turn to interiority as the re-appropriation and ruination of alterity.[93] While this protects negativity from contamination by positivities, it does so at the cost of returning it to a metaphysical 'outside' indistinguishable from negative theology. Foucault's fear of interiority is dictated by his fear of the dialectic as a machine of appropriation and interiorisation of negativity. This fear is not simply wrong. In Žižek, the contemporary theorist who has done most to rehabilitate negativity, we find that it is conceived as a self-relating negativity that appears too often to return to the sovereign individual subject – even if Žižek argues that this involves the traversal of our usual substantial models of subjectivity towards the model of the subject as 'empty' container or the Hegelian 'night of the world'.[94] While there are counter-currents in Žižek's work which would blunt this charge, the risk of making the individual subject the sole place-holder of negativity is courted. Instead I am suggesting that there are other vectors of a *collective* negativity, which does not rely on the figure of the subject but can figure a plural agency.

Debord's filmic *détournement* tries to recover a 'pure' temporality of negativity. Discussing *In Girum* Badiou remarks that it reveals a 'pure temporal moment [that] speaks to the glory of cinema, [and] which may very well survive us humans'.[95] A slightly strange remark, but one suggestive that negativity does not have to be simply correlated with human subjectivity. The difficulty is to make this negativity more precise, rather than reifying it into absolute alterity. What concerns me is the thinking of this negativity as an immanent voiding, which can be referred to what Edgar Morin calls the 'autological form of Nothingness': 'an acentric and polycentric universe, a world without aprioristic laws since our known laws of the universe develop with the world cotemporally and coextensively'.[96] This is a non-providential universe, without guarantees. Thinking negativity in this non-guaranteed form requires that it does not form a 'pure' temporal moment, which would seem to return us to the Bergsonian problematic of duration, but is thought as the interruptive and irreversible effect of a necessarily impure appearance of the negative. Obviously, in terms of the politics of negativity I am setting out, it is true that I am *primarily* concerned exactly with a correlationist problematic of human agency, and more precisely collective human agency. I also want to suggest, however, that this negativity dictates a thinking of an atheological universe – one denuded of the supposed comfort of God(s), laws or networks, which would save us.[97]

NOTES

1. Nietzsche, *Ecce Homo*, p. 80.
2. Latour, *We Have Never Been Modern*, p. 40; Latour, 'Let the dead'; Latour, 'We are all reactionaries'.
3. Latour, 'Response'.
4. Jensen, 'A Nonhumanist Disposition', p. 248.
5. Latour, 'The Enlightenment', pp. 88–9.
6. Latour, 'Never too late'.
7. Latour, *We Have Never Been Modern*, p. 9.
8. Ibid. p. 2.
9. Ibid. p. 10.
10. Ibid. p. 34.
11. Quentin Meillassoux's *After Finitude* (2008) offers a similar characterisation to Latour, in his argument that modern post-Kantian philosophy is dominated by 'correlationism', in which reality only figures secondarily by its correlation to human presence. Graham Harman, in *Prince of Networks* (2009), has explored the tense relation between Latour and 'correlationism', and argued that despite '*flashes* of correlationism' (p. 163) Latour is one of the few contemporary philosophers who can escape this charge.
12. Perhaps the most extreme example of the anti-modern tendency, unmentioned by Latour, is the work of the 'anarcho-primitivist' John Zerzan. In *Elements of Refusal* (1999) Zerzan is not content with the usual dating of the 'catastrophe' of the modern to the origin of capitalism or the birth of the state. He goes back beyond even the Neolithic revolution, which introduced agriculture, to date the 'fall' to the 'invention' of language and symbol formation. The extremity, and inadequacy, of such a position has been criticised from within the anarchist milieu by David Graeber, in *Fragments of an Anarchist Anthropology* (2004) (pp. 53–4), and by En Attendant in their pamphlet *John Zerzan and the Primitive Confusion* (2004).
13. Badiou, *The Century*; for a more nuanced defence of the modern project, in the style of Walter Benjamin, see Owen Hatherley's *Militant Modernism* (2009), which attempts to recover the utopian possibilities for an egalitarian politics within a fidelity to socialist modernism.
14. See Latour, *Reassembling the Social* (2005).
15. Latour, *We Have Never Been Modern*, p. 3.
16. Ibid. p. 5.
17. Graham Harman has used the term 'flat ontology' approvingly to describe the work of Manuel DeLanda in his article 'DeLanda's Ontology' (2008). His work on Latour implies a characterisation in similar terms.

18. Latour, *The Pasteurization of France*, p. 156. 'Irreductions' was published as a separate book in French in 1984; it is included as the second part of *The Pasteurization of France* (1988) in English.
19. Harman, *Prince of Networks*, p. 15.
20. Latour, *The Pasteurization of France*, p. 173; my emphasis.
21. Latour and Callon, '"Thou shall not calculate!"'.
22. Ibid.
23. Latour, 'We are all reactionaries'.
24. Ibid.
25. Žižek has repeatedly called for a politicisation of the economy, against, for example, Alain Badiou's tendency to leave the economic as a site outside of politics. He conceives this politicisation in re-worked Marxist terms:

    The class struggle is thus a unique mediating term which, while mooring politics in the economy (all politics is 'ultimately' an expression of class struggle), simultaneously stands for the irreducible political moment in the very heart of the economic. (Žižek, *In Defense of Lost Causes*, p. 293)

26. Marx, in the *Grundrisse*, states that: 'as soon as capital has become capital as such, it creates its own presuppositions' (p. 460).
27. Marx, *Capital vol. 1*, Appendix 'Results of the Immediate Process of Production', p. 1021.
28. Ibid. p. 1021.
29. Latour, 'Let the dead'.
30. Latour, *The Pasteurization of France*, p. 173; my emphasis.
31. See Latour, 'Turning Around Politics'.
32. Harman, *Prince of Networks*, p. 131.
33. Ibid. p. 131.
34. Latour, *The Pasteurization of France*, p. 158.
35. Serres with Latour, *Conversations* (1995); originally published in French as *Eclaircissements* (1990).
36. Serres with Latour, *Conversations*, p. 1.
37. Serres, in Serres with Latour, *Conversations*, p. 52.
38. In the terms of Albert Hirschman's analysis in *The Rhetoric of Reaction*, Latour combines the 'perversity' and 'futility' arguments against radical change.
39. Latour, 'The Enlightenment', p. 85.
40. Ibid. p. 89.
41. In Descombes, *Modern French Philosophy*, p. 13.
42. Latour, 'The Enlightenment', p. 91.
43. Ibid. p. 92.
44. Serres with Latour, *Conversations*, p. 15.
45. Latour, 'The Enlightenment', p. 93.
46. Ibid. p. 96.
47. Latour, 'Why Has Critique Run out of Steam?', p. 232.

48. Serres with Latour, *Conversations*, p. 26.

49. Jensen, 'A Nonhumanist Disposition', p. 254; Latour's own formulation of this stylistic pragmatism is that: 'The only effect to consider is the effect upon the public of this or that alliance of words: "No, he's exaggerating," or "it's well written," or again, "very illuminating," "very convincing," "how full of himself," or "what a bore."' (*The Pasteurization of France*, p. 178).

50. See Latour, 'Socrates' and Callicles' Settlement'.

51. Latour, *We Have Never Been Modern*, p. 5.

52. Harman, *Prince of Networks*, p. 132.

53. Latour, *Reassembling the Social*, p. 244.

54. Ibid. p. 245.

55. Ibid. p. 132 note 187.

56. Cohen, 'Science Studies and Language Suppression', p. 340, p. 354.

57. Serres with Latour, *Conversations*, p. 5.

58. Žižek, *In Defense of Lost Causes*, p. 197.

59. Slavoj Žižek remarks that: 'one should never forget that Hegel's critique [of the Terror] is immanent, accepting the basic principles of the French revolution' (*In Defense of Lost Causes*, p. 208). This point is driven home in the excellent article by Rebecca Comay, 'Dead Right: Hegel and the Terror' (2004), and for a historical account of the patterns of terror, revolution and counter-revolution in both the French and Russian revolutions see Arno J. Mayer's *The Furies* (2000).

60. Héritier, *Two Sisters and Their Mother*, p. 17.

61. Boltanski and Chiapello, *The New Spirit of Capitalism*, p. xvi.

62. In the article 'Violence', Étienne Balibar provides an invaluable survey of Marxist theorisations of the role of violence.

63. Latour, 'Let the Dead'.

64. Hardt and Negri, *Empire*, pp. 396–407.

65. Marx, *Early Writings*, p. 251.

66. Žižek, *In Defense of Lost Causes*, p. 159.

67. Ibid. p. 159.

68. Beckett's formulation captures, rather precisely, this negative conception of habit: 'Habit is the ballast that chains the dog to his vomit' (*Proust*, p. 19).

69. To give a trivial example, any car driver who tries to follow exactly the speed limit soon finds out how disruptive this is to the usual routines of road travel.

70. Hegel, *Phenomenology*, p. 330.

71. On this utopian moment see, in particular, Richard Stites, *Revolutionary Dreams* (1989) and John Roberts, *Philosophizing the Everyday: Revolutionary Praxis and the Fate of Cultural Theory* (2006). For an intriguing attempt to rehabilitate these utopian interventions in the present, see Owen Hatherley, *Militant Modernism* (2009).

72. In *Cold World* (2009), Dominic Fox argues that this unmooring can be understood as the production of a 'cold world', in which sadness or

desolation poses the world as frozen – a stasis that can lead to parox-
ysms of destruction (violence as it is usually understood) or towards new
worldly commitments and another logic of existence (violence felt as such
from the position of the existent world).

73. The Situationist International, *Situationist International Anthology*,
p. 153.
74. Clark and Nicholson-Smith, 'Why Art Can't Kill the Situationist
International', p. 473.
75. Nancy, *Being Singular Plural*, p. 52.
76. Ibid. p. 51.
77. The Situationist International, *Situationist International Anthology*, p. 22.
78. Vaneigem, *The Book of Pleasures*, p. 4.
79. Clark and Nicholson-Smith, 'Why Art Can't Kill the Situationist
International', p. 479.
80. Debord, *Complete Cinematic Works*, p. 147.
81. Ibid. p. 220.
82. Ibid. p. 182.
83. The Situationist International, *Situationist International Anthology*, p. 55.
84. Ibid. p. 176.
85. Debord, *Complete Cinematic Works*, pp. 223–4.
86. Benjamin, *Illuminations*, p. 261.
87. Debord, *Complete Cinematic Works*, p. 182.
88. Debord and Sanguinetti, 'Theses', #41.
89. Ibid. #29.
90. Colletti, *Marxism and Hegel*, p. 164.
91. Bhaskar, *Dialectic*, p. 3.
92. Foucault, 'Maurice Blanchot'.
93. Ibid. p. 21.
94. As Žižek puts it: 'This "nothing", of course, is *the subject itself*, the subject
qua \$, the empty set, the void which emerges as the result of contraction
in the form of expansion: when I contract myself outside myself, I deprive
myself of my substantial content' (*The Indivisible Remainder*, p. 44).
95. Badiou, 'Rhapsody for the Theatre', p. 188.
96. Morin, 'Approaches', p. 85.
97. See Brassier, *Nihil Unbound* and Meillassoux, *After Finitude*.

4. Immeasurable Life: Negri

> The good, the infinite, are nothing less than pure construction. Let's dare hope, let's dare build something!
>
> Antonio Negri[1]

Antonio Negri is the philosopher who has done most to re-tool an affirmative thinking of immanence for the contemporary conjuncture. This work was formed in the matrix of the 1970s; in the situation of grasping the rebellious subjectivities of Italy's 'long '68' (from 1968 to the repression of 1979) through a meeting between the conceptuality of a 'Marx beyond Marx' and the currents of French thinking in the 1970s (Foucault, Deleuze, Guattari). As Negri puts it: 'I went to wash my clothes in the Seine!'[2] The well-known result of this synthesis is his work with Michael Hardt: *Empire* (2000) and *Multitude* (2004) – the recto and verso of contemporary power. Empire composes a new '*decentered* and *deterritorializing* apparatus of rule that progressively incorporates the entire global realm within its open, expanding frontiers'.[3] Hardt and Negri argue, in line with the accelerationist thinking of the 1970s, that '[w]e must push through Empire to come out the other side'.[4] Rather than simply being a hymn to capitalist power, however, Hardt and Negri read Empire as the production of the power of the multitude: resistance 'is entirely positive'.[5] It is this positive power of resistance that has forced capitalism to transform itself from an imperial system anchored in the nation-state into this new global form. At the same time it will be the power of the resistant multitude that will allow us to push through Empire towards a new global communism. In Hardt and Negri's political analysis the negative is squeezed out between these 'two' positive powers.

I want to return to the slightly earlier formation of Negri's position in *Insurgencies: Constituent Power and the Modern State* (1992). Negri uses his own development of the concept of constituent power, distinguished from juridical and legal constituted power, as the key concept that distinguishes him from his contemporaries. This is not merely a matter of intra-theoretical novelty. For Negri his initial grasping of this positive constituent power in the 1970s took place as a result of 'the exponential intensification of political struggles, the expansion of the political movement throughout the social terrain as a whole'.[6] His continuing insistence on that concept in the 1990s is a matter of tracking the re-composing of this collective political power in the wake of the collapse of state socialism in 1989 and neo-liberal counter-attack. This re-articulation of collective agency would be partly borne out by the 'movement of movements' triggered by Seattle in 1999, which provided *Empire* with its agential basis and, in part, its audience.

For Negri, then, thought is always a matter of politics. Constituent power is not just a political concept, but is the result of a political experience – of the power of the postmodern multitude born in 1968, and coming to fruition in the new wave of global struggles unleashed in the 1990s. I am not so concerned here with the narrative of Negri's own political development, and his debts to the Italian political currents of *Operaismo* and *Autonomia Operaia*.[7] Instead, I want to consider Negri's work of the 1990s and 2000s in terms of a re-activation and re-working of the immanent thought of the 1970s, notably Deleuze and Guattari. Negri notes that Deleuze provided the means 'to break the structural horizon' in terms of the power of singularities,[8] but that the Deleuzian event 'is never identified with the Doing of movements in history'.[9] The possibility of the singular event is identified, but, according to Negri, never given its full collective articulation. Negri returns to the conjuncture of Deleuze and Guattari's work of the 1970s to re-conceptualise their thinking of immanence, not solely in terms of lines of flight that risk being identified with the powers of capitalism, but in terms of collective acts of resistance – 'the Doing of movements'.[10] It is entirely appropriate that Negri should carry out this project in collective terms.[11]

Despite this collective articulation and collective activity I will treat Negri as a more singular figure, as a philosopher in fact.[12] This treatment is not intended to minimise the collective or political dimensions of his work. Instead I am following Negri's own self-characterisation of his thinking, which joins together metaphysics and politics through the concept of constituent power. This power articulates the constitution of reality through the political exercise of the revolutionary power of the multitude. The advantage of this reading is that by isolating Negri in this way we can identify his articulation of the strong case for the affirmative subordination of negativity as the condition for collective communist political action. Such a case, of course, poses an acute test for my insistence on the political valence of negativity. It is only by traversing and critiquing Negri's thinking that I can further refine the necessity of negativity to the aim of collective political acting.

CONSTITUENT POWER

The difficulty with identifying constituent power is that it is constantly sublated within the juridical and political frames of existing consti-tuted power; from the viewpoint of constituted power, constituent power is figured as an 'extraordinary power' that 'has to be closed, treated, reduced in juridical categories, and restrained in administrative routine'.[13] In a Copernican reversal Negri traces the emergence of this 'extraordinary power' as *primary*, instantiated at moments of revolu-tion (the English, American, French and Russian). In these moments we witness the struggle of constituted power to contain and restrain the ever-present, but often hidden, explosive force of constituent power. This, in a sense, is Negri's lesson. We take revolutions as particular moments of emergency but, to paraphrase Walter Benjamin, we have to realise that the state of emergency is the normal state of affairs. What would happen to our conception of constituent power if we were to suspend the viewpoint of constituted power? What emerges, accord-ing to Negri, from this viewpoint of crisis or emergency is a view of constituent power as a disutopia: 'an overflowing constitutive activity, as intense as a utopia but without its illusion, and fully material'.[14] Not an ideal, constituent power is a material rupture of the regime of constituted power.

Although this power is regarded as 'fully material' and, as we shall see, fully positive, some ambiguity plays over Negri's language in accounting for its emergence in these emergency moments: 'Constituent power is defined emerging from the vortex of the *void*, from the abyss of the *absence* of determinations, as a totally open need'.[15] Here we can see a certain deployment of the language of the negative – void and absence – coupled to a language of fullness in the emergence of constituent power. In contrast to Derrida's use of the negative to hold open the gap, which is then affirmed as a positive opening, Negri leaves the gap as negative to affirm the 'fullness' of power which surges through that gap. Constituent power, *qua* multitude, comes to realise the fullness of its power at 'the point of crisis and *negativity*',[16] and 'only resistance, refusal, and *negativity* can weave together and shape positively [the threads of historical reality]'.[17] This appearance of nega-tivity is, however, deceptive. The void of negativity is only a point of crisis for constituted power, which offers an ideological and disfiguring interpretation of constituent power 'as a negative substance'.[18] This is the 'dialectical' interpretation of constituent power, which merely reduces it to the negative 'double' of constituted power available for sublation within constituted power. So, the moment of negativity plays as the effect of rupture, still seemingly given a valorising interpretation by Negri, and then as an ideological mutilation of constituent power.

In this reversal to the viewpoint of constituent power we can grasp it as 'originary productivity'.[19] It is the full power of 'rebellion, resistance, transformation, [and] the construction of time'.[20] Conceived as such constituent power is no longer capable of being assimilated by constituted power, and an asymmetry emerges in the dualism. In this form of argumentation Negri is following the seminal pathway opened by Mario Tronti's 'Lenin in England' (1964).[21] Tronti wrote:

> We too have worked with a concept that puts capitalist development first, and workers second. This is a mistake. And now we have to turn the problem on its head, reverse the polarity, and start again from the beginning: and the beginning is the class struggle of the working class.[22]

Here the asymmetry is that it is the labour-power of the working class in struggle that: 'set[s] the pace to which the political mechanisms of capital's own reproduction must be tuned'.[23]

Negri, however, wants to avoid the possible reading that would associate this new power with a *negative* rupture from capital; such a rupture would, for Negri, remain too bound to capital. Instead this Copernican reversal has itself to be taken further, to the point where the subject (i.e. the multitude) is '*[n]o longer negative but constitutive*'.[24] While Tronti opens up a gap for the power of the working class he casts this in the form of the opposition of two subjects – workers and capital – permitting the re-dialectisation of this relationship. Instead we have to go further – to the 'constitutive dimension'[25] – to the point at which we find the 'originary productivity' of rebellious subjectivity that creates and exceeds constituted power. Instead of an oppositional negativity, which would carry the risk of synthesis and sublation, we find an affirmative, productive and constitutive monism.

Certainly, in line with Tronti, Negri insists that constituent power is a class concept: 'constituent power is established politically on that social cooperation that is congenital in living labour, . . . [on] its productivity or, better, its creativity'.[26] As Negri specifies in his later interview with Cesare Casarino, what lies behind the development of the concept of constituent power is the development and overcoming of the concept of class; constituent power:

is an attempt to revitalize the rational nucleus of the concept of political class through a new concept of corporeal singularity, to update such a rational nucleus by forcing it to confront the world of the immaterial, that is, the world in which the body is given a priori as wholly constructed and artificial, as always a labour instrument.[27]

This remains enigmatically phrased. If, however, we trace the question of constituent power to the linked concepts of the multitude and its Spinozan correlate absolute democracy (which have a relatively minor presence in *Insurgencies*), we can grasp more clearly what this revitalisation consists of.

In the text 'Towards an Ontological Definition of the Multitude' (2002) Negri makes matters clearer concerning the nature of multitude as a class concept.[28] He argues this is in continuity with, but different from, the concept of the working class. In fact, Negri is here faithful to his continual political re-working of the concept of class under changing conditions of class struggle and capitalist re-composition. In the 1970s he had passed from the conception of the 'mass worker' (the worker of the Fordist factory) to the 'socialised worker' (the new composition of the worker of casualisation, intellectual labour and work outside the factory). The multitude is another name, or another figure, for the radicalisation of the 'social worker'. As Negri explains the multitude is not constrained to the field of production (industrial workers) or particular forms of labour. Instead, the multitude is a field of cooperative singularities and therefore subject to exploitation as the exploitation of the 'networks' of cooperation.[29] The multitude has, however, an immeasurable power, hence the link back to constituent power. Class exploitation no longer functions directly through the exploitation of industrial labour-power, but through the imposition of command on this immeasurable ontological surplus or excess of power.

We can see a thread of continuity in Negri's work: from his analysis of class composition, to the thinking of constituent power, and on to the ontological and political thinking of the multitude. At work is the underlying schema of an asymmetrical opposition between forces, tracked through to that between constituent and constituted power. This schema persists into one of the missing inserts from *Empire*: 'Totalities'.[30] Hardt and Negri counter-pose themselves to the conception of totality as revolutionary in Lukács and totality as domination in Adorno. Drawing away from what they regard as this redemptive paradigm, in which the totality is what must be redeemed either positively or negatively, Hardt and Negri argue for two conceptions of totality: the totality of right and the State and the totality of insurgency. The juridical and legal totality is the domain of the political scientist, who is concerned with the organisation and production of obedience and 'assumes power as totality'.[31] On the other hand, there is the 'insurgent science' that is concerned with totality as the democratic absolute, which 'assumes disobedience and rebellion as its sole objects'.[32] It should be obvious that these correspond to constituted power and constituent power respectively (and they are identified as such). These two totalities are not, however, simply opposed but are asymmetrical and atopic – they constitute different places. The science of politics occupies the place of transcendence, while insurgent science occupies the place of immanence.

This positioning reflects the terms of the dispute between Negri and Giorgio Agamben. In *Homo Sacer* (1995) Agamben singled out Negri's *Insurgencies* as failing to provide any true criterion 'by which to isolate constituting power from sovereign power'.[33] In the interview with Cesare Casarino, Negri admits perplexity in the face of the criticism. For Negri, Agamben's point is banal: of course there can be no separate concept of constituent power from the point of view of constituted power.[34] In effect Agamben takes up the position of the political scientist sketched above. What he cannot do is take the position of insurgent science as the Copernican reversal in which '[c]onstituent power does not need to ask itself whether or not it exists: it does exist, and it leads a parallel life with respect to constituted power'.[35] It is no longer a matter of extracting a concept of constituent power from constituted power, but vice versa: of challenging constituted power to account for the necessity of this insurgent constituent power. By refusing to take up this question Agamben's critique not only misses the point, according to Negri, but it also evades the question of the constitution of the political.

We remain in what appears as a dualism of constituent and constituted power. This effect is not much helped when Hardt and Negri resort to the language of a 'dogmatic and savage separation', an anti-dialectical opposition between constituent and constituted power.[36] We have to be aware, however, as Deleuze points out in regard to Bergson, that: 'Dualism is therefore only a moment, which must lead to the reformation of a monism'.[37] Negri prefers Spinoza to Bergson, but the point is the same, and his new monism requires the radical subordination of negativity. The tendencies of constituent power and constituted power are actually resolved when we realise that there is only *one* power: constituent power. As Negri states:

> Spinozism is a system of thought that knows no mediation: on the one hand, there is this power [*potenza*] that creates life, that produces and reproduces, that defines the styles of life in which freedom, love, and knowledge continuously interact in the constitution of such a process

of production, and, on the other hand, there is nothingness – the power [*potenza*] of the nothing.[38]

The 'interaction' between constituent power and constituted power is not dialectically mediated, but rather concerns 'a subtraction of power, and this is how the dualism turns into an infinity of concrete relations'.[39]

Again this seems somewhat enigmatic. Negri specifies that constituted power has no separate 'power' of negation or the negative: it is the limit of our power that has no positive reality but is always produced by constituent power. Drawing an analogy with Augustine's conception of evil as privation, Negri notes that Augustine retains his early attachment to the Manichean heresy by conceding too much to evil as a separate power of negation. Rather, following Spinoza, we find there is only one power, constituent power, and its limit. The radical conclusion is the elimination of the negative except as the figure of our own failure to realise our own power: 'our desire reaches a limit, which then we identify with the State, et cetera. In other words, this limit is a negative reality that is actually produced – and it is produced at once by our need to develop and our inability to do so'.[40] To quote the young Marx: '*I am nothing and I should be everything*'.[41]

How do we overcome these limits? In true Spinozan fashion we do so through love rather than any of the negative passions. It is love and the positive passions that: 'increasingly constitute us collectively, that is, as collectivity'.[42] What then does this do to our initial conception of the dualism of constituent and constituted power? Well, despite initial appearances, it is not a matter of a Manichean struggle between two forces but 'a question of capturing the relation between these powers [*potenza*] – intended as a relation between life and its real limits – in each singular nexus'.[43] So, it is (finally) a matter of life. The 'relation' of *two* powers is actually a *singular* nexus in which life as constituent power faces constituted 'power' as the negative limit which it has produced.

This 'life', as Hardt and Negri have made abundantly clear, is a matter of biopolitics. In an unconvincing fashion Negri is insistent that his evocations of the immeasurable powers of life are not a vitalism but rather 'a multitude of singularities' conceived collectively.[44] Why choose life as the term instead of singularities? We could risk an answer to this question through the link that Negri makes between life and the Marxist concept of living labour: 'I always try to bring concepts to bear on labor – which is why I still call myself a Marxist'.[45] Therefore the choice of life bears a triple determination: derived from Deleuze's thinking of immanence in terms of 'a life',[46] from Foucault's thinking of biopolitics, and (over-determined by) Marx's thinking of living labour in the *Grundrisse* (1857–61).

Tracing this predominantly through the last two references we can see how Negri takes up and twists Foucault's concept of biopolitics to give it a positive ontological significance through the Marxist reference to labour. For Foucault biopolitics is conceived as the dispersed productive operation of power, that seizes both the collective subject of the population and the individual subject by investing life with power.[47] The key operator of this double movement of power – both collective and individualising – is sexuality, which forms the intersection point between collective questions of population, reproduction and existence, and the individual question of sexual identity. In *Empire* Hardt and Negri radicalise this thesis. They insist that 'when power becomes entirely biopolitical, the whole social body is compromised by power's machine and developed in its virtuality'.[48] This total investment of biopolitics in the social field is correlated with Marx's thesis of the passage from formal to real subsumption (outlined in the 'missing' sixth chapter of *Capital*, 'Results of the Immediate Process of Production').[49] In formal subsumption capital integrates external non-capitalist or pre-capitalist formations, whereas in real subsumption capital integrates labour into itself and, to quote Hardt and Negri, 'society is ever more completely fashioned by capital'.[50]

Matters seem worse than even Foucault thought – we face not only the integration of sexuality as the form of power, but of all labour under an expanded capital. Hardt and Negri argue that this is not to concede to a 'one-dimensional' vision of total power, because this power that 'unifies and envelops within itself every element of social life' at the same time reveals a new context of the 'milieu of the event'.[51] As capital *qua* biopolitics penetrates the (re-) production of labour so it becomes vulnerable at every point to the vital, productive, biopolitical elements it has integrated. They distinguish this position from both Foucault and Deleuze and Guattari. On the one hand Foucault cannot account for 'who or what drives the system, or rather, who is the "bios," his response would be ineffable, or nothing at all'.[52] On the other hand, Deleuze and Guattari 'seem to be able to conceive positively only the tendencies towards continuous movement and absolute flows . . . and [so] the radical ontology of the production of the social remain[s] insubstantial and impotent'.[53]

What is required is a reading through Marx's concept of labour, expanded through his conception of Marx's idea of the general intellect, outlined in the *Grundrisse*, and the linked concept, developed by later post-Autonomist thinkers, of immaterial labour. These expansions of the concept of labour, which integrate the capitalist requirement for the deployment of scientific intelligence and machines in production, can be further expanded to include life itself as the site of reproduction and production. When biopower integrates the entire context of production – including reproduction (in the sense of the reproductive labour of birth, care-giving, etc.) and vital relationships (affective labour) – then life becomes directly and immeasurably productive. We return here to the same structure we outlined with constituent power. In the first instance we have the viewpoint of biopolitics as biopower in which the body is captured and integrated into power. We need, however, to split this concept into two: 'biopolitics, on the one hand, turns into biopower [*biopotere*] intended as the institution of a dominion over life, and, on the other hand, turns into biopower [*biopotenza*] intended as the potentiality of constituent power'.[54] We find a new 'bio-potential' that (again) drives and produces the effect of biopower as domination. (More commonly in his texts Negri splits this concept between 'biopower' as equivalent to constituted power and 'biopolitics' as equivalent to constituent power.)[55] The integration of this bio-potential of life reveals that it must be regarded as a presupposition: *naked life* as productive power and the wealth of virtuality comes first.[56]

Negativity is subordinated but at the cost of scepticism. We appear to have a more thoroughgoing version of the accelerationist politics of the worst. The more capital dominates in real subsumption, right down to the roots of existence, the more potential there is for resistance; the worse the better. More than this, this penetration of capitalist relations right down into the body is in fact a sign of the immeasurable power of naked life – reversed from its Agambenian signification of powerlessness into a pure, productive potential. This is achieved by Negri's re-inscription of naked life in terms of poverty. While poverty might be expected to imply privation, lack and negativity, for Negri 'it is the possibility of all positivity, because it is lacking in all determination of wealth, of inclusion and of liberty.' [57] In what Negri himself admits is a 'creative paradox' poverty now signifies 'the power of metamorphosis'.[58] This dictates that 'capitalist relations' figure only as the self-imposed limit of the multitude to its own powers: they are its own powers. The collapse of negativity into reversible moment of re-valorisation leaves us at risk of a monism of positivity, in which, despite all the evidence, capital is mere expression of the underlying power of the multitude. In the words of Alexander Pope, in 'An Essay on Man' (1733–4), 'whatever is, is RIGHT',[59] or in Voltaire's mocking re-formulation, '*Tout est bien*'.

Critics have not been slow to seize on this reversal. The insurrectionalist anarchists Chrissus and Odotheus argue that: 'In fact, it is this being [the multitude] that has power even when everything would seem to bear witness to the contrary. All that domination imposes is really what this being has desired and won'.[60] This is, as they point out, the schema of the most traditional orthodox Marxism. In fact it is precisely the schema of that German Social Democracy that Benjamin contested because of its severance from the negative moment of the dialectic.[61] Despite claiming to put all power on the side of the multitude, and thereby evade what had seemed to be the accelerationist vulnerability to simply finding themselves in agreement with the deterritorialising power of capital, Negri (and Hardt and Negri) re-composes the same error in more absolute terms.

Badiou argues that this conceptualisation of the power of the multitude is only a 'dreamy hallucination'[62] and that:

> As is well known, for Negri, the Spinozist, there is only one historic substance, so that the capitalist empire is also the scene of an unprecedented communist deployment. This surely has the advantage of authorizing the belief that the worse it gets, the better it gets; or of getting you to (mis)take those demonstrations – fruitlessly convened to meet wherever the powerful re-unite – for the 'creation' and the 'multiform invention' of new petit-bourgeois proletarians.[63]

Badiou's refinement is that this 'hallucination' cripples any conception of political agency by making the agency of the multitude appear *everywhere*. If everything that happens, including any capitalist relation, is an effect (finally) of the power of the multitude then we have no way to distinguish the 'power' of the multitude from what is.

The result, as with Pope, is a theodicy. In this case for Negri all 'evil' is a reactive form of power, or to be more precise the limit of the power of the multitude. What we have with the elimination of the negative is the refusal to think the reality of capitalist power – it loses any of its 'positivity'; except it gains an absolute positivity because such relations are the effect of the multitude, because, after all, they are 'really' communist if only we know how to realise this communism. In Thesis XI of his 'Theses on the Philosophy of History' Benjamin noted that:

> The conformism which has been part and parcel of Social Democracy from the beginning attaches not only to its political tactics but to its economic views as well. It is one reason for its later breakdown. Nothing has corrupted the German working class so much as the notion that it was moving with the current. It regarded technological developments as the fall of the stream with which it thought it was moving.[64]

The key symptom of this conformism was the establishment of labour as the value to be defended by the working class movement – a symptom already present in the early labour movement, and the subject of Marx's 'Critique of the Gotha Programme' (1875). For Benjamin this emphasis is consonant with fascism and with the exploitation of labour, and he counter-poses to it Fourier's conception of a new form of 'labour' which would release the bounty of nature. We could also counter-pose it to Marx's insistence on the proletariat as the agency of negation and the *'actual* dissolution' of the world order founded on labour.[65]

Of course it is somewhat ironic that Negri emerges from the tradition most associated with the refusal of work, and also for his own insistence on proletarian sabotage.[66] Even in 'Domination and Sabotage' (1977), however, Negri had argued that 'Sabotage is the *negative power [potenza] of the positive*'[67] and that there is 'a positivity that commands the negative and imposes it'.[68] Where the negative had emerged in the work of Tronti, Negri would quickly re-absorb it into a new positivity via the concept of labour-power.[69] Even in Negri's work of the 1970s, however, Steve Wright has pointed to its tendency to 'collaps[e] the intricacies of social conflict into a one-dimensional thematic of power'.[70] Of course, as Wright is indicating, this is *not* the usual Western Marxist tendency to conceive of a one-dimensional power of capital, but the contrary error to attribute a one-dimensional power to the working class or multitude. The effect of the negative, as we saw previously, is confined to the brief effects of rupture that permit the emergence of constituent power. Negri's earlier, violent, emphasis on the necessity for the *negation* of labour through workers' counter-power in the forms of refusal becomes magically re-coded as the expression of an unlimited positive power. Eliminating this conception of violent relation (as a relation of rupture), Negri leaves us with a self-relating multitude only ever relating to its self-imposed limits that it must continually burst through rather than destroy.

This one-dimensional conception of the multitude's power can lead to opposing interpretations of the absent place of the negative in Negri's work. For Turchetto, Negri remains too dialectical,[71] while for the British political collective Aufheben, Negri, and related thinkers like Paolo Virno, are not dialectical enough.[72] This seeming opposition indicates symmetry. Negri is too dialectical for Turchetto because, as an Althusserian, she takes dialectics (vulgarly) to mean the teleological 'progress' of historical stages; not dialectical enough for Aufheben if we take the dialectic as tracing the oppositional formation of differential 'moments' consisting of the positive and the negative. To take Benjamin's charge we can say that Negri cuts himself off from the *'destructive element'* of the dialectic, either in the form of the 'creative destruction' of capitalism or in the form of the proletarian negation of the existing world order. The result is a fatal 'tailism' – the conception that the historical process will mechanically produce communism out of capitalism.

We have a symmetrical subordination of negativity. Capitalism presents itself as a seamless ontological fabric composed, finally, out of the ontological power of the multitude. Capitalism in this way loses any contradiction, any points of weakness or strength, and any points that are not subject to real subsumption.[73] We lose any point of intervention, whether that is conceived as breaking the 'weakest link' in the chain (Lenin) or the 'strongest link' (Tronti). Capitalism has no negative moment. On the other hand the multitude has no interventional moment of negativity properly given. It never disrupts the existence of capitalist relations but affirms and exceeds them, and the similarity to Deleuze's affirmative reading of Marx is evident. While maximalising the conception of class agency this formulation minimises any effect of disruption – except 'disruption' conceived of as exceeding or accelerating of existing tendencies.

Negri's reading of this situation is that capital's investment of the whole of life allows intervention at any and all points – an entirely undifferentiated analysis: 'If anything, the problem is how to take action, from *any one of the points* of Empire, in order to open scenarios of global destabilization'.[74] As Negri himself admits such a conception of the multitude means that: 'the actual location of the confrontation becomes problematic'.[75] He is perfectly explicit in regarding Empire and the multitude as homologous in their lack of a centre or 'place'. The result, for Negri, is that this permits intervention at any point, but in contradiction he also argues for the retention of privileged points of intervention: 'there are always liberated spaces within globalization – holes and folds through which an exodus of resistance can take place'.[76] Again, negativity returns in the language of holes, but this 'negativity' is only ever a moment towards the composition of a positive resistance in the form of exodus or poverty. There is no doubt that Negri has good reason to distance himself from 'the obsession with the negative and . . . [with] the weakness of resistance.'[77] On the other hand, in the desire to avoid any thematics of weakness and destitution, Negri bends the stick too far to an absolute positivisation and ontologisation: 'resistance is always [the] positive affirmation of being.'[78]

It is the restriction of negativity to a mere moment or moments folded within positivity that, I contend, deprives us of the interventional 'holes' of intervention by re-coding them into surreptitious and expressive positivities. What goes missing is the possibility of the identification of agency. Negri's point is that there is only *one* agent and that is the multitude. While taking the multitude as the 'radical negation' of state and capitalist sovereignty,[79] this negation is in the service of an existent set of positive singularities. Contra Hardt and Negri's insistence on raising the level of struggles, which mirrors capitalist accumulation,[80] Chrissus and Odotheus insist on absolute rupture with 'Empire'. They strive for a world that is *absolutely other*, imagined 'in negative terms, as a world without money, without laws, without work, without technology and without all the numberless horrors produced by capitalist civilization'.[81] While drawing attention to the problems of Negri's language of production and accumulation, and the necessity of negation, this ultra-leftist negativity appears as undifferentiated as Negrian positivity. Instead, it is necessary to pose negativity that does not conform to the usual clichés, neither weakness nor irrepressible power.

THE ART OF THE MULTITUDE

Negri's minimisation of negativity leaves us in an impasse in terms of both sites of intervention and agencies of intervention. To re-pose this problem of agency I want to take a detour through Negri's recent reflections on art.[82] Art is a particularly acute site for the thinking through of the relation between agency (usually conceived of in terms of the artist) and the world (usually conceived of as the formation of the art object). The reason for this is that art deploys a working-over of the ontological fabric of capital composed of real abstractions; as Negri puts it: 'artistic development transforms the abstraction of the social relations in which we are immersed into corporeal figures'.[83] Negri's writing on art offers a more precise account of this transformation at the local level of particular relations than his more speculative discussions of the collective agency of the multitude.

Negri, of course, links the production of art directly to this collective mass productivity of the multitude. For Negri the situation of art under capitalism is one that has to be located within the functioning of capitalist culture considered as a response to the power of the multitude. In the same schema we saw with biopolitics, capitalism has performed the real subsumption of art and culture – there is no external point of resistance that exceeds the ontological fabric of culture (at least from the viewpoint of Empire). In his essay 'Art and Culture in the Age of Empire and the Time of the Multitudes' (2007) Negri therefore begins from accepting the most totalising critique of post-war culture: that made by Adorno and Horkheimer. Negri's argument is that they were correct to see a kind of generic fascism invading the mass media in the wake of the defeat of actual fascism. This invasion takes the form of a mass aestheticisation of existence, in particular through the media. The twist is that this analysis is surpassed because Adorno and Horkheimer's model exhausts itself in its *realisation*.[84] Once again, we must not take this judgement negatively. Hardt and Negri had already argued that the conception of postmodernity 'as a closed totality of repression' leads to the illusory response of a negative dialectics, whether in Adorno's aesthetic and mystical form, or in the theological and deconstructionist forms of Lévinas and Derrida.[85] While they note the moment of refusal in these gestures, for Hardt and Negri all they offer is a futile 'genteel manipulation'.[86]

Adorno had, in fact, offered a necessarily tortured defence of the possibility of a minimal negative thinking in the very torsion of 'absolute' capitalism. This occurs at the point that the absolute artwork meets the absolute commodity, in which the autonomy of the artwork at once figures its status as complete commodity and its status as the immanent contradiction of the commodity form.[87] Not so much 'genteel manipulation', or retreat into a semi-transcendent niche of negativity, Adorno's thinking of art is a working through of precisely the question Negri avoids: capitalist commodification *qua* relation. Instead Negri collapses the question of relation in two ways: by making all art and culture (and all life, as we have seen) completely penetrated by capitalism, and then by reversing this perspective to argue that this is a result of the power of the multitude permitting a new re-composition. In this way relation is voided in the one-way determination of the power of the multitude. This position is quite close to the cultural studies dissolution of the autonomy of art into the more encompassing field of culture, coupled with those strands in cultural studies that stressed the creative power of mass culture or the consumer. The usual, and false, opposition between a mandarin Adorno contemptuous of mass culture and the cultural studies celebration of the potentials of mass culture is realised in Negri's vision as two sides of this underlying ontological power of the multitude.

The very worst appears to become the best: the quasi-fascist aestheticisation of life created by the culture industry is merely the effect of the resurgence of the 'insurgent spirit' of the multitude on this terrain of completely 'perverted signs'.[88] Basquiat's 'infantile signs and utopian descriptions' are the 'simple signs of truth' indicating the linguistic production of the multitude.[89] Exactly as we saw with the biopolitics of life the complete invasion of capitalism is actually the sign of communism – the realisation of a 'new production of desire' taking place 'on a new terrain, that of the multitude and of postmodernity'.[90] The complex negotiations of Adorno's negative dialectics are replaced by a more magical reversal. This recalls Heidegger's tendency to repeatedly quote Hölderlin's line: '*But where danger is, grows / The saving power also*' ('*Wo aber Gefahr ist, wächst / Das Rettende auch*').[91] In Heidegger this 'saving power' would eventually come to be figured through the mysterious return of a God, as 'only a God can save us'.[92] In Negri this 'God' is the immanent power of the multitude – which realises both the danger and the saving power.[93]

Where does this power of the multitude appear in this culture dominated by a quasi-fascist aestheticisation of existence? For Negri we re-find the power of the multitude in their own counter-media; in the fact that now the multitude has cameras and can film police violence: 'The multitude rebelled by means of its own capacity to produce images, rendering rebellious the abstraction of signs'.[94] The inadequacy of this account is obvious. While I would not concede to an absolute pessimism that denies any power to the production of such images, it would be foolish to ignore the constraints of this 'counter-media'. The Internet may be a useful site for the distribution of dissident images, but it hardly breaks up or disrupts the hold over image production and distribution held by large media conglomerates. Also, we might question the power of such images in relation to collective action. To make a Debordist point: do these images not merely constitute further spectacle of resistance, or even worse spectacles of failed resistance? To view such images may inspire or instruct, but could it not also enforce the alienation of the spectator?

A supplementary question is: what form should these counter-images take? What precisely is an art of the multitude? Negri is surprisingly silent on this question, invoking only one actual artist – Basquiat – in this essay. Perhaps this is apposite given the collective power of the multitude, but how is this to be instantiated artistically? Negri's answer is to coordinate his thinking on art with the immeasurable power of the multitude. Life is the key term, as 'this great transformation is taking place within life, and . . . it is within life that it finds new figures of expression; figures without measure, formal immeasurabilities – monsters'.[95] The art of the multitude is the art of producing new immeasurable beings, which from the perspective of the constraints of the constituted power of Empire can only appear monstrous: 'what, then, does it mean to act artistically? It means constructing new being; it means making a global space reflect back on itself, re-directing it towards the existence of singularities'.[96] In an article co-written with Éric Alliez a slightly more precise sense of what this artistic action might be is given through the concept of Exodus, as 'the name for a transmutation of the values of resistance into the constitutive power of a biopolitics that would finally exhibit an other postmodernity'.[97]

Art, as one of the sites of this production of an 'other postmodernity', functions through an exodus 'as the only *possible* creative event'.[98] The creativity of this event lies in the flight of the multitude from the existent partition of identities. On this line of flight socially-sanctioned identity, artistic or otherwise, is dissolved by 'cosmic immersion' in the creative and immanent power of exodus – 'the aesthetic anticipation of a communist future'.[99] The un-working of these existent identities is what exposes the artist to the power of sensation,[100] which is then linked to the power of the multitude as an exit from the constraints of the art world. The difficulty is the relative lack of any direct exemplifications or instantiations of what this new political creation might look like. We can find some help in Negri's 'Towards an Ontological Definition of the Multitude', where he insists:

> Today we need new giants and new monsters who can join together nature and history, labour and politics, art and invention in order to show the new power attributed to humanity by the birth of the General Intellect, the hegemony of immaterial labour, the new abstract passions and the activities of the multitude. We need a new Rabelais, or, better, many of them.[101]

In terms of agency this art is collective rather than the work of a singular artist. The material of art, its 'primary matter' is the 'flesh' conceived of as the point of a 'common living substance' in which the body and intellect coincide.[102] Negativity, in terms of the negation or destruction of existent materials to open the space of creation, is denied through an immanent collective productivity incarnated in the monstrous production of the figure of this very excess.

Art is then the exercise of power. In a counter-intervention to this purely positive conception of artistic power the post-autonomist thinker Franco 'Bifo' Berardi has indicated the psychopathologies of social relations under capitalism that result from the integration of the new 'cyberspace' technologies within the subject.[103] Again, we should note the role of financialisation here, which both relies on such technologies and integrates them within the subject in the form of constant risk calculation – resulting in the de-realisation of the subject. In a way analogous to Fredric Jameson's well-known account of postmodern subjectivity as 'schizophrenic',[104] Berardi is signalling that, contra Deleuze and Guattari circa *Anti-Oedipus*, we have to recognise the negative side of this experience. Berardi is suspicious of the uncritical deployment of signifiers such as 'creativity' and 'activism' in post-Autonomist thought, which he regards as commensurate with a new social organisation of the '*Prozac economy*'.[105] In particular the social closure of such possibilities makes Berardi far more sceptical about the emergence of any new wave of revolutionary or radical subjectivation. The result is a highly pessimistic stance in which all that remains is 'withdrawal into inactivity, silence and passive sabotage'.[106] Although couched in the terms of absolute impasse, the flip side of Negri's absolute optimism, Berardi's signalling of this psychopathological situation offers an indication of the hidden economy of negativity *qua* negative affect denied by Negri.

Taking this point further, following Alain Badiou, we can note how Negri's own optimistic reading of artistic practice with biopolitical production is simply, more or less, the ideology of contemporary capitalism.[107] The crucial problem, stripped out by the stripping out of negativity to mere moment, is any possible distinction between the material art of the multitudes and the existing accepted 'cultural' art of capital. Contra to Badiou's implicit suggestion that Negri's position is identifiable with the identitarian differential logic of capitalism – in which art expresses particular experience – Negri insists on the flight and abolishing of particular identities. This, however, only serves to re-compose a more literally global identity of the multitude, which as we saw in the previous section appears fundamentally indistinguishable from capital. What Adorno had maintained as a speculative task of thinking through the identity of the absolute commodity with the absolute artwork as both identity and difference is abolished in a both hyper- and un-dialectical immediate reversal of the immeasurable power and dispersion of the media into the power of the multitude. What goes missing is a true consideration of the fabric of capital composed as real abstraction, and so we cannot identify any criteria for distinguishing the collective power of the multitude from capitalist action. This leaves us, to quote Hegel's inaccurate criticism of Schelling, in a night in which all cows are black.

THE ONTOLOGICAL FABRIC OF EMPIRE

> [T]he metaphysics of American power is a metaphysics of the unlimited.
> Alain Badiou[108]

Italian *Operaismo* and *Autonomia* always displayed a fascination with America. Mario Tronti argued that American labour struggles of the 1930s were a 'red sun that comes from the West' and 'more serious than European ones in that they obtain more results with less ideology'.[109] The International Workers of the World ('Wobblies') were a constant reference for 'autonomous' workers' resistance,[110] and Marx's remarks on the Westward migration of American workers in the final chapter of *Capital Vol. 1* formed the model for the political strategy of exodus.[111] America then is the positive reference for new forms of class struggle and radical politics supposedly 'uncontaminated' by the Stalinism of European Marxism – 'a history without ideological mediation, violent and concrete.' [112]

This is America as site of resistance, but what about America as site of power – as, for Badiou, the uncanny mirror of Negri's constituent power? And what implications does this mirroring effect have for Negri's flattened conception of the unlimited, or immeasurable, power of the multitude? For Badiou the ideological referent for Negri's politico-ontological concept of constituent power is not simply the mirroring of capitalist power in the abstract, although Badiou makes this charge also, but American power in particular.[113] Of course this 'metaphysics of the unlimited' is a fantasmatic metaphysics – a metaphysics of capitalism through its own self-perception as the operator of unlimited accumulation.[114] One reason for this flawed identification is that Hardt and Negri have rushed to avoid the charges of anti-Americanism that have regularly been hurled at the left since 2001 (although such accusations have a longer Cold War history). The desperate attempt to avoid an obviously facile anti-Americanism (more alive in the minds of those making such accusations than in reality) leads Hardt and Negri to sidestep the issue of *any* identification of America as a hegemonic site of capitalist power.

The problem of the place of America in *Empire* has been regularly noted by critics, and also answered repeatedly by Negri and Hardt.[115] In another of the missing inserts from *Empire* they remark that: 'The US government is not the centre of Empire and the president is not its Emperor'.[116] While it is true that 'the USA certainly occupies a privileged position in the global segmentations and hierarchies of Empire',[117] this is only a fleeting moment as we exit the 'imperial' twentieth century for Empire 'proper'. The questionable empirical nature of this thesis is self-evident, and certainly much of the critical debate which Empire has attracted has been focused on the inadequacy of this element of it to account for the situation since its publication – with the US war on, and on-going military occupation of, both Afghanistan and Iraq. Thus critics have continually recurred to the fact that arguing for the surpassing of the nation-state by contemporary capitalism is to ignore the modes in which capitalism accumulates around and through the nation-state, as well as to ignore the concentration of military hyper-power in the US.

By taking Empire as 'the ontological fabric in which all relations of power are woven together' Hardt and Negri disperse capitalist power and so refuse to analyse any elements of its concentration.[118] When we do see or find such cases of concentration they can then be dismissed as the passing phase of the old imperial model of capitalism before the full realisation of Empire. This problem is also compounded when it comes to the matter of the resistance to Empire. One mechanism by which this dismissal of American power is produced is by assimilating the recognition of the concentrations of the power of nation-states to the position which 'work[s] to reinforce the sovereignty of nation-states as a defensive barrier against the control of foreign and global capital'.[119] Certainly this is a common position among certain elements of the left, especially in its remaining official and sanctioned forms. The question remains, however, whether the identification of certain loci of power necessarily leads to this position. Is the stark alternative between national liberation and democratic globalization one that exhausts the political conjuncture? This is particularly true when this opposition is overlaid by the organisational contrast between 'parties' and 'networks'.[120] To accept any element of the national or imperial function of capitalist power and resistance to that power is taken to lead to the paleo-Leninist errors of anti-imperialism, national chauvinism and party organisation against the new 'good' form of the 'always overflowing, excessive and unknowable' multitude.[121]

To take matters at a more abstract level, and to refine Badiou's point, we might suggest that Hardt and Negri appear to impose an overly simplistic model of 'decentred' power derived from Derrida and Foucault. This ontological or metaphysical claim that no centre can fully function as a centre is deployed to license the failure to analyse the actual organisation of power. The 'absent centre' of US power places America at the centre of *Empire* as the new polycentric model of decentred model of power – currently occupied by capital but soon to be seized by the multitude. This, however, is the 'centre' conceived as network, and so the actual US has no central place to play. In many ways Negri (with or without Hardt) offers the flip side of Latour's modelling of networks. Both agree on the fundamental positivity of networks, but while Latour uses this to constrain political activity and to resist any conceptualisation of capital, Negri simply takes it as the sign of an immanent and imminent communism to come. This is not only an *ontologically* flattened network, but also a *politically* flattened network. In the case of Negri it functions to give capitalism a false consistency to all the while accrue the true consistency of the side of the multitude. 'Power is everywhere' is a banal truism, especially when it leaves us with a multitude that is everywhere without intervening anywhere.

DOWNGRADING THE NEGATIVE

Negri's downgrading of negativity dictates the valorisation of power, production and accumulation, which does not break with the horizon of capital but mirrors it in an inverted form. His smoothing out of capitalism, in the same manner as Deleuze and Guattari, is designed to multiply interventional ruptures, but functions at the expense of replicating capital's own self-image. In fact it is considerably more naïve than the deployment of the network model by the Israeli and US militaries to intervene in the 'fractalised' space of the global slums.[122] These articulations of networks, which borrow from Deleuze and Guattari, and other poststructuralist theorists, use that model to precisely manage the application of military force, rather than treating the network as simply a globally-given actuality of power. The same could be said of the operations of neo-liberal capitalist 'networks'.[123] Military and capitalist agencies might find it congenial to ideologically present themselves as incarnations of positive power, but they display a commitment to recognising or even inciting the 'friction' of negativity when it confronts their operations. Rather than gliding over a smooth space it might be better to say they constantly and actively *smooth* space. To do so they deploy negativity as the motor of their own violent accumulatory logic, recoding it back into positivity.

What is also lost by Negri is, as Finn Bowring points out, 'a conception of the interiority and negativity of the class subject. Without this conception, the prospects of transcending the alienating conditions of class determination look unnecessarily bleak'.[124] Of course Negri is usually praised for his optimism, even by his critics. The problem here is a terminological one. In everyday parlance the negative is usually correlated with failure, inadequacy and the inability to act. So-called 'negative thinking' is inevitably contrasted with the 'power of positive thinking', or, at a more sophisticated level, met with cognitive and behavioural adjustment to eliminate 'negative framings' or 'negative thoughts'. Instead, negativity speaks of a conception of agency and struggle which disrupts positivities, and so to deny or repress negativity in the name of a reified 'negative' is to limit capacties of agency. While Negri may hymn the powers of the multitude and the imminent achievement of communism, his subordination of negativity robs his theory of the ability to articulate agency in a meaningful fashion.

Negativity takes multiple and overlapping forms: reified into stasis, failure and the pathos of suffering; taken as the sign of the suffering produced by existing social forms – the ways in which capital is inscribed on the body and the mind; and negativity as the disruption

and contestation of existing positivities. I am most concerned with
the third form of negativity, and with Benjamin's suggestion that such
negativity – 'the destructive side' – is essential to act on the world
that would otherwise slide into barbaric self-destruction. Of course
Benjamin is often identified with a melancholic conception of the negative, and describes himself as 'born under the sign of Saturn'.[125] Here
again negativity slips back into the first sense of failure, depression or
catastrophe. While Benjamin referred to Kafka as offering the 'purity
and beauty of a failure',[126] we must remember in what sense this is
meant: a failure in terms of the mystified form of capitalist success, and
a failure who is failing contests and negates those forms. Failure here
signifies a *refusal* of capitalism – precisely because capitalism is the bar-
barous accumulation of catastrophe in which 'culture' is only another
false positivity piled on top of us as the victims of history.

The failure to fully tease out these forms of negativity is what
leads to the radical simplifications of Negri's theses, in which the
most radical gesture of contemporary thought fatally folds back into
a 'tailism' of capital. This is not, of course, Negri's intention. His
intention is to envelop the negative, usually coded as the void and as
poverty, within a positive ontological power. This strange twist on
the dialectic of the 'negation of negation', resolutely posed as non-
dialectical, admits negativity only as the site of superior affirmation.
His resistance to the dialectic comes from his identification of the
dialectic with capital, in which negativity is only ever the motor of
capital with no real alternative form. It also comes from his objec-
tions to the various forms of deconstructive 'weak thought', which he
argues, and I would agree, reify negativity on the model of a quasi-
mystical 'liminal transcendence': a conception of the negative as
marginal to capital, as a limit-point that somehow transcends existence.[127] To avoid these fates the waning moments of negativity have
to be re-stiched to the ontological fabric of affirmative positivity in a
Spinozist style. Instead, as we will see in the next chapter, there is an
alternative to this division between negativity as transcendence and
positivity as immanence.

Capital operates through its own form of negativity – the enclos-
ing of commons, the alienation of the worker's time, life and labour,
ecological and social destruction, and so on – coupled to accumulation. Also this never unfolds, despite Hardt and Negri's claims about
Empire, as a smooth global deterritorialised power without a centre or
limits. The very need for precision in capitalist negation, in its 'creative destruction', creates a more heterogeneous and stratified 'space'
(and time) of struggle. Hardt and Negri recognise a certain tendency

of capitalism to globalised 'smoothing', and the tendency of capital to produce what Marx called 'real subsumption'. The problem is that they extrapolate the tendency to an achieved state of capitalism's own fantasy of itself, and so overwrite this realised fantasy back onto its existent forms. In doing so they neglect the contradictory tendencies of subsumption, in which formal and real subsumption do not simply form discrete historical stages, but also heterogeneous ensembles and strategies. Certainly I agree on a general dominant tendency to real subsumption, as what Stewart Martin calls 'an imminently approaching horizon',[128] however the global and local absoluteness of this process is overstated by Hardt and Negri. In doing so they omit to properly consider new deployments of formal subsumption – the return of absolute surplus value extraction – within the general frame of real subsumption. The importance of these moments is that they often depend on the destruction of previous moments of real subsumption, for example the destruction of factory space, to begin a new cycle of accumulation, say in the conversion of such spaces as sites for creative industries.[129] The result is that the assessment of points of intervention and forms of negativity contesting capitalism are occluded. If capital is everywhere then it is also nowhere, and although this seems to encourage struggle at every point it completely loses any strategic sense of the possibilities of negation and intervention.

This abandons the key point of Marx, which was seemingly recognised in Negri's work of the 1970s in terms of the refusal of work; namely, that proletarian negativity, the negation or dissolution of labour and of production, is the key stress point in the reproduction of capitalist accumulation. Of course, as the debates of the 1970s prove, part of the reason for Negri's disengagement from this insight was to avoid a pure concentration on the workers of the large factories and to map the multiplicity of struggles across the social field. I am not arguing for us to jettison this insight and return to a classical workerism or labourism in the 'bad' sense. What I want to recover from Negri's complete positivisation of Marxism is his earlier radically anti-productivist and anti-teleological Marxism. Therefore it is not so much a return to the factory per se as a closer mapping of the negations of labour *in all its forms*, including the necessity of the articulation of negativity with the persistence of the factory form.[130] I doubt that the expansive concept of immaterial labour can really serve this need of articulation, which it instead prefers to replace with an undifferentiated concept of expression. In a sense, and this is the attraction of Negri's work, all the elements are there – notably tendency, immanence and refusal of work. It is their persistent ontological and affirmative articulation, as well as the exaggeration and flattening of both temporal and spatial coordinates, that leaves them fatally compromised.

Of course the value of negativity I am arguing for is what is usually taken as its source of failure: the fact it merely negates particular instances and forms of positivity, and so cannot stand on its own two feet. In the Nietzschean atmosphere of affirmationism this immediately leads to the charge of *ressentiment*. Two points: first, as Fredric Jameson points out, '*Ressentiment* is the primal class passion'.[131] There is a material hatred that emerges from the effects of alienation and negation: 'the fear of modern people that they have not really lived, not yet lived or fulfilled their lives, in a world organized to deprive them of that satisfaction'.[132] *Ressentiment* is not just the sign of a failure to become truly active, but the sign or beginning of a passion to negate the negation of life imposed on us. It is a precise and local recognition of an experience of suffering imposed on us through a negation passing itself off as a positivity. Second, as I have just suggested, it is this *ressentiment* which gives precision to the negation of positivity, in which an internal negativity disrupts positivity. Rather than remaining in Berardi's 'intellectual potency of depression', which remains both too pessimistic (in its correlation of negativity with depression) and too optimistic (in its valorisation of potency), we can seek an alternative form of courage that might re-work suffering and hatred in a truly political direction.

NOTES

1. Negri in Negri and Fadini, 'Materialism and Theology', p. 668.
2. Negri in Casarino and Negri, 'It's a Powerful Life', p. 153. After repeating the same metaphor in another context, Negri explains:

   in other words I created a hybrid between my workerist Marxism and the perspectives of French post-structuralism. I had already begun to do this during my years in prison (from 1979 to 1983), working on Spinoza, an excellent terrain of ontological encounter for this operation. (*Reflections on Empire*, p. 13)

3. Hardt and Negri, *Empire*, p. xii.
4. Ibid. p. 206.
5. Ibid. pp. 361–2.
6. Negri in Casarino and Negri, 'It's a Powerful Life', p. 152.
7. For contextual readings of Negri's development see Steve Wright's *Storming Heaven* (2002), and Finn Bowring's article 'From the mass worker to the multitude' (2004).
8. Negri in Casarino and Negri, 'It's a Powerful Life', p. 153.
9. Ibid. p. 155.

10. Éric Alliez has insisted that Deleuze and Guattari's work will be mis-understood unless we note that they trace an '*absolute* form of deter-ritorialisation' that can 'cause the capitalist process of valorisation itself to flee' ('*Anti-Oedipus* – thirty years on', p. 8). We can see Negri's own work as a development of this point, and Alliez's own work with Negri suggests this convergence (see Alliez and Negri 'Peace and War').

11. Negri has continued his politically collaborative practices of the 1970s working on the journals *Futur Antérieur* (1990–7), *Posse*, and *Multitudes*, as well as his co-writing with Michael Hart and Éric Alliez.

12. There is a precedent for this approach to Negri as a philosopher set by the collection edited by Murphy and Mustafa, *The Philosophy of Antonio Negri Volume Two: Revolution in Theory* (2007).

13. Negri, *Insurgencies*, p. 2.

14. Ibid. p. 14.

15. Ibid. p. 14; my emphasis.

16. Ibid. p. 320; my emphasis.

17. Ibid. p. 321; my emphasis.

18. Ibid. p. 317.

19. Ibid. p. 23.

20. Ibid. p. 24.

21. Tronti, 'Lenin in England'; and see Negri's comments on Tronti in *Reflections on Empire*, pp. 36–7.

22. Tronti, 'Lenin in England'.

23. Ibid.

24. Negri, *Reflections on Empire*, p. 38.

25. Ibid. p. 48.

26. Negri, *Insurgencies*, p. 33.

27. Negri in Casarino and Negri, 'It's a Powerful Life', p. 160.

28. In Negri, *Reflections on Empire*, pp. 114–25.

29. Hardt and Negri, *Multitude*, pp. xiv–xv.

30. Hardt and Negri in Brown et al., '"Subterranean Passages of Thought"', p. 195–7.

31. Ibid. p. 196.

32. Ibid. p. 196.

33. Agamben, *Homo Sacer*, p. 43.

34. Negri in Casarino and Negri, 'It's a Powerful Life', p. 177.

35. Ibid. p. 177.

36. Hardt and Negri in Brown et al., '"Subterranean Passages of Thought"', p. 202.

37. Deleuze, *Bergsonism*, p. 29.

38. Negri in Casarino and Negri, 'It's a Powerful Life', p. 168.

39. Ibid. p. 168.

40. Ibid. p. 170.

41. Marx, *Early Writings*, p. 254.

42. Negri in Casarino and Negri, 'It's a Powerful Life', p. 170.

43. Ibid. p. 172.
44. Ibid. p. 168.
45. Ibid. p. 167.
46. Deleuze, 'Immanence: A Life', in *Pure Immanence*, pp. 25–33.
47. Foucault, *The History of Sexuality vol.1*.
48. Hardt and Negri, *Empire*, p. 24.
49. Marx, *Capital vol. 1*, pp. 941–1084; for the distinction between formal and real subsumption see pp. 1019–38.
50. Hardt and Negri, *Empire*, p. 255.
51. Ibid. p. 25.
52. Ibid. p. 28.
53. Ibid. p. 28.
54. Negri in Casarino and Negri, 'It's a Powerful Life', p. 167.
55. Negri, *Reflections on Empire*, pp. 73–4.
56. See Negri, '*Kairòs,* Alma Venus, Multitudo'.
57. Ibid. p. 221.
58. Ibid. p. 246.
59. Pope, 'An Essay on Man', p. 280.
60. Chrissus and Odotheus, *Barbarians: disordered insurgence*, p. 17.
61. Ibid. p. 17.
62. Badiou, 'Beyond Formalisation', p. 126.
63. Badiou, *Polemics*, p. 45.
64. Benjamin, *Illuminations*, p. 258; and see Chrissus and Odotheus, *Barbarians: disordered insurgence*, p. 21.
65. Marx, *Early Writings*, p. 256.
66. Negri, 'Domination and Sabotage' (1977), in *Books for Burning*, pp. 231–90. On proletarian self-activity in this period see in particular Nanni Balestrini's novel *The Unseen* (1989).
67. Negri, *Books for Burning*, p. 258.
68. Ibid. p. 259.
69. There was another tradition that held on more strongly to this moment of 'negative' thought emerging from *Operaismo*, notably in the work of Manfredo Tafuri and Massimo Cacciari, see Matteo Mandarini, 'Not Fear but Hope in the Apocalypse' and Gail Day's 'Strategies in the Metropolitan Merz'. In fact, it was Negri's discomfort with the results of this movement that in part led to his suspicion of the negative, see Mandarini, 'Beyond Nihilism'.
70. Wright, *Storming Heaven*, p. 157.
71. Turchetto, 'The Empire Strikes Back'.
72. Aufheben, 'Keep on smiling' and 'The language of retreat'.
73. This question has been raised by a number of thinkers and activists (Massimo De Angelis and Peter Linebaugh, for example, and also see the journal *The Commoner*). They have argued that capitalist accumulation is not a one-off moment belonging to the origins of capital, but an ongoing and continuous process. Rather than real subsumption being

fully completed capitalism engages in a constant struggle to absorb its 'outside', in the form of the 'commons' (now generalised to include everything from knowledge – the 'knowledge commons' – to the capitalist capture of nature – eco-accumulation). Aufheben (in 'Value struggle or class struggle?') have pointed out the tendency of a dangerous symmetry to arise between the Negrian conception of capital having no outside and the undialectical invocation of a 'pure' outside. Instead they insist on the more complex mediations of the relation of the proletariat to capital, which involve both the negative moments of our experiences of alienation and exploitation and the positive moments of our experiences of struggle. While broadly in agreement with this conception I would also argue that struggle forms a moment of negativity, posed against capitalist negativity.

74. Negri, *Reflections on Empire*, p. 25; my emphasis.
75. Ibid. p. 106.
76. Ibid. p. 26.
77. Negri, '*Kairòs,* Alma Venus, Multitudo', p. 241; see Mandarini, 'Beyond Nihilism', for a detailed contextual reconstruction of some of the reasons for Negri's wariness.
78. Negri, '*Kairòs,* Alma Venus, Multitudo', p. 179.
79. Negri, *Reflections on Empire*, p. 107.
80. Negri explicitly uses the term 'ontological accumulation' (*Reflections on Empire*, p. 137), when referring to the production of struggle.
81. Chrissus and Odotheus, *Barbarians: disordered insurgence*, p. 78.
82. See Toscano, 'The Sensuous Religion of the Multitude' for a contextualisation of the range of Negri's writing on art.
83. Negri, 'Metamorphoses', p. 22.
84. Negri, 'Art and Culture', p. 50.
85. Hardt and Negri, in Brown et al., '"Subterranean Passages of Thought"', p. 201.
86. Ibid. p. 201.
87. Martin, 'The Absolute Artwork', and Roberts 'Art and Its Negations'.
88. Negri, 'Art and Culture', p. 49.
89. Ibid. p. 49.
90. Ibid. p. 50.
91. Quoted in Heidegger, *The Question Concerning Technology*, p. 28, and for this motif recurring in Hardt and Negri see Turchetto, 'The Empire Strikes Back', p. 35.
92. Heidegger, '"Only a God Can Save Us"'.
93. This theological reading of Negri is, of course, pre-empted to a degree by his own turn to theology, as he states:

> I have never had anything against religion, I am simply against transcendence. I absolutely reject every form of transcendence. But certain aspects of religion, especially certain religious experiences, truly have

the capacity to construct, not in a mystical form but in an ascetic manner. (quoted in Stolze, 'Marxist Wisdom', p. 129)

Negri has pursued this 'materialist' re-inscription of religious experience most in texts written during his periods of imprisonment: *The Labor of Job*, begun in 1982 or 1983, and '*Kairòs*, Alma Venus, Multitudo' (2000). See also the interview Negri and Fadini, 'Materialism and Theology', and the sympathetic discussion of this re-inscription by Stolze, 'Marxist Wisdom'.

94. Negri, 'Art and Culture', p. 49.
95. Ibid. p. 51; see also Negri, *Reflections on Empire*, pp. 24–5.
96. Negri, 'Art and Culture', p. 55.
97. Alliez and Negri, 'Peace and War', p. 115.
98. Ibid. p. 114.
99. Ibid. p. 114.
100. See Deleuze, *Francis Bacon*.
101. Negri, *Reflections on* Empire, p. 118.
102. Ibid. p. 118.
103. Berardi, *Precarious Rhapsody*, pp. 108–22, p. 131.
104. Jameson, *Postmodernism, or The Cultural Logic of Late Capitalism*.
105. Berardi, *Precarious Rhapsody*, p. 126.
106. Ibid. p. 127.
107. Badiou, *Logics of Worlds*, p. 2.
108. Badiou, *Polemics*, p. 45.
109. Tronti, 'Workers and Capital'.
110. Alliez, 'Hegel and the Wobblies'.
111. Virno, *A Grammar of the Multitude*, p. 70.
112. Marazzi in Lotringer and Marazzi, 'The Return of Politics', p. 11.
113. Gregory Elliott makes the most acerbic version of this charge, when he argues that *Empire* 'is ultimately a mutant Browderism: Americanism is, after all, Communism' (*Ends in Sight*, p. 118). The reference to 'Browderism' is, for those unfamiliar with the history of the communist movement, to the policy of Earl Russell Browder, General Secretary of the Communist Party USA. In 1944 he argued that American capitalism could peacefully evolve towards Communism, and identified American capitalism with an embryonic communism with the slogan 'Americanism is Communism', and for this reason was expelled from the party in 1946.
114. Žižek, *The Parallax View*, p. 263.
115. Hardt and Negri, *Empire*, pp. 179–80; See also Negri, *Reflections on Empire*, pp. 16–18.
116. Hardt and Negri, in Brown et al, '"Subterranean Passages of Thought"', pp. 210–11.
117. Ibid. p. 211.
118. Hardt and Negri, *Empire*, p. 354; for a more sympathetic reading

of Negri's dispersion of struggle across the social field see Toscano, 'Factory, Territory, Metropolis, Empire' (2004).

119. Hardt, 'Today's Bandung?', p. 114.
120. Ibid. pp.116–18.
121. Ibid. p. 117.
122. Weizman, *Hollow Land*, pp. 185–218; Monk, 'Hives and Swarms'; and Croser, 'Networking Security'.
123. Mitchell, 'Dreamland'.
124. Bowring, 'From the mass worker to the multitude', p. 127.
125. See Susan Sontag, 'Under the Sign of Saturn'.
126. Benjamin, *Illuminations*, p. 145.
127. Negri, '*Kairòs*, Alma Venus, Multitudo', p. 192.
128. Martin, 'Artistic Communism', p. 493.
129. Benedict Seymour has identified this return of formal subsumption in economies dominated by real subsumption as 'surreal subsumption'. This is to indicate its distance from original processes of accumulation. See Seymour 'Drowning by Numbers'.
130. For such a mapping see John Roberts, 'Productivism and Its Contradictions'.
131. Jameson, 'Marx's Purloined Letter', p. 39.
132. Ibid. p. 40.

5. On the Edge of the Negative: Badiou

Alain Badiou places his philosophy unequivocally under the sign of affirmation, insisting that: '[philosophy] must break with whatever leads it through nihilistic detours, that is, with everything that restrains and obliterates affirmative power'.[1] This affirmative philosophy was originally politically conditioned by May '68, which derailed Badiou from the expected bourgeois coordinates of his life.[2] The difference between Badiou and many of the other thinkers of his generation is that he has always, to use his own term, retained fidelity to this inheritance.[3] The nostalgic or dismissive image of Badiou as the last *soixante-huitard* is, however, deceptive. What matters more is Badiou's effort to *maintain* a thought of rupture, not by simply repeating revolutionary dogma but by adapting his thinking to persist in unpropitious times. His affirmative conception of philosophy was explicitly formulated in terms of maintaining resistance in the face of the weakening of thought associated with the 1980s (and dating for Badiou from 1976).[4] Although Badiou's thinking was initially conditioned by an external event of rupture he has developed and elaborated that thought in the seeming *absence* of such events. To hold on in this state of absence, Badiou implies, requires an affirmative thinking unwilling to concede to the *doxa* of 'weak thought' or to a negative dialectics that finds itself all too consonant with contemporary ideology.[5]

Sustaining a radical philosophy of rupture in this context demands the insistence that 'to be on the side of creation, affirmation and an egalitarian collective future' requires the affirmative appeal to events.[6] Badiou styles himself as an unabashed affirmationist and because of this, despite his hostility, the 'secret sharer' of Antonio Negri – another radical affirmationist who survived the 'polar night' of the 1980s with his politics intact. In both cases, I am suggesting, affirmationism becomes the source of resistance, although in very different forms. No doubt this characterisation reflects the dominant orientation of Badiou's thought, and yet it might then come as a surprise that in an interview given in 2007 Badiou insisted that we re-think the categories of critique and negation 'beyond the concept of a negation taken solely in its destructive and properly negative aspect'.[7] He also conceded 'our contemporary need to produce a non-Hegelian category of negation'.[8] This is not a simple *volte-face*. Badiou's two-fold orientation, which insists both on affirmation and the need to re-invent the negative in the face of what he calls 'this crisis of negation today',[9] is explicable if we return to his sequential analysis of contemporary thought. Badiou's own historical probes reveal that the shifting emphasis between negation and affirmation must itself be understood as historically and politically conditioned. Instead of taking the somewhat forbidding and abstract appearance of Badiou's thought at face value we need to grasp his insistence that philosophy is conditioned from outside (by art, science, politics and love), and that philosophy provides a conceptual framework for grasping its own conditions.[10]

Badiou's affirmationism, I contend, is historically conditioned by the desire to resist the experience of defeat occasioned by the restoration of the 1980s (and of course continuing still, despite various points of resistance).[11] In Badiou's periodisation, given in the Preface to the English edition of *Metapolitics*, the period 1976 to 1995 is characterised as 'counter-revolutionary'. This is then succeeded by a more obscure period, dating from the protest movements in France of 1995, characterised by reactionary phenomena (racism, the crisis in the Middle East, aggressive defences of the capitalist status quo) and by signs of a progressive recovery, especially among youth.[12] For Badiou it is a point of justifiable pride to have conceded nothing to the betrayal of the cause of an egalitarian politics. This resistance, this ability to hold on, is partially conditioned by affirmation, which provides the prescriptive point of resistance against the disintegrative 'organized disorientation'[13] of contemporary capitalism. While respecting the political imperative that drives Badiou's thinking, although not agreeing with all his formulations, it is exactly this kind of stabilisation of the possibility of philosophy and grand politics by affirmation that I have been contesting. That said, Badiou's own sympathetic return to possibilities of the negative is crucial for the re-orientation of theory which I am attempting. If Derrida remained a liminal figure for the entrance into affirmationism, Badiou is a liminal figure for an exit from it.

HISTORICISING THE NEGATIVE

Badiou's seemingly contradictory attitude to the negative makes sense only if located against his own periodisation of the twentieth century. In *The Century* (2005) Badiou argues that the 'short' twentieth century (1917–1989), the communist century conditioned by revolution and war, is dominated by *'the passion for the real'*.[14] This is the passion to realise the utopias of the nineteenth century through the programme of 'changing man, of creating a new man.' [15] It is this programme that forms the meta-condition of the four 'conditions' of politics, art, science and love. In each case the aim is to extract and purify the real 'from the reality that envelops and conceals it.' [16] This purification involves attention to form – the real is not some concealed content disguised by existent forms, but is only reached through a radical formalisation (not a formalism) that can serve to extract it.[17] Perhaps the best example here is from science. Quantum physics – which profoundly destabilises our usual sense of reality to render the 'Real' of the quantum realm – is achieved through an extreme mathematical formalisation. The various well-known exemplary thought experiments associated with quantum physics, such as Schrödinger's cat, are merely imaginary (in the Lacanian sense) guides compared to the density of this formalisation, although, of course, also useful sites for further development and formalisation.[18]

Badiou identifies two privileged procedures to achieve this access to the real: destruction and subtraction. The first proceeds by unmasking copies and discrediting fakes; it is dedicated to the authentic, and to an endless and violent process to achieve this truth. In art we could reference Dada and certain tendencies in Surrealism as its supreme instance, in which the desire to dwell in the purity of the absolutely real finds its final correlate in suicide – what we might call absolute terror directed against the self. In contrast subtraction is 'a differential and differentiating passion devoted to the construction of a minimal difference, to the delineation of its axiomatic'.[19] Badiou's example is Malevich's *White on White* (1918), which 'opposes minimal difference to maximal destruction'.[20] Here is a contemporaneous avant-garde strategy that does not try to render the real directly as an identity, but to render the real as an *opening*. I leave aside the question whether this is an exhaustive description of the twentieth century, and especially its artistic production.[21] I am more concerned with the question of the coordination of these two forms of the passion for the real, especially considering Badiou's identification of destruction with negation.

First, in terms of dating and the overall contours of analysis, Badiou implies that these two forms arise simultaneously. And yet it is obvious in Badiou's own account that he privileges subtraction over destruction. Whereas destruction is 'doomed to incompletion, a figure of the bad infinite', subtraction permits 'the staging of a minimal, albeit absolute, difference'.[22] Here Badiou is staging a self-criticism in relation to his own embrace of destruction circa *Theory of the Subject* (1982) as the 'torsion' that 'ravages its places, in a laborious duration.'[23] Now that embrace is re-cast in the terms of Hegel's critique of the Terror, in which destruction is correlated with the bad infinite of trying to track the real to a final, pure and ineliminable identity that always remains out of reach and so which thus fuels further cycles of destruction.[24] In contrast subtraction does not produce the real as an identity, but as a gap to always be kept open – so Malevich's *White on White* stages the real as the 'gap' between the two squares. In making subtraction contemporaneous Badiou can at once claim fidelity to the twentieth century as the century of the 'passion for the real', while at the same time distancing himself from it as a sequence of destruction. Also, considering Badiou's identification of destruction with negation, the privileging of subtraction implies, at best, the radical subordination of negation.

Despite his caveats Badiou also appears to imply a definite periodisation in which the twentieth century is dominated by destruction, and now this must be surpassed to achieve a recovery of the 'minor' (in the Deleuze-Guattari sense) current of subtraction.[25] While Badiou does not disavow destruction, after all as he remarks 'many things deserve to be destroyed',[26] we may feel a little suspicious of the implicit teleology of the transition from (now bad) destruction to (good) subtraction. Let us take the case of politics. Badiou argues that the Marxist and Leninist tradition of the twentieth century was dominated by the idea 'that destruction alone was capable of opening a new man, and so on'.[27] On the contrary, Badiou argues, 'I think we must assert that today negativity, properly speaking, does not create anything new'.[28] Marxism, it appears, is ironically confined to its own metaphoric trash-can of history. Again, the claim that subtraction is synchronous with destruction allows Badiou to rescue communism from this ignominy by arguing that we can recover it from the discourse of war and destruction and so figure a 'subtractive' communism.[29] Today, Badiou argues, to stay faithful to communism requires an 'originary subtraction capable of creating a new space of independence and autonomy from the dominant laws of the situation'.[30] In common with a number of contemporary thinkers and theorists Badiou puts his faith in the creation of independent 'zones' or 'spaces' of resistance that can be subtracted from the laws of capital and the state.[31] Destruction still has a place here, but only a strictly secondary one – as the necessity of the defensive function of violence necessary to defend these new independent spaces, as a 'protective force, capable of defending something created through a movement of subtraction';[32] once again, destruction or negation cannot create anything new on its own.

Badiou applies much the same argument to art. While destruction may have been a justifiable impulse of the avant-gardes, which also drew on the model of war to figure artistic practice, today we must return to subtraction. What is required for art is that it resist the forces of the state and capital by subtracting its works from them through an 'an independent affirmation'.[33] Creativity is lodged in this independence of affirmation, with negation becoming correlated with a dependent and reactive, in the Nietzschean sense, practice, which cannot invent anything new. If we link this temporal and conceptual mapping of art to the development of Badiou's own work then we can more clearly grasp his dismissal of negation, assimilated to destruction, and the endorsement of subtraction. The explicit Maoist phase of Badiou's work, which we can date from 1968 to *Theory of the Subject*, is dominated by the thematic of destruction.[34] The new phase of his 'mature' philosophy, summarised in *Being and Event* (1988), is marked by the dominance of subtraction and affirmation. This transition takes place in the reactionary context of the 1980s, as Badiou loses faith (no doubt with justification) in the applicability of the Maoist-Leninist model and seeks out a new model of affirmative politics that can resist the retreat into 'weak' and 'negative' thought. Badiou's mapping of the century is then also a reflexive self-mapping, and his new appreciation of the negative still, as we will see, subordinated to the subtractive.

We can refine this historicisation further by paying a little more attention to the local conditions of Badiou's re-thinking of destruction and subtraction. In the 1970s Badiou articulated his dialectic of destruction in terms of history and politics, especially the history of the masses, figured in Maoist terms as the agents of history ('the masses make history'), via a coupling to the party.[35] This entailed, in the context of French radical politics, a classically Maoist position of occupying the correct line of the 'centre-left' against right-wing and left-wing deviations.[36] Badiou's organisation – the *Groupe pour la Fondation de l'Union des Communistes de France Marxiste-Léniniste* (UCFML) – defined itself in struggle against two Maoist groups: the *Parti Communiste de Marxiste-Léniniste de France* (PCLMF) on the right and *Gauche Prolétarienne* (GP) on the left.[37] The PCLMF represented a retrograde hyper-Stalinist configuration, obsessed with a doctrinal purity that prevented any innovation, while GP incarnated an adventurist 'ultra-leftism' that failed to grasp the true political contradictions of the period. Outside of this micro-Maoist context the UCFML defined themselves more widely against the right-wing deviation ('modern revisionism') of the *Parti Communiste Français* (PCF) and its associated union the *Confédération Générale du Travail* (CGT),[38] regarded by them (with some justification) as atrophied Stalinist forms, and against the left-wing deviation of the various libertarian groupuscles, who completely rejected the party form. This political identification was overlain with a theoretical one. In illegitimate theoretical terms, considering the disputes between Althusser and the PCF, the right-wing deviation was identified with a static structuralism that regarded social relations as fixed in places. On the other hand, the left-wing deviation was identified with Deleuze and Guattari's model of free-floating desire, regarded by Badiou as a model of pure force inattentive to the structural effects of place. The dialectical solution was the mutual interlocking for force and place, mediated through the party as operator, which would allow actual revolutionary intervention.[39]

In this context destruction functioned as a mechanism of division, used both against the stabilising and accomodationist PCF, and to distinguish the UCFML from 'weightless' neo-libertarian positions. We might suggest that the difficulty in sustaining this position in the early 1980s did not come solely from being, as Peter Hallward argues, 'confronted by the historical wreckage of actually-existing Maoism',[40] which the unsympathetic could easily suggest had been self-evident before that time. Instead, I want to suggest that the crisis of destruction (and so negation) in part comes from the crisis of its targets on the left – with the waning of both the PCF and the neo-libertarian groupuscles as political forces. While destruction had a polemic force in its insistence on a proletarian negativity against these tendencies, it had rather less traction when not cashed out in terms of changes in capital's regime of accumulation and the class composition of the working class. Badiou's relative blindness to questions of political economy left his own articulation of negativity merely 'political' and gestural – linked to some future Maoist party that never materialised. And yet, the very destructiveness of capital in its new forms of accumulation, and the widespread retreat into styles of 'negative' thought in the 1980s, gave subtraction coupled to affirmation a new attractiveness.

There is no doubt truth to Peter Hallward's contention that the path of Badiou's work, from *Theory of the Subject*, to *Being and Event*, to *Logics of Worlds* (2006), is one marked by a 'qualification of [revolutionary] expectations'.[41] For Hallward this sequence is characterised by an increasing recognition of the penetration of state power into appearance, and a concomitant trust only in what is inconsistent, non-apparent or disappearing. This distrust of representation can produce highly dubious political results – at once sustaining resistance, but only in the form of what is always subtracted and never appears: 'Badiou's motto has in effect become: trust only in what you cannot see'.[42] This apparent waning of political hope has, however, been accompanied by an increasingly bullish affirmationism, which reaches its apogee in Badiou's 'Third Sketch of a Manifesto of Affirmationist Art' (2005).[43] Without wishing to minimise all their obvious points of dispute one can note a convergence between Badiou's insistence on an irreducible inconsistency that always evades capture by power and Antonio Negri's insistence on the ontological irreducibility of potentiality. In both cases this tone emerges out of trying to hold on through an experience of defeat. The collapse of political representation on the left, even of those actors to which one may have been opposed (such as the PCF), renders invisibility a political virtue, attesting to a potential for rupture, instead of being a sign of defeat.[44] Now *all* forms of political representation come under suspicion as never measuring up to some primary and irreducible resistance, encoded in a subtractive (Badiou) or expressive (Negri) ontology of force.

The obvious difference between Negri and Badiou is that even at his most affirmative Badiou insists that the eruption of inconsistency be figured as emerging from the void point of the event, and not from the positivity of Spinozan ontological substance. And yet even this apparent difference conceals convergence: Negri too correlates the affirmation of the new to its emergence at the edge of being through exposure to the void,[45] while Badiou insists on the positive construction and affirmation of the event contrary to a thought of negativity. This convergence indicates the attraction of affirmationism in an inhospitable political environment. Certainly Badiou allows a larger 'space' to negativity than Negri, and it is possible to reconstruct Badiou's classical thought of the event as a thinking of negativity.[46] I prefer to analyse Badiou's more recent, and direct, reconsideration of the negative and its relation to politics and art. Although made in scattered essays this re-consideration is to be the subject of a future book by Badiou. It suggests, at the very least, the qualification of his affirmationism, and is also an indication of the necessity of negativity in a new phase of political and historical reflection.

No longer does it appear that we must simply make a teleological transition from destruction to subtraction, or from negation to affirmation. Instead, Badiou has begun to re-articulate together the relations between destruction and subtraction.[47] The reason for this re-emergence of negativity is that Badiou's thinking is always responsive to, and conditioned by, its times, despite the often austere appearance of his 'system'. In the current context of capitalist crisis and the global 'war on terror', Badiou has started to register the limits of affirmationism and the necessity for the 'adjustment or calibration between the properly negative part of negation and the part I [Badiou] call subtractive'.[48] The question is what form this calibration will take.

FORMALISING THE NEGATIVE

Badiou argues, in his article 'Three Negations' (2008), that the question of politics, cast in the Schmittian distinction of the couplet friend-enemy, is fundamentally a matter of the complex relation dictated by the action of negativity. To specify this complex relation Badiou gradates and analyses the different levels or 'strengths' of the negative, correlating these with different forms of logical description – he formalises the negative. The common and most accepted formulation of the negative is that of the absolute destruction of what is negated. Badiou notes that in this case negation obeys the classical logical of the principle of non-contradiction – if proposition P is true then proposition non-P is false. In Badiou's terms this speaks to his philosophy of the event, in which we have something new only in the complete interruption or rupture with the existing laws of the world. The event, developed as a multiplicity composed of its consequences, has a two-fold existence: first, as a part of the world and so immanent to it, and second, as the negation of the world, subtracted from the laws of the world. Therefore negation is an essential operator of the truth-process which instantiates and develops an event. This would seem to attest to the subterranean efficacy and primacy of the negative secreted within Badiou's subtractive affirmationism.

When it comes to a description of the action of negation, however, Badiou continues to put affirmation first. The example he chooses, which is key for his whole philosophy, is that of political revolution as the exemplar of the event. What is dubious is that Badiou does not choose to analyse an actual revolution, which one would have thought would be the usual procedure in tracing such an event, but Marx's *theorisation* of revolution. For Badiou, Marx's theory of revolution requires a first affirmative revelation of 'hidden laws of society', which is then coupled to a second 'destructive transgression of all these laws'.[49] But, of course, it might seem that the practice of revolution usually works in the opposite direction: first, the transgression or destruction of existing laws which, second, reveal the hidden laws of society. Instead, Badiou puts theory before the event, reversing his usual understanding. Putting this aside, to explicate this 'coupling' requires that we follow Badiou in his more exact specification of the form that negation takes in the rupture, or as Badiou prefers 'transgression', of the law. He specifies these forms by defining the various logical forms of negation in terms of their departure from Aristotle's laws of thinking, particularly his second law (the principle of non-contradiction), and his third law (the principle of the excluded middle). These two 'laws of negation' will provide us with a grid through which to specify the relative strengths of different negations.

The grid is constructed in relation to which of the two principles the forms of negation obey and this gives us four possibilities: that negation obeys both principles; that negation obeys the principle of contradiction, but not the excluded middle; that negation obeys the excluded middle, but not the principle of contradiction; that negation obeys neither of the principles. Ruling out the last as the elimination of any effective negation, that leaves us with three forms, gradated in terms of decreasing strength.[50] Badiou identifies these forms not only with particular 'strengths', but also with particular forms of logic, and, in line with his system, a particular philosophical status and a particular evental implication. The question of philosophical status follows the distinction that Badiou has developed in *Logics of Worlds*, between ontology – in which things are pure multiplicities without determination – and the logic of appearance – in which multiplicities exist as relational objects in the world. He summarises that: 'There is a sort of univocity of being, but an equivocity of existence'.[51] In the world of ontology, which obeys classical logic, we can have a 'pure' negation, a univocal switching from one state to another. In the world of appearance matters are more complex as 'a multiplicity can appear more or less'.[52] The equivocal nature of appearance results in a domain that is stretched between the maximal and the minimal degrees of appearance. In terms of logic the world of ontology is classical, while the world of appearance is intuitionistic.

To complicate matters further we not only have to take into account ontology and appearance, but also the event – the implication of the negative. Badiou had specified in *Being and Event* that the event is 'the arrival in being of non-being, the arrival amidst the visible of the invisible.'[53] Where ontology is always presented in the form of the state of the situation, which is to say regulated and ordered, the event emerges from the edge of the situation, at the void point of pure inconsistency or multiplicity. The appearance of the event throws ontology out of joint; at the same time the event is an immanent possibility to ontology and also the sign of its impossibility. In the case of the event we have a change in intensity from the minimal – which Badiou describes as the 'inexistent' – to the maximal – the singularity. The various 'levels' of the degree of rupture and appearance of the event are therefore linked to the three forms of negation. In this way negation is built back in to Badiou's theory of the event, to track the 'level' and 'impact' of the event, or to be more precise wherever a happening or change reaches the level of the event.

To summarise Badiou's investigation, the first negation obeys classical logic. This is the strong negation because the negation of P excludes P and any other possibility. Such a strong negation implies a maximal intensity, and a maximal change from inexistent to the new 'law' of a situation. The world in this case is classical, as we only have two degrees of intensity – inexistent and maximal. Therefore, we can suppose that the 'true' event is one that produces this maximal negation of P: 'the world turned upside down'. This then is the true revolutionary change, or what Badiou calls a singularity. The second negation, which obeys the principle of contradiction, but not the excluded middle, is correlated with the intuitionistic logic of Brouwer and Heyting. Here the negation of P excludes P itself but not other possibilities that lie between P and non-P. In terms of the implications of the event we have here an intermediate change, which is neither minimal nor maximal. Something new does appear, but it does not change the law of the situation. In this case, to use Badiou's political terminology, we face a situation of reformism rather than revolution. This is the situation of a 'weak singularity', as the existent hierarchies are not seriously troubled and absorb and delimit the inexistent. Finally, the third negation, which obeys the principle of the excluded middle but not the principle of contradiction, is correlated with the paraconsistent logic of Da Costa. This is the weakest form of negation, in which the negation of P excludes the space between P and non-P, but not P itself. Badiou points out that this form of logic is similar to Hegelian dialectics, as P lies inside the negation of P (the (in)famous 'negation of the negation'). Whereas for Hegel this involves the necessary inscription of negativity as the force of change, Badiou regards this kind of change as making no perceptible difference at the level of the inexistent. Rather than any kind of decisive change something does happen but we cannot identify it – everything is identical. Badiou summarises the results of this inquiry: 'The lesson is that, when the world is intuitionistic, a true change must be classical, and a false change paraconsistent'.[54]

While Badiou specifies these different logics of negation he does not appear to offer much instruction concerning the relation of negation to affirmation; all we have learnt is that true negation obeys classical logic and offers an absolute rupture with the existent (P > non-P). Badiou's only political examples in this article offer little that exactly seems to match up exactly to these various forms of negation, or with his own wider theory of the event. His final example is telling in this regard. Discussing the selection of presidential candidates in France and the United States, Badiou argues that their 'logic' is paraconsistent, and so false. He does, however, accept that you can treat them as intuitionistic, and so open to change.[55] What is left unsketched is what would be a classical negation in this context? Presumably, in light of Badiou's other work, such a negation would be the refusal of the electoral process.[56] This option is left absent. What is also lacking is a more precise sense of the articulation or shading between the three forms of negation. If the logic of appearance is intuitionistic how can we truly impose a classical logic of negation without falling back into intuitionistic or paraconsistent logics? How can we go about making transformative negations that would track back from paraconsistent negations to classical negations? So, it seems impossible to imagine how an event would appear in the world of appearance, which is to say how could a classical negation appear in an intuitionistic world?

In *Logics of Worlds* this problem is answered by Badiou's theory of points. A point is the localisation of a tension or contradiction: the instantiation in the world of appearance of a moment of decision in a Kierkegaardian 'either / or'. Although a point instantiates a positivity, it also invokes the insertion of a classical negation in the world of appearance as the moment of decision that makes possible a negation of the world as it is. The difficulty still remains, however, of the *identification* of such a point, or points, of decision. This problem is compounded by Badiou's argument that the number of such points in a world is variable, and that we can have an atonal world in which the transcendental is devoid of points – in fact our world under capitalism.[57] This voiding of points can be the result of a world being presented as so nuanced and so complex that no point can be definitively extracted, or so homogeneous that no point can be identified.[58] These positions nicely reflect our analysis of Latour and Negri respectively, and also give some confirmation to our suggestion of a convergence between them. Of course, as we traced in our analysis of real abstraction, capitalism constitutes a world regime of appearance that is both complex and homogeneous at the same time: creating a proliferation of differences as sites of accumulation, coupled to a 'smoothing' or voiding of any and every content. In this situation the eventual possibility seems to disappear, although Badiou invokes the possibility of an overcoming of atony 'into a sufficiently resistant isolate, capable of anchoring an active point'.[59] This possibility of forcing the appearance of a point in an atonal world is left under-specified and quasi-voluntarist, in an uncomfortable position between the subjective decision and objective localisation. This discomfort, I will argue, results from the subordination of negativity.

Badiou's own answer to the question of the appearance of the negative, and the relation of negation to affirmation, can be found in a lecture he delivered in 2007, titled 'Destruction, Negation, Subtraction – on Pier Paolo Pasolini'. Here Badiou defines, in a series of lapidary statements, the precise relation of negation to affirmation. First, he admits that negation is necessary to provide the means to rupture with the objectivity of the situation. This would seem to imply the major concession of the priority and necessity of negativity to permit change, denied or minimised by Badiou elsewhere. But Badiou goes on to define novelty and creation as *the affirmative part of negation*. In this way affirmation is again accorded priority within negation, because, for Badiou, while negation provides the necessary force of rupture it remains bound to what it negates. This is the usual problem of the mutual dependence of transgression and law, given its most pithy formulation by Paul: 'And where there is no law there is no transgression'.[60] While 'the very essence of a novelty implies negation', for such a novelty to be truly novel it 'must affirm its identity apart from the negativity of negation'.[61] Once again, as with Badiou's reflections on politics, the negative is given a subsidiary or defensive position, protecting the primacy of affirmation or clearing the ground for its emergence. What is striking, however, is that now it appears that negation insinuates itself directly, as the essence of novelty.

Badiou clarifies this relationship between negation and affirmation in terms of the relation between destruction and subtraction. To do so he, appropriately enough for an ex-Maoist, divides the concept of negation into two. We have destruction now defined as the *negative part of negation*, which requires the complete disintegration of the old world. This correlates with Badiou's classical 'strong' negation, which leaves nothing in its wake and no alternative to the destruction of P, but non-P. The difficulty is that this would leave the event in the state of pure negativity, which Badiou regards as characteristic of the paroxysmal nihilism of the attacks on the World Trade Center, and the violence of Takfirist and Salafist Islamic groups more generally.[62] To avoid this collapsing into the negative destruction (as the negative part of negation) must be coordinated with subtraction as the *affirmative part of negation*, as the new systemic coherence which takes place on the ground cleared by destruction. For the event to be the event it must combine destruction and subtraction, which again leaves destruction, or negation proper, as mere ground clearing before affirmation. The twist, or torsion, here is that affirmation itself becomes a subordinate part of negation. Badiou's preference, which I would consider to be under-determined, is that this, in fact, re-codes negation as affirmative via the correlation of affirmation with subtraction: the 'fundamental idea of the beginning century must be that the very essence of negation is subtraction'.[63]

As we have seen repeatedly in this work the struggle to subordinate negation and negativity is a fraught one, and often staged in the manner of a fundamental decision that has no intrinsic necessity. In fact, it would easily be possible to argue that Badiou's insistence that negation has an affirmative part which determines and guides the destructive to a new order seems to return to the Hegelian 'negation of the negation' that he had earlier tried to circumscribe as a moment of paraconsistent logic.[64] To recapitulate Badiou's reading of negation via Pasolini, with his political correlations, might allow us to refine a little this seeming impasse. First, we have negation without destruction. This is the paraconsistent logic of 'capitalist-parliamentarianism', in which negation is so weakened that it fades into nothing, a mere virtual opposition. Paired with this is the second option of negation dissociated from subtraction, which (as we saw above) Badiou characterises as nihilist will-to-destruction – or what he calls in the text on Pasolini 'the hard side of negation'.[65] For Badiou these two forms of negation form a Deleuzian 'disjunctive synthesis',[66] pairing together the paraconsistent logic of the state with the violent attempt to disrupt that logic for the sake of nihilist destruction. This composes something like what Baudrillard had called 'the mirror of terrorism' – that self-reinforcing 'spiral' of violence staged between the state and the terrorist.[67]

Third, we have subtraction dissociated from destruction or negation, which results in despair, or what Badiou calls in *The Meaning of Sarkozy* (2008) an 'omnipresent affective negativity'.[68] What this certainly seems to do is to modify, to say the least, some of Badiou's claims concerning a politics of subtraction. Here subtraction finds itself caught up in the field of the inconsistent and, we can presume, not far away from a mere logic of 'dropping out', or the disgust at the world characteristic of the Hegelian beautiful soul. Once again we find a tangled situation in which the more Badiou formalises the negative the more it becomes crucial, and then the more Badiou tries to ward off the implications of this by trying to reterritorialise this negativity within subtraction. The result is his uncomfortable assertion that: 'The way of freedom is a subtractive one; but to protect the subtractive itself,

to defend the new kingdom of emancipatory politics, we cannot radically exclude all forms of violence'.[69] Leaving aside the eschatological
language, we find that the concession of the necessity of negation is
re-mapped onto violence to then ensure its subordination. This is a reification of negativity by making it isomorphic to violence, which then
tends to be taken in its most spectacular and mediated forms. Certainly,
unlike in the case of Latour, Badiou does not dismiss violence out of
hand. The difficulty is that Badiou leaves his 'positive' conception of
violence rather too tied to traditional 'grand' forms (i.e. Revolution),
and that his gestures towards other forms of 'defensive' violence fail, it
seems to me, to grasp other forms of 'violence', or I would prefer negativity, immanent to capitalism. Hence I want to return to the problem
of destructive negation through a tangential reading of Badiou's admission of the necessity of negation, before going on to explore certain
resources in Badiou's work for the thinking of forms of agency that
might correlate with a re-configured negativity.

ACTIVE NIHILISM

I want to pause a little longer over the option that Badiou dismisses out-
of-hand as the effect of our current impasse: a 'pure' destruction, which
for Badiou involves 'falling for the paroxysmal charms of terror'.[70] Set up
in these terms such a manoeuvre can only appear as tasteless posturing,
or the endorsement of the most retrograde and desperate forms of contemporary political violence. In Badiou's commentary on Pasolini's poem
Vittoria he notes the impasse Pasolini sketches between the 'father' – the
figure of political and cultural authority – who has subtraction without
destruction, abandoning the field to despair, and the 'sons' – the next
political generation – who respond with destruction without subtraction,
and are left only with the 'destructive part of negation'.[71] For Badiou,
Pasolini's poem is a description of 'terrorist subjectivity' in advance.
Abandoned by the father the sons are left awaiting 'an orientation, for
a negation which, under some paternal law, reconciles destruction and
subtraction'.[72] When that does not arrive nihilism blooms. Now, I have
no desire to play the part of one of the 'sons' in this psychodrama, even
figuratively at the level of theory. Some kind of reconciliation between
negation and the construction of the new is no doubt necessary, although
whether this entails immediately placing and ordering this process by
affirmation is what I have been questioning. To displace Badiou's identification I want to return to a number of comments he makes on a figure
of destructive or active nihilism, which do not allocate this position to
'terrorist subjectivity' but to a position on the libertarian left.

Badiou, in *Theory of the Subject*, regards Guy Debord and the Situationist International (SI) as exemplars of active nihilism, an ethics of the impasse which is structured by the discourse of discordance: 'The active nihilist is particularly odious and particularly promising'.[73] On the one hand, active nihilism has a certain virtue, as it has never succumbed to belief and 'valorises only itself.'[74] On the other hand, the activist nihilist is always at risk of squandering this capacity through an indifference to re-composing the world (perhaps we could say an indifference to affirmation). This indifference, for Badiou, is an indifference to the discipline and patient labour of organisation. It is the title of Guy Debord's final film – *In girum imus nocte et consumimur igni* – that is the motto of active nihilism. This reference to being consumed by fire is the sign that: 'We place all our hopes in the fact that this fire may consume the world, having once again become Prometheus' fire through the mediation offered by political confidence'.[75] Without organisation, or by ignoring the different organisational forms and debates which the SI practised, we are left only with hope in some world-cleansing destruction.

This figuration is achieved by severing Debord's film from its own dialectic, which, as we saw in Chapter 3, is actually organised through the primacy of water over fire. It is 'water', as the element of time, which metaphorically 'douses' this Promethean fire. Instead of a hope in purely formless raging destruction, the very strategies of contestation must constantly adapt and re-develop themselves in time – hence the finitude of such strategies. Of course, we could easily argue that this confirms Badiou's point in another form. Instead of an active nihilist desire to consume the world we have merely the simulacrum of that desire, always held in check by the certainty of defeat.[76] In this way active nihilism would constantly risk returning to passive nihilism, to the role of the 'realist, packing his bags for the posts and places of social fate'.[77] While, of course, Debord refused this fate, the pessimism of his later *Comments on the Society of the Spectacle* (1988) would seem to confirm Badiou's insight that the active nihilist swings from absolute revolt to *de facto* accommodation.

I wish to dispute Badiou's diagnosis, and his later leap to equating active nihilism with the ideology of terrorist subjectivity. In fact, Badiou himself offers slightly different nuances in his discussion of this position. Whereas he usually condemns Debord and the SI in these terms, although not without admiration for Debord's intransigence, in 'Rhapsody for the Theatre' (1990) he offers a different judgement. Describing *In girum* as a superb film, Badiou, in a remark we noted in Chapter Three, argues that the film produces: 'This pure temporal moment [that] speaks to the glory of cinema, [and] which may very well survive us humans'.[78] Now this may be simply an 'aesthetic' judgement, and elsewhere Badiou questions the artistic status of cinema – depicting it as the paradigmatically mixed art, and therefore particularly difficult to purify.[79] That said, Badiou is arguing that Debord has achieved this purification, and in political terms. What is also noticeable is that this achievement is analysed in terms of time, exactly the dimension that Badiou occludes in his previous reading of the film as a, literally, incendiary tract.

Of course, it is not a matter of merely deferring to the authority of Badiou on this issue. I think, however, it is telling that Badiou too has to concede the possible production of something new – an inhuman cinema of time, in fact – out of that kind of active nihilism he elsewhere regards as incapable of novelty. This attests, from within a position deeply hostile to Debord's Hegelian Marxism, to an appreciation for the possibilities of *détournement* as a strategy of negativity that is not condemned to sterile repetition, or to so-called 'mindless' destruction. In fact, once again, the negative converges on the possibility of time thought as negativity, as the interruption of what Benjamin called 'homogeneous, empty time'. It is no longer dependently transgressive, which conforms to the libertine image of Debord and the SI (which they did nothing to discourage), nor is it simply ground-clearing destruction prior to a true politicisation (vectored through the formation of the Maoist party for the Badiou of the 1970s). This new image of negativity suggests the need to think a new set of strategies, via *détournement*, which do not simply repeat those of the SI (the staple of many of those claiming the SI's mantle). Instead, negativity, correlated with an inhuman 'experience' of time, opens a new fluidity of intervention. While this could easily be followed down the speculative and anti-correlationist path of detachment from the subject, here I want to pursue, still through Badiou, the question of its strategic *attachment* to the subject.

THE SUBJECT OF COURAGE

The continuing resonance of active nihilism in the current context is that it poses the problem of action in a situation of impasse and discordance. Our present, as Badiou has insisted on in a number of places, is a time of disorientation.[80] In such a conjuncture we feel compelled to act, but with no orientation as to how we might act successfully. Of course such a diagnosis can easily overestimate the clarity of previous 'sequences' of politics, which may have been clear from the point of view of Badiou's Maoism but were not always as self-evident as he supposed. Rather than re-hash the past, however, I would agree that Badiou's most insightful description of the present moment is as one of 'organized disorientation'.[81] The reason for this is that such a characterisation does not imply that disorientation is simply the result of Nietzscho-Heideggerean global nihilism, or the crisis of Western metaphysics. Stressing the *organisation* of this disorganisation, or disorientation, allows us to consider it better as the result of a capitalism that produces, structures, organises and orders such disorientation. I have argued that Badiou's affirmationism is structured by the desire to stabilise a point of resistance against this 'organised disorientation', anchored not in ontology but in the event as the moment of the exception to ontology. This is vital because, for Badiou: 'the interval between an event of emancipation and another leaves us fallaciously in thrall to the idea that nothing begins or will ever begin, even if we find ourselves caught in the midst of an infernal and immobile agitation'.[82] According to Badiou it is exactly that interval which we now live in after May '68, and with no strong signs of a new political event in sight, although certainly we do not lack for signs of agitation, if not catastrophe (ecological, most notably). In accordance with this analysis Badiou has re-affirmed affirmationism in *The Meaning of Sarkozy* (2008), where he argues that the task of resistance requires the courage to be 'on the side of creation, affirmation and an egalitarian collective future'.[83]

At the same time, however, Badiou has also attempted to re-integrate negativity within his thinking. This indicates a new flexibility, which now recognises the necessity of negativity under changing political and social conditions. The obscurity of these new conditions implies, contrary to the usual strident claims made for affirmation, that philosophy play the more modest role of clarification of the present and the preservation of an alternative to the present order.[84] In an argument still tinged with affirmationism Badiou argues that today: 'philosophy is like the attic where, in difficult times, one accumulates resources, lines up tools, and sharpens knives.' [85] I would even suggest the complexity and impasses of Badiou's historicisation and formalisation of the negative respond to this situation of obscurity: incarnating a recognition of the necessity for negation, but only under the condition of an affirmative orientation to preserve us from the 'omnipresent affective negativity' which surrounds us. In a sense affirmationism indicates the initial necessity to hold on to what had been gained in the revolutionary sequences of the twentieth century and to resist the waves of restoration. As, however, this mode of restoration has shifted, and as new political possibilities of resistance have been signalled, no matter how faintly, Badiou has come to a new appreciation of the necessity of destruction and the negative. We are, as he puts it, 'in the context of a new interval phase'.[86] What can be made of this, in terms of a more full-blown rehabilitation of the negative and its use for a re-thinking of the conditions of agency?

Badiou is renowned for running against the grain of Continental philosophy in his emphasis of the role of the subject. In terms of politics this subject is always collective and conditioned by political events. Commenting on the work of his comrade Sylvain Lazarus, Badiou endorses, if in a fashion that integrates it into his own philosophy, the aim of Lazarus 'to authorise a thought of subjectivity which is strictly subjective, without passing through any type of objective mediation'.[87] Badiou's own formulation is that this is the possibility of an '*objectless subject*', defined as arising from a singularity (an event) that is prescriptive, sequential and precarious.[88] Although insisting on the rarity of political subjectivity, which in the absence of an event can seem to imply its disappearance, there is no doubt that Badiou strongly insists on the retention of the category of the subject as the form of activated political agency. I want to suggest, however, that a certain irony results. Despite his insistence of the necessity of the subject Badiou charts the coming-to-be of the subject in a form which entails a fundamental passivity of agency.

In his commentary on his own subjectivation by the events of May '68 Badiou argues that the embrace of this moment of political becoming requires the courage to accept passivity as the condition of being worked-over by the event:

> Passivity is in effect nothing but the dissolution of the 'I', the renunciation of any subjective identity. In the end, in order to cease being a coward one must fully consent to becoming. The crucial issue is this: *the reverse of cowardice is not will, but abandonment to what happens.*[89]

In an unlikely moment Badiou's insistence on an 'almost ontological passivity',[90] which is the effect of an 'unconditional abandonment to the event',[91] converges with the formulations of passivity associated with Maurice Blanchot or Emmanuel Lévinas. Of course the crucial distinction is that for Blanchot and Lévinas the subject is passive hostage to the force of absolute alterity, whereas for Badiou the subject's passivity is what opens them to the actual event. But does this difference make enough difference when it comes to thinking agency?

In fact, Badiou's version of passivity is actually closer to that of Deleuze and Guattari. They suggest the necessity for a certain passivity in the reception of the virtual possibilities of becoming, which is required to allow the actualisation of these possibilities in new forms of collective activity and new 'lines of flight'.[92] The similarity to Badiou is that they share the reference to rupture cast in terms of *immanence* rather than transcendence. This is why Badiou can agree with Deleuze on the necessity of affirmationism for the actualisation of the new. The difference is that in Deleuze and Guattari passivity, especially in their more accelerationist moments, is figured as the acceptance of the deter-ritorialised forces of desire, in which the subject becomes the accelerator of the de-coding effects of capital. Badiou, by contrast, argues for the passivity of the subject as the operator to accept or accede to the event, which in the political context is incarnated as the universal egalitarian demand *interrupting* the law of the world. So, it is not capitalist flows which do the work, but the evental interruption of those flows. What I still want to question is the fundamental inscription of passivity in this model of the subject, and to contrast this with the possibility of agency.

   To do so I want to return to Badiou's political affect of courage as the means to challenge his passive and affirmative conception of the subject. Of course Badiou insists that courage is affirmative and that to be cou-rageous requires not activity but consent to becoming. Therefore it will be necessary to *détourné* Badiou's concept of courage, to place it under the sign of negativity. The reason for this is not only to correct a fault in Badiou, but also to revise our usual image of the affective dimension of negativity. Critics of Badiou's downgrading of negativity, such as Simon Critchley and Andrew Gibson, try to re-inject this quality through the pathos of finitude and suffering.[93] Challenging what Critchley calls the 'tragic-heroic' paradigm of contemporary theory,[94] they argue for the necessity of negativity in exactly those bodily terms that, to my mind, Badiou has correctly problematised. After all, the essential refer-ence of tragedy for Badiou is Aeschylus's *Oresteia*, in which the cyclical concept of vengeance – the *lex talionis* ('for hatred hatred / For every fatal stroke a fatal stroke'[95]) – is eventually broken by 'the *interruption* of the infinite debt'.[96] Badiou explicitly rejects, in advance, the fasci-nation with heroic failure and pure rupture, which he correlates with the preference for Sophocles's *Antigone* as the drama of the anguished quest that leads only to 'the vortex of terror'.[97] In contrast, Aeschylus offers the drama of 'the contradictory advent of justice by the courage of the new'.[98] This requires no concession to finitude, weakness or the comic, but rather courage as 'the anticipation of justice'.[99] I want to take up this argument, but rather than correlate courage with affirma-tion instead argue that it can be used as the model for the political virtue of negativity *qua* agency – detached from both the pathos of the heroic (i.e. active nihilism) and the pathos of finitude (i.e. passive nihilism).

In fact, Badiou himself inscribes courage in an ambiguous fashion. On the one hand, his affirmative conception of courage *does* have a reference to the heroic: 'Courage, in the sense in which I understand it, has its origin in a heroic conversion, and is oriented towards a point that was not there, a Real woven out of the impossible'.[100] On the other hand, he also insists (as we previously noted in Chapter 1) that courage is the refusal to 'live dangerously', a virtue of 'endurance in the impossible' that is contrasted with heroism as a 'posture'.[101] In the first instance 'heroism' seems to fall on the side of the passive acceptance of the event, whereas what interests me more is the second form of courage, as a virtue that orients itself to a point, to a Real, in the intervallic period of the *absence* of the event. Rather than either the simple reference to a past event or the hope in a future event, I regard courage as the subjective operator of negativity – the very persistence of the negative – that is oriented to this point, or points, of the real. For this reason I would agree with Badiou that 'courage orients us locally amid the global disorientation'.[102] In fact, I would argue that Badiou's renewed interest in the negative, a historicised and formalised negative rather than the negative of pathos and finitude, is precisely calibrated as a means to deal with the 'disorientation' of the present. Again, I would not wish to over-state this disorientation, which can become a self-serving motif. That said, courage offers a non-heroic political virtue, a stubborn insistence against the vacuities of affirmation, in the name of negativity – woven out of political memories which are not mere nostalgia, but also critique and re-formulation.

THE LINE OF THE NEGATIVE

To flesh out the subject of courage we can refer to what might appear a minor moment in Badiou's articulation of courage. In *The Century* he argues that:

> Perhaps the greatest contribution of the United States to the thematic of the century is to have placed at the heart of its cinema the question of the genealogy of courage and of the intimate struggle against cowardice. This is what makes the western – in which this struggle is permanent – a solid, modern genre, and what has enabled it to yield an inordinate number of masterpieces.[103]

This is a surprising gesture, considering the usual positioning of the classical western as a reactionary genre – often regarded as racist and sexist in content.[104] An exhaustive survey and analysis of this form, let alone a defence, is beyond the limits of this work. Instead I want to focus on one example of the form to re-chart this genealogy of courage in terms of a subjectivation that can produce something new and which is not locked into purely nihilist negation.

My example is an admittedly minor and little-known, and little-regarded, example of the genre: *Valdez is Coming* (1971).[105] The film demonstrates, in a precise fashion, the virtue of courage as the persistence of negation. The Mexican lawman Bob Valdez (played by Burt Lancaster) is forced into killing an ex-soldier and supposed fugitive when his attempt to apprehend him is deliberately de-railed by a gunman working for Frank Tanner – a local business man and quasi-criminal gang leader. The accused man, who was innocent, 'happened' to be African-American and his wife Apache. Valdez, himself previously an 'Indian hunter', pursues compensation for the man's wife. Offered an initially derisory sum of a few dollars by the town's notables, Bob insists on two hundred dollars. They promise to pay half this sum if Bob can get the rest from Frank Tanner – knowing full well that Tanner, an evident racist, will never agree. Asking Tanner, and in a soft-spoken fashion insisting on the sum, Valdez is punished for his impudence by being tied to a makeshift cross and forced to walk back to town. Eventually freed from his bonds – oddly by the racist hired gun man who had originally forced Valdez to kill – he dons his old military uniform and announces 'Valdez is coming'. He negates the existent racist obscene underside in which he (described by Tanner and his men as a 'greaser'), his Mexican friends, the ex-soldier and the ex-soldier's wife, are all worth less than the whites and their accepted associates. Valdez is the hero of the film, but a hero who is not overtly heroic – merely displaying the courage of polite, even servile, insistence. The radical subversion of his gesture is to continue to demand the one hundred dollars, nothing more and nothing less, and in this way to register the real antagonism of racism.

Valdez pursues Tanner's gang, and is eventually led to kidnapping Tanner's fiancée. Again, despite the racist and sexist fantasies of Tanner's men, Valdez behaves in a perfectly reasonable fashion towards her – all the while killing his pursuers. The film ends with a final confrontation as Bob is run to ground. In the stand-off which follows Tanner's own Mexican gang leader, El Segundo, refuses to shoot Valdez, or to allow any of his men to do so, insisting that Tanner must do it himself. It ends at this point, as Tanner blusters, revealing his cowardice, but with no resolution – leaving us simply, in the style of Leone, with a geometric image of the stalled shoot out. Now, of course, this appears to be a typical heroic Western, if a late example more reflective on the racism often found in the genre. What interests me, however, is the galvanising effect of Valdez's courage – which is pure insistence rather than absolute or suicidal heroism – on those around him. Tanner's wife, despite being kidnapped, stands with Valdez at the end of the film, as does, in his own way, El Segundo. Valdez, despite seeming to become the typical 'lone hero' of the western, is, in fact, the incarnation of the collective dimension of the law through his 'internal' negation of the law's obscene underside.[106] This is what Badiou, in *Theory of the Subject*, calls 'strong consistency': 'the principle of the real in the collective excess and the adherence'.[107] Valdez, almost despite himself, subjectivates those around him by his gesture and then draws them into this subjective process of consistency. This is a 'collective excess' as this process forces all the characters out of their normal and normalised place.

This notion of a 'strong consistency' suggests that courage correlates with negativity, but not with the 'negative passions' of finitude, suffering or depression. These affective features are present in the film, but they are subordinated to a collectively articulated negation of the existing regime of law in the name of justice. Valdez insists on the empty signifier of the one hundred dollars, effectively politicising the void-point of money as a lack / excess that de-stabilises the structure of justice – at once indicating the lack of justice, and being in excess of the 'correctly' racist amount to be paid. Valdez steps into this gap of negativity as the 'structuralist hero', creating an intervention as a 'mutation point' that disarticulates the positivity of the social through an inhuman and infinite negativity. At the same time it is crucial that this is a *self*-negation: Valdez *détourné* his own previous identity as an 'Indian fighter' by taking up the uniform and weapons, but this time in the name of a justice that refuses the racism that subtended his own previous identification. Negation is the negation of a previous socio-political identity, of the licensed violence of the 'Indian fighter', and a re-alignment of identification through the hollowing-out of that previous identity. It is figured in the 'weak' self-presentation of Valdez, who even in his hunting down and killing of the gang only kills when necessary and offers every opportunity for justice to be done. This is precisely not a vengeful fantasy of extermination, which would leave Valdez in the position of the furies of the *Oresteia*, but rather already an anticipation of justice, no less implacable for its very meekness.

What Valdez figures is not, therefore, the grand destructive gesture of some ultra-leftist fantasy of absolute social rupture (what Badiou calls 'speculative leftism'), but a patient and courageous practice that dissipates and corrodes the positivity of the social. In *Theory of the Subject* Badiou argues that: 'Courage is insubordination to the symbolic order at the urging of the dissolutive injunction of the real.'[108]

This insubordination is not the valorisation or reification of the real as a 'pure' transcendent moment of negativity that can never be captured by, or subordinated to, any social formation, but only fantasmatically, romantically or suicidally dwelt in.[109] Instead, it is the begining of a praxis that treats or renders the real through the symbolic to produce a new law or justice.[110] In this case that point of the real which can be forced to produce justice is precisely the empty, mobile, abstraction of money. This is also a praxis, to switch to a Deleuzian register, that creates a new assemblage by the negative transversal linking of a series of 'subjects'. In a figurative sense Valdez's own journey is just such a 'savage line' of the negative, not simply as a line of flight, although it could be read as such, but rather a line of confrontation, refusal and negation. The new – in the sense of the novelty of justice – emerges from the negation or *détournement* of the 'bad new' – Tanner's service of the social and market good(s).

This is only one filmic example of course, and thereby might be thought to reside at merely the level of the aesthetic – deliberately detached from any actual political valence. I want to argue, however, that it is suggestive of a courage articulated in a time of reactionary restoration, a linkage between the myth of the western and the film's own contemporary context of the articulation of racism and imperialism (especially the Vietnam War). Rather than the thesis of the irreducible contamination of the western by racism it *détourné* this form, and negates its racism. No doubt this can always be read as really indicating the primacy of affirmation – in this case, perhaps, a Derridean insistence on 'undeconstructible' justice, or Badiou's insistence on an 'independent affirmation'. What I want to suggest is that it proffers a model of agency which is at once collective, active, courageous and negative. It is the intervention of such an agency that opens the passage to the 'sublated' negativity that is also encoded within existent positivities. The static geometric ending of the film is not simply a frozen image of the impossibility of resolution, but the necessary figuration of a pure temporal moment of negativity *in* the image.

This admittedly allegorical reading allows us to start to grasp the lineaments of the line of the negative, which traverses and exceeds the subject. It does not do so by reference to a grand evental rupture, or through an exacerbation of the worst, or through a quasi-mystical reversal of an abject subjectivity into a new messiah or saviour (despite the Christological elements of the film). It begins, instead, from the negation or *détournement* of an existent set of positivities, specifically in the instance of the film the positivity generated through the coordination of racism with business, a coordination obviously not without resonance in the present – in which the resistance to financial crisis and capitalist business-as-usual has often predicated itself on nativism and racism. This negation generates the new of the collective agency of courage in the absence of the event, an intervallic resistance that predicates itself on disarticulation and ruptural 'violence', by turning back a previously reactionary violence towards liberation. What it excavates are the possibilities that exist if we do not subordinate negativity, if we think it beyond and against the disjunctive synthesis of active and passive nihilism which are nothing more than meagre reflections of the everyday violence of capitalist creative destruction. The line of the negative is looped through the agency which operates the destruction of those real abstractions that govern us.

NOTES

1. Badiou, *Polemics*, p. 35.
2. Badiou, *The Century*, pp. 125–6.
3. Badiou, 'The Crisis of the Negative', pp. 646–7; for Badiou's comments on his peers who took that path of renegades see the interview, 'Roads to Renegacy'.
4. Bensaïd, 'Alain Badiou', p. 100.
5. Badiou argues that Adorno's 'negative dialectics', with its critique of identity as the fundamental principle of enlightenment rationalism, its suspicion of universalism as the imposition of the One, and its respect for alterity, exemplifies in advance the themes of contemporary ideology; see '*De la dialectique négative*', session one (8 January 2005).
6. Badiou, *The Meaning of Sarkozy*, p. 94.
7. Badiou, 'The Crisis of the Negative', p. 652.
8. Ibid. p. 652.
9. Ibid. p. 653.
10. Badiou, *Being and Event*, p. 4.
11. In *The Meaning of Sarkozy* Badiou lists these points of resistance, since 1977, as: the first two years of the Portuguese revolution, the beginning of the Solidarity movement in Poland, the first phase of the insurrection against the Shah in Iran, the creation of *L'Organisation Politique* (Badiou's own group) in France, and the Zapatista movement in Mexico. In more contemporary terms Badiou suggests the need to analyse Hezbollah and Hamas, to pay attention to peasant uprisings in China, and to look at the actions of 'Maoists' in Nepal and India (p. 111 note 6).
12. Badiou, *Metapolitics*, p. xxxv.
13. Badiou, *The Meaning of Sarkozy*, p. 18.
14. Badiou, *The Century*, p. 32.
15. Ibid. p. 8.

16. Ibid. p. 64.
17. Badiou, 'Beyond Formalisation', p. 116.
18. John Polkinghorne points out in *Quantum Theory: A Very Short Introduction* that 'the full articulation of the theory requires the use of its natural language, mathematics' (p. i).
19. Badiou, *The Century*, p. 56.
20. Ibid. p. 56.
21. See Noys, 'Monumental Construction'.
22. Badiou, *The Century*, p. 56.
23. Badiou, *Theory of the Subject*, p. 131.
24. In fact, in *Theory of the Subject*, Badiou argued that Terror was correlated with the superego and that a truly radical revolution 'participates in the courageous tipping of the scales into destruction and the just audacity of recomposition' (p. 172; see also pp. 292–4).
25. Badiou, 'Beyond Formalisation', p. 119.
26. Badiou, *The Century*, p. 56.
27. Badiou, 'The Crisis of the Negative', p. 653.
28. Ibid. p. 652.
29. As Badiou states: 'this politics of subtraction is no longer immediately destructive, antagonistic, or militarized', Ibid. p. 650.
30. Ibid. p. 653.
31. Ibid. p. 654.
32. Ibid. p. 654.
33. Badiou, *Polemics*, p. 143.
34. On this period of Badiou's work, as well as reading *Theory of the Subject* (especially pp. 111–76), see also the excellent account by Bruno Bosteels in his article 'Post-Maoism: Badiou and Politics', and for further detail on Badiou's valorisation of destruction see Alberto Toscano's article 'Religion and Revolt'.
35. Badiou, *Theory of the Subject*, p. 198; Hallward, 'Order and Event', p. 100.
36. Nina Power and Alberto Toscano, in 'The Philosophy of Restoration', provide a useful account of Badiou's philosophical and political position in the 1970s (pp. 35–40), including Badiou's own diagram of the field of theory at this time (p. 39).
37. Badiou, 'Roads to Renegacy', p. 131.
38. UCFML, 'Maoism', p. 517.
39. Badiou, *Theory of the Subject*.
40. Hallward, 'Order and Event', p. 100.
41. Ibid. p. 120.
42. Ibid. p. 122.
43. Badiou, *Polemics*, pp. 133–48.
44. This emphasis on indiscernability also links Badiou to Jacques Rancière. In *Logics of Worlds* Badiou remarks on the 'very real affinity' between him and Rancière, which is the ground on which their 'unending

dispute takes place' (p. 561) (for that dispute see Rancière, 'Aesthetics, Inaesthetics, Anti-aesthetics', and Badiou, *Metapolitics*, pp. 107–23).

45. Negri, '*Kairòs,* Alma Venus, Multitudo', p. 154.
46. See Gillespie, *The Mathematics of Novelty: Badiou's Minimalist Metaphysics* and Noys, 'The Powers of the Negative'.
47. Bosteels, 'Post-Maoism', p. 619.
48. Badiou, 'The Crisis of the Negative', p. 652.
49. Badiou, 'Three Negations', p. 1878.
50. This analysis can be read as a return to Badiou's earlier analysis of degrees of contradiction and force outlined in *Theory of the Subject* (p. 25).
51. Badiou, 'Three Negations', p. 1880.
52. Ibid. p. 1880.
53. Badiou, *Being and Event*, p. 181.
54. Badiou, 'Three Negations', p. 1883.
55. Ibid. p. 1883.
56. See Badiou, *Polemics*, pp. 75–97.
57. Badiou, *Logics of Worlds*, p. 420.
58. Ibid. p. 420.
59. Ibid. p. 423.
60. Rom 1. 4: 15.
61. Badiou, 'Destruction, Negation, Subtraction'.
62. Badiou, 'Of Which Real is this Crisis the Spectacle?', p. 143; for a more nuanced use of Badiou's recent work to explore the subjective forms of political Islam see Alberto Toscano's essay, 'The Bourgeois and the Islamist'.
63. Badiou, 'Destruction, Negation, Subtraction'.
64. John Roberts, in his essay 'On the Limits of Negation in Badiou's Theory of Art', has argued that Badiou's 'interplay' of destruction and subtraction risks only producing an '*incomplete or deflected* Hegelianization of the avant-garde and negation' (p. 277). In fact, we could return, as Bruno Bosteels suggests, to Badiou's *Theory of the Subject*, where Badiou argues that Hegel remains in 'a circular completion' (p. 34) that requires a further scission of the dialectic towards force and the historical.
65. Badiou, 'Destruction, Negation, Subtraction'.
66. Badiou, 'Of Which Real is this Crisis the Spectacle?', pp. 158–62.
67. Jean Baudrillard, *The Transparency of Evil*, pp. 75–80.
68. Badiou, *The Meaning of Sarkozy*, p. 11.
69. Badiou, 'Destruction, Negation, Subtraction'.
70. Badiou, *The Century*, p. 65.
71. Badiou, 'Destruction, Negation, Subtraction'.
72. Ibid.
73. Badiou, *Theory of the Subject*, p. 329.
74. Ibid. p. 329.
75. Ibid. p. 330.

76. In *Being and Event*, Badiou diagnoses this active nihilism as 'speculative leftism', the belief in the absolute event that all too easily folds over into accepting the unalterable reign of power (pp. 210–11); see also Bosteels, 'The Speculative Left' and 'Radical Antiphilosophy'.
77. Badiou, *Theory of the Subject*, p. 329.
78. Badiou, 'Rhapsody', p. 188.
79. Badiou, 'Of Which Real is this Crisis the Spectacle?', pp. 110–11.
80. See, in particular, Badiou, 'The Caesura of Nihilism'.
81. Badiou, *The Meaning of Sarkozy*, p. 18.
82. Badiou, *The Century*, p. 140.
83. Badiou, *The Meaning of Sarkozy*, p. 94.
84. Badiou, 'The Crisis of the Negative', pp. 646–7.
85. Badiou, 'Of Which Real is this Crisis the Spectacle?', p. 163.
86. Badiou, *The Meaning of Sarkozy*, p. 112.
87. Badiou, *Metapolitics*, p. 27.
88. Ibid. p. 34.
89. Badiou, *The Century*, p. 125.
90. Ibid. p. 126.
91. Ibid. p. 125.
92. See Deleuze and Guattari, *Kafka*.
93. See Critchley, '"Fault Lines"', and Gibson, *Beckett & Badiou*; cf. Badiou, 'On Simon Critchley's *Infinitely Demanding*', p. 161.
94. Simon Critchley, 'Comedy and Finitude'.
95. Aeschylus, *The Oresteia*, p. 106 (in Ted Hughes's translation).
96. Badiou, *Theory of the Subject*, p. 163.
97. Ibid. p. 167.
98. Ibid. p. 165.
99. Ibid. p. 330; and see the diagram on p. 328.
100. Badiou, *The Meaning of Sarkozy*, p. 75.
101. Ibid. p. 72.
102. Ibid. p. 76.
103. Badiou, *The Century*, p. 124.
104. Contrary to the usual image of the western as racist and patriarchal Gilberto Perez, in the first half of his chapter 'American Tragedy' on the western (*The Material Ghost*, pp. 233–51), argues that it is not politically univocal, but a sophisticated reflection, in the mode of romance or allegory, on the foundational role of violence in the formation of community.
105. The film was directed by Edwin Sherin and scripted by Roland Kibbee and David Rayfiel from an Elmore Leonard novel of the same name.
106. Žižek often refers to the racism of the Klu Klux Klan as exemplary of the 'obscene underside' – the licensed or sanctioned 'transgression', which actually functions as the necessary support of official law, See *Violence*, p. 143, p. 149.
107. Badiou, *Theory of the Subject*, p. 232.

108. Ibid. p. 160.

109. Lee Edelman's *No Future* (2004) is the emblematic work of such an abso-lutised real *qua* negativity, which is defined in terms of an anti-political queer negativity that ruptures completely with any social reproduction (what Edelman calls 'reproductive futurism'). For a critique of Edelman's irrationalism see Nina Power's excellent article, 'Non-Reproductive Futurism'.

110. In *The Four Fundamental Concepts of Psycho-Analysis* Lacan remarks that psychoanalysis is a praxis 'which places man in a position to treat the real by the symbolic' (p. 6) and insists that: 'The analyst's desire is not a pure desire' (p. 276); see also Badiou, *Theory of the Subject*, p. 129.

Conclusion

I

If philosophy, as Gilles Deleuze claims, is about posing the right problem rather than finding the correct solution then, contra Deleuze, we have argued that the correct problem is the problem of *negativity*. To conclude requires some clarification of this problem, and especially its dissociation from a number of common confusions. Negativity is all too persistently associated with a pernicious abstraction, whether in the form of the violent abstractions of a communist politics that would disrupt and destroy the true density of the life-world or, symmetrically, in the form of the abstractive creative destruction of capitalism, which itself is an equally utopian project of violently re-making the life-world.[1] Reflecting this *doxa*, Simon Critchley argues that the radical politics of the 1960s was doomed by a 'politics of abstraction . . . attached to an idea at the expense of a frontal denial of reality.' [2] Critchley's call for a new self-abnegating 'politics of love'[3] is at one with a number of contemporary attempts to solve this antinomy of abstraction by recourse to 'warmer' affirmative abstractions,[4] whether they be found in the 'richness' of the material density of the world, in an immanent ontological point of resistance, in the exception of an event or in Christian mysticism. Such 'solutions' merely compound the problem of abstraction by the creation of a pseudo-concrete 'point' of affirmation somehow external to real abstraction. Instead, I have argued for the return to negativity as the means for the immanent of traversal of these real abstractions. It is the abstractive potential of negativity that allows us to re-pose the problem of agency in terms of rupturing with this aporetical structure.

An initial difficulty for this concept of immanent negativity is raised by Slavoj Žižek: the necessity 'to transpose revolutionary negativity into a truly new positive order'.[5] This demand for transposition results from the collapse of a really meaningful communist politics, and so the collapse of the antinomy or aporia between the violent abstraction of communism and the violent abstraction of capital. In this situation we face the monism of capital itself, and a monism in which the negative is completely correlated with, and subsumed by, the destructive and abstract force of capital. Žižek provocatively suggests that the Chinese Cultural Revolution, which could be regarded as a singular attempt to incarnate, from within a Stalinist configuration, a politics of permanent revolution and perpetual negativity led, by the cunning of reason, to the implantation of capitalism as 'permanent revolution'.[6] In this situation the question of the transposition from a fruitless oppositional negativity which mimics capital's creative destruction to a new 'positive' conception of an alternative social order becomes crucial. Badiou and Žižek have repeatedly, and provocatively, insisted on the necessity of discipline and order as the essential virtues for such a positive project, against the false novelty of capitalist negativity.[7]

The politics of negativity once used to figure a resistance to the sclerotic positivities of the official labour movement and the institutions of social democracy. Perry Anderson, writing in 1964, contrasted the institutionalised British Labour movement, as the 'monument to the positivity of the oldest working class in the world', with the negativity of the working class, 'whose end is to abolish class society and so effectively itself'.[8] Negativity had the therapeutic effect of dissolving the tendency of social-democratic forms to 'lock' the working class in place by valorising it as 'labour'. At the same time, Anderson also insisted on a dialectic of negativity and positivity, because if we take the working class as 'pure negativity, it would be immolated in a perpetual uprising'.[9] Now, the values have been inverted. In the wake of the collapse of the social-democratic compact negativity is identified with the *perpetuum mobile* of capitalism, and a purer and superior positivity with the necessary affirmation, order and discipline to disrupt the 'capitalist reappropriation of revolutionary dynamism'.[10] If we are to rehabilitate negativity it is necessary to *separate* it from this particular ambiguous identification with perpetual revolution.

To begin to do so I want to briefly reflect on Deleuze's essay 'Coldness and Cruelty' (1967), which can be read as a reflection on the politics of negativity. In contrasting Sade and Masoch, Deleuze argues that: 'Underlying the work of Sade is negation in its broadest and deepest sense.'[11] This negativity operates in two forms: a secondary partial negativity associated with the rupture of existing social laws through criminality, perversion and transgression, and a primary negativity, which takes the form of the perpetual flowing negativity of

'Nature' itself, fundamentally indifferent to all human laws and values. Of course, the aporia is that we can only reach primary negativity by means of secondary negativity, and so the pure negativity of Nature seems a fleeting and disappearing 'transcendental illusion'. The political correlative of this work of negation is Sade's radicalised Republican political programme of 'anarchic institutions of perpetual motion and permanent revolution'.[12] Such institutions, however, recapitulate the aporia. They mimic an endlessly receding primary negativity, and remain bound to a perpetual incitement of secondary negations that never cohere into anything like a new order. Deleuze also defines this politics of sadism in accelerationist terms, as based in 'quantitative techniques of accumulation and acceleration, mechanically grounded in a materialistic theory'.[13] Unlike Deleuze's own later accelerationism, here this dynamic is posed as deeply problematic. The implication is that the repeated and structural failure of the politics of sadism is all too close to the accumulative dynamic of capital itself.

Deleuze contrasts this politics of sadism with a politics of masochism that is 'frozen', suspenseful, and secures an ideal in fantasy. Against the perpetual abstract frenzy of negativity in sadism, in masochism we have an:

> operation that consists neither in negating nor even destroying, but rather in radically contesting the validity of that which is: it suspends belief in and neutralises the given in such a way that a new horizon opens up beyond the given and in place of it.[14]

Implicitly we could say masochism already ciphers for Deleuze a *properly* affirmative politics, not correlated to Sade's rather po-faced hyper-republicanism, but to the humorous subversion of the law through the parodic use of the contract. Whereas Sadian negativity remains bound to a continual and futile transgression of the existing law, masochism's suspensive disavowal of the law permits the constitution of a new law, and in particular a new place for the people to come.[15] Deleuze's implicit preference is for the politics of 1848 over the politics of 1789, for Masoch's parodic politics of 'agrarian communism' over Sade's abstract republican universality.[16]

My own inscription of negativity in terms of *détournement* is designed to subvert exactly this kind of identification. Negativity no longer lines up with a purely destructive will, the desire to reach an impossible diabolical evil, and the impotent acting-out which results from trying to bridge between a secondary partial negation and a primary pure negativity. This is the usual ideological image of negativity as absolute destruction, which we have repeatedly encountered. Instead, the persistence of the negative undermines exactly this structure by excavating a negativity that is suspensive and preservative, rather than one dreaming of a fantasmatic apocalypse. Such a politics of negation refuses the identification of negativity with the supposed 'abstractions' of an ideologically-determined revolutionary politics, at least in the traditional model of Terror, and the symmetrical displacement of such a politics onto capital as a perpetual-motion device driven by negativity. This is a negativity that defies the terms of Deleuze's schema; neither sadist nor masochist, republican nor agrarian communist, but a new contemporary communism.

II

A second critical question concerns the relation of this suspensive politics of negativity to capitalist real abstraction. Can a politics of negativity truly grasp the function of these real abstractions? According to Roberto Finelli, Marxism has typically treated the relationship abstract-concrete in terms of opposition-contradiction, and so in terms of a dialectical politics of the negative. Unpacking this re-coding he argues that a 'Marxism of contradiction' presupposes a humanist and anthropocentric political subject, classically the proletariat, which is the concrete producer of wealth subject and so in *contradiction* to an abstract and alienating capital. In contrast he proposes a 'Marxism of abstraction', which analyses the dynamic of capital in terms of abstraction-emptying out rather than opposition-contradiction.[17] This form of Marxism recognises that the abstractive force of capital is one that goes all the way down and which is able, in Marx's strategic use of Hegelese, to presuppose and posit any element for further accumulation. In Finelli's argument we do not have two subjects – the concrete proletariat versus abstract capital – but rather: 'the abstract occupies and itself invades the concrete, filling it according to the exigencies of its expansive-reproductive logic'.[18] In this way, as presciently noted by Fredric Jameson, Marxism provides the means for grasping postmodernity as the deepening of the logic of capitalist abstraction.[19] All the familiar tropes of the postmodern – simulacra, depthlessness, loss of affect, fragmentation, etc. – refer to the realisation of abstract and impersonal wealth and the concrete dissimulated as the surface.

For Finelli, then, the true function of dialectical negation is the motor of capitalist abstraction.[20] Real abstraction creates a topsy-turvy world by this emptying out, in which the more labour is de-personalised and abstracted the more it appears as creative and personalised. Walter Benjamin noted in his study of Baudelaire that while the principle of creativity 'flatters the self-esteem of the productive person, it effectively guards the interests of a social order that is hostile to him'.[21] The social order produces the ideology of creativity that imputes powers to the artist or worker which she no longer possesses, dissimulating the intensified production of capital by making the abstract disappear. In this situation negativity appears, at best, superfluous or, at worst, commensurate again with the logic of capital. As we have seen, however, the creative ideology produces exactly those models of ontological creativity and primacy that we have been contesting under the name of 'affirmationism'. It is not a matter of abandoning negativity; what is required is its re-figuration away from the dialectical conception that obeys the logic of abstraction. In this way negativity itself has to be *détourné*, no longer conceived of as corresponding to an externalised and absolutised duality of 'Being and nothingness' or 'Capital and proletariat', but now as the means to contest the universalising power of the abstract *from within*. Without this effect of negativity we risk falling back into the most pessimistic of sub-Baudrillardian positions.

The clue for this re-figuration of negativity can, again, be traced back to Benjamin and his retention of it as an operator of critique. In his commentary on Karl Kraus, Benjamin argues that:

> For far too long the accent was placed on creativity. People are only creative to the extent they avoid tasks and supervision. Work is a supervised task – its model: political and technical work – is attended by dirt and detritus, intrudes destructively into matter, is abrasive to what is already achieved, critical toward its conditions, and is in all this opposite to that of the dilettante luxuriating in creation.[22]

In Benjamin's argument the rupture comes not from disindentification with capital by a supposedly 'superior' principle of creativity, whether that is ontological or evental. Instead it comes through an immanent *over-identification* with labour in terms of political and technical work that is conceived as a negative and disruptive intervention.

This should not be mistaken for a re-valorisation of 'real' work against the supposedly 'abstract' form of creative or cognitive labour. Such a manoeuvre would find itself in consonance with the valorisation of labour against capital posed by the traditional workers' movement, or with the current retrograde celebrations of productive labour in opposition to sterile speculation. This would restore a Marxism of contradiction, and in doing so feed into capital's own valorisation of labour as the source of value. What I am suggesting via Benjamin is a complex re-inscription and *détournement* of work against work as it is usually conceived. Rather than a superior workerism I take Benjamin to be re-posing the need for tasks and supervision as means of breaking the ideology of creativity, an ideology that has only taken greater hold since he wrote. Negativity is crucial to this re-inscription because it is only the access to such negativity, to such 'dirt and detritus', that enables the splitting of work from within, by the disruptive working-over of 'abstract labour'.

III

How are we to negate real abstractions? Over-identification in this case explicitly refuses the positing of any exceptional or irrecuperable element. Contra to contemporary *doxa*, resistance does not, necessarily, come first. Instead, the negation of real abstractions is a matter, to use Lacan's terminology, of *traversal*. This implies a relational engagement with real abstractions, rather than an insistence on a non-relational principle, whether immanent, transcendental or transcendent. This relational engagement is, however, a relation of rupture. What might this mean? Žižek offers a clue in his discussion of how we should read Kafka:

> Reading Kafka demands a great effort of abstraction – not of learning more (the proper interpretive horizon of understanding his work), but of *unlearning* the standard interpretive references, so that we become able to open up to the raw force of Kafka's writing.[23]

In a reverse of a homeopathic model it is *greater* abstraction that leads to the rupture of real abstraction. It is the line of the negative, I am arguing, which forms this greater abstraction that gives us purchase of the real abstractions that govern us. It is a matter of probing the 'truth' of real abstractions as concrete appearances through their negation.

To give some more precision to this prodecure I want to refer to one of Althusser's lesser-known articles, 'Cremonini, Painter of the Abstract' (1966). Although deeply antithetical to Hegel, and perhaps *because* Althusser is so deeply antithetical to Hegel, it is this work that gives us the lineaments of a possible negation of real abstractions. The importance of Cremonini, a friend of Althusser's, is that he is not an *abstract painter* but a *painter of abstraction*: '"painting" in a sense we have to define, real relations (as relations they are necessarily *abstract*) between "men" and their "things", or rather, to give the term its stronger sense, between "things" and *their* "men"'.[24] The work of his painting is one that falls on these relations and hence, for Althusser, has to be detached from the normal ideological models of the creative subject and aesthetic consumption. These models are symmetrical: the ideology of creation insists on the category of the subject as producer and consumer, while the ideology of consumption insists on the work of art as *object*. Instead, in Cremonini, we find the painting of relations that allows us to see the relation between a 'work' and *its* painter – mimicking the actual effect of real abstraction.

What Cremonini paints, according to Althusser, is history, which for humans is marked by 'the *abstraction* of their sites, spaces, objects, i.e. "*in the last instance*" by the *real abstraction* which determines and sums up these first abstractions: the relations which constitute their *living conditions*'.[25] It is not that he paints 'living conditions', or social relations or 'class itself', but that he does paint, through visible connections, 'the *determinate absence* which governs them'.[26] What is traced in this tracing of visible connections is the structure that governs us, and which never appears as such, and so can be depicted 'only by traces and effects, negatively, by indices of absence'.[27] The negativity of the structure, defined as a differential structure without positive terms, as the content-free and differential structure of capital, can only be rendered in the re-tracing of the negative absence of relations. We have no image of capital, capital itself is a kind of pure relationality, a pure abstract relation of value, labour and accumulation, which can only be 'seen' in negative. This is why the negation of real abstractions demands further abstraction, as abstraction is the only possible means to reveal this pure relationality which conceals itself in plain sight, in the value-form which is free of content and so can 'hold' any content.

Focusing on Cremonini's depiction of human faces – the ideological proof of the individual human subject – Althusser stresses how he subjects them to '*determinate* deformation',[28] another name for what we have been calling *détournement*, or what is usually referred to as determinate negation. What this deformation disrupts is the expressiveness of the face, its form of individuality, which places the individual as the creator of objects and the world – precisely the disruption of what Meillassoux calls a correlationist position.[29] Instead of being creators the subjects are left as the mere trace of their gestures:

> They are haunted by an absence: a purely negative absence, that of the humanist function which is refused them, and which they refuse; and a positive, determinate absence, that of the *structure* of the world which determines them, which makes them the anonymous beings they are, the structural effects of the real relations which govern them.[30]

What is marked is the subject as structural effect, the ideological effect of the dominance of real abstraction, in which we are governed, oddly enough, by the absence of structural relations.

This rendering of abstraction is materialist and anti-humanist because it absents the subject, and in doing so denies us the complicity of consumption and enjoyment. It is 'the refutation *in actu* of the ideology of creation'.[31] This includes the absenting of the painter himself, who sacrifices his own expressiveness to remain 'present' in his paintings only in the form of relations, and more precisely in the absence of the human subject from those relations. What we find, as a result, is that we cannot recognise ourselves in the image – we have none of the satisfaction, always tinged with aggression and rivalry, of the Lacanian imaginary. Instead, we are led to *knowledge* of our subjection to real abstractions. The result is that: 'we know that "consciousness" is secondary, even when it *thinks*, in the principle of materialism, its derivatory and conditioned position'.[32] What Cremonini proposes, in Althusser's reading, is a traversal of real abstractions that does not reveal the hidden subject beneath, whether individual or collective, but the structural absence of the subject. We might suggest that the passage through real abstractions leads to a kind of practical rupture of correlationism: a downgrading, or degrading, of creativity and the subject as the principle of politics or philosophy. In its place we have the subject as the agent of negativity.

IV

We still do not appear to have fully explained how this suspensive politics of the negative might perform the 'transposition' of negativity onto positivity. My slightly oblique and negative approach to this question is one dictated by Marx and Engels's anti-utopian definition of communism as 'the *real* movement which abolishes the present state of things'.[33] I am suggesting that this 'real movement' is one of traversal, and that this traversal is not only negative, in the usual sense, but also preservative – and hence 'positive'. In this way it corresponds to Deleuze's invocation of a politics that 'radically contests the validity of what is', that 'neutralises the given' and so 'opens a new horizon'. To be more precise, and more concrete, I want to suggest that such a politics involves the preservation not merely of utopian moments or fantasies within the 'smooth space' of capitalist ideology, but rather the memories and re-actualisations of forms and modes of struggle – including the achievements of those struggles in curtailing the demands of the market and carving out areas of non-commodified life. Negativity is therefore not simply correlated with the violent dissolution of existing positivities, but also with the ruptural preservation of past and existing negations of capitalist relations.

To more precisely specify this 'preservative' function of negativity I want to refer to the biblical *katechon* – a deeply enigmatic figure, which occurs only once in the bible, as 'that which restrains' the coming of the Antichrist.[34] The *katechon* has a strange dual status, because, as Paolo Virno explains: 'By impeding the triumph of the Antichrist, *katechon* impedes, at the same time, the redemption to be accomplished by the Messiah'.[35] In this way the *katechon* 'delays the end of the world',[36] and so for an eschatological Marxism the *katechon* may be any reform that delays the final reckoning and so the ushering in of the new communist society. In fact, the figure has been more often deployed by conservative political thinkers – notably Carl Schmitt – as a figure for the state's function in restraining human 'evil', or, as Perry Anderson acerbically notes, restraining 'the risks of democracy'.[37] In Virno's re-figuration the *katechon* becomes the power of the 'negation of negation', the ability to disrupt the negative power of language that can define certain groups as 'not human' by negating the negation – 'not not human'.[38] Again, as in Freud ('Negation'), here negativity is confined to the linguistic and given a particular negative (in the bad sense), form.

Instead, I want to suggest giving the *katechon* a more empirical and concrete form as those social institutions and forms which restrain the commodification of existence. In a very difference sense to that of Virno's the *katechon* does embody a kind of 'negation of negation', in terms of indicating the disruptive 'preservation' of those social forms that restrict and erode the colonisation of the life-world by real abstractions. Contrary to an accelerationist insistence on radicalising existing lines of capitalist flight, our thinking returns to Benjaminian insistence on putting the brakes on such forces.[39] It involves resisting the generalised anarchistic form of the market, which has too often bewitched the forms of resistance to capital.[40] Fredric Jameson argues: 'Today, . . ., the most urgent task seems to me the defense of the welfare state and of those regulations and entitlements that have been characterized as barriers to a completely free market and its prosperities'.[41] While this would seem to run up against the problem of reformism and the restraint of revolution, Jameson's elegant solution is to claim that: 'We must support social democracy because its inevitable failure constitutes the basic lesson, the fundamental pedagogy, of a genuine Left'.[42] The difficulty with such a position, however, is its cynicism: we are not genuinely defending what remains, but merely temporarily instrumentalising it.

In an interview with Timothy Brennan, Moishe Postone agrees on the necessity of recognising how the state can offer partial containment of the market, and that to reach even a pre-revolutionary situation would require 'a series of reforms'.[43] One of the signs of the contemporary 'anarchistic mood' is a suspicion of the state among many activists and theorists that would refuse such an accommodation as reformist, while often making demands to the state. My position is, perhaps, similarly uneasy. The negation of the value-form, and the assault on the accumulative logic of capital, requires the non-cynical use and recognition of the *katechon* of those regulated, and often state-directed, forms of re-embedding. While there has been a common tendency in a number of critical traditions, especially that of the Frankfurt school, to argue for utopian traces of resistance within the commodified forms of capital, images of the good life, I want to also suggest that there are more concrete non-utopian social forms of resistance. In the UK, for example, one notable example, which has been steadily and cynically eroded, is that of the National Health Service (NHS). Hardly a revolutionary measure, and, of course, hardly immune to the stratifications of class society, it has, however, provided an essential point of resistance in the political imaginary, and, of course, as an actual experience, of the relatively non-commodified.[44]

Radicalised theoretical forms, both affirmative and negative, have often had a disavowed and complicated relation to the post-war achievements of social democracy (and state communism): at once dependent on them as a point of reference, but also highly critical. With the continuing destruction and erosion of those achievements it becomes possible to see the need for a flexibility of thinking, and, I am suggesting, the detachment of the thinking of negation from a purified and absolute politics of abstractive destruction. This does not imply acceptance of the state as the mechanism of liberation, but rather a closer probing of the negation of state-forms, and a refusal to reify or suppose an isomorphy between those forms and the forms of the capitalist market. This thinking of negativity is also oriented against the tendency of value-form Marxism, such as Finelli's or Postone's, to compose an 'automatic' capital without any forms of counter-agency – such a conception mirroring, in an inverse form, accelerationism. While we need to be aware of the immanent grounding of our critique, we should not transform capital into the 'untranscendable horizon' of our times. The necessity is therefore for a cartography of negativity, which can identify and map the neuralgic points of capitalism – the fact, as Postone recognises but does not adequately theorise, that capital: 'is characterized by a complex interplay of what we might regard as positive and negative moments, all of which are historically constituted'.[45] This is particularly evident as we witness a series of overlapping crises that fall, as Perry Anderson has indicated, exactly at the points of commodification that Polanyi argued constituted the 'fictitious commodities' essential to capitalism: labour, nature and money.[46]

This problem of *détournement* as *katechon* cuts across the question of the state because only in such a way is it possible to engage with the geopolitical and macroeconomic issues raised by this series of crises.[47] To confine *détournement* to a cultural strategy is to confine it to the field saturated with the ideology of creativity. Instead, I am trying to figure the negativity of 'expropriating the expropriators' as a potential model for social, political and economic forms of re-appropriation. The point of a *relation* of rupture is that it forms such a relation with *all* forms of ideological dominance, but in particular with real abstraction as the operator of capitalist valorisation. While the ultimate aim of such a strategy is the abolition of the law of value, it also constantly aims at preserving, in its traversal, the ruptural points in-built to capitalism as a field of antagonism. Contra Badiou, the negative is no longer correlated with a defensive function. Instead that function falls to the 'positive' moment of the *katechon*, while negativity as traversal is correlated to the function of strategic attack.

Such reflections may seem deeply out of place in a book of theory or philosophy, however the rehabilitation of negativity I have embarked upon is dictated by the relation between forms of thought and social forms, and so includes the necessity not only to think forms of thought out of social forms, but also how forms of thought might engage or re-engage with social forms – how they might find 'their' social forms. In particular, as I have suggested, theories not only mimic social forms, but also *imply* particular social forms. An immanent critique of theory is therefore a matter of tracing and drawing out these implications to make them available for traversal. As I previously remarked, part of the character of my rehabilitation of negativity is a certain vulgarity of thought, something like a *détourné* form of Brechtian *plumpes Denken*.

V

The crux of the problem of negativity is agency. Malcolm Bull has noted that the most intractable problem for contemporary radical politics, and, I would add, radical theory, is not a lack of positive pro-posals, but 'who is going to make it happen?' [48] I have traced the oscil-lation in affirmationist theory between deflationary and inflationary conceptions of agency, which all seem to founder in finding purchase on the ideological, political and economic forms of contemporary capitalism: Derrida's deconstruction of subjectivity radically attenu-ates agency, to the point of leaving it commensurable to capital's own 'hauntological' operations;[49] Deleuze's accelerationism disintegrates the subject to release and radicalise capital *qua* subject; Latour both inflates interventional capacities of agency and restrains them within the confines of networks; Negri also inflates agency by making the multitude co-extensive with capitalism and the sign of an incipient communism; Badiou, meanwhile, inflates the necessity of subjectivity through a deflationary strategy of leaving such subjectivation dependent on the passive acceptance of events. This veering between thinking agency as all powerful or completely evacuated is perhaps best seen in Giorgio Agamben's oscillatory conception of agency as 'bare life', which is at once the misery of a completely denuded existence and the glory of an entirely redeemed subject.[50] This antinomy replicates the fact that, as Postone points out: 'Marx analyzes capitalism as a society in which there is a great deal of individual agency and a great deal of historical structural constraint'.[51]

In the contemporary context Bull argues that this structural constraint takes the unholy form of a feedback loop between two types of agency: market globalisation, which then leads to populist assertions of sovereignty, which then, paradoxically, exacerbate the market form, so that: 'All agents seem trapped within this cycle of unintended effect and ineffectual intent'.[52] The passivity of market forms of agency, which are, as Polanyi suggests, actively structured and reinforced by the activity of the state, generate their own active responses, but as false alternatives to capital. What has concerned me is how affirmationist concepts of subjectivity, which stridently assert the necessity of activity and agency, all too often replicate this structure by leaving the effects of real abstractions unthought. In this way they may have an energising political effect, which is certainly better than the usual conformism, but this is vitiated by their lack of specificity and abstract character. Instead, I am suggesting that if we do not think capitalism then capitalism will certainly think us.

The theoretical rehabilitation of negativity is not an off-the-shelf solution to this new aporia of agency. I have argued, however, that it permits a better re-posing of the problem, and the means to start to think the rudiments of forms of agency that could traverse and contest the dominance of real abstractions, and the structural and geopolitical pressures of the present. Part of the necessity for the posing of this problem is to regard capitalism itself as an ontological, metaphysical and philosophical form. In this way we can more accurately assess our own philosophical and theoretical concepts of agency. At the moment, of course, no substantial *actual* agents stand in this place. The promise of negativity, we could say, is a largely empty one and modesty is no doubt necessary, rather than the inflation of theory as the site of solution. That said, the incorrect posing of the problem of agency has severely constrained the forms of affirmative theory and the wider affirmationist consensus. In particular these theoretical models often remain tilting at reified models of the state and capital derived from the previous social-democratic consensus, while reproducing in their alternative conceptions the dynamics of a deterritorialising and disembedding capitalism. Although modest, sceptical and suspicious of grandiose claims for novelty or theoretical invention, the rehabilitation of negativity is crucial to negotiating the inhospitable climate for radical theory. A first step is the negation of capitalism as the untranscendable horizon of our time.

NOTES

1. See Polanyi, *The Great Transformation*.
2. Critchley, 'Mystical Anarchism', p. 300.
3. Ibid. p. 304.
4. Alberto Toscano, in 'The Culture of Abstraction', notes that 'recent conceptual production has sought to circumvent the customary reproaches against abstract thought by promoting concepts that are ever more vital, supple, pliant: flows, rhizomes, the virtual, scapes, the diagram, and so on' (p. 56). The implication of this approach is, as he goes on to state, that: 'The cold abstractions of yesteryear must be replaced by what we could call warm abstractions' (p. 56).
5. Žižek, *In Defence of Lost Causes*, p. 194.
6. Žižek, 'Mao Tse-Tung', pp. 25–6; in his revised presentation of this analysis in his *In Defence of Lost Causes*, Žižek argues that the Cultural Revolution functions at two levels: as inherently inconsistent passage to capital *and* as an Event, as the incarnated idea of egalitarian justice which is not exhausted in its reversal into capitalist transformation (p. 207).
7. Badiou, 'Crisis of the Negative', p. 650; Žižek, 'Divine Violence and Liberated Territories'.
8. Anderson, *English Questions*, p. 36.
9. Ibid. p. 36.
10. Žižek, 'Mao Tse-Tung', p. 27.
11. Deleuze, 'Coldness and Cruelty', p. 26.
12. Ibid. p. 87.
13. Ibid. p. 70.
14. Ibid. p. 31.
15. Deleuze's analysis of masochism prefigures his own later endorsement of a politics of the minor in which the 'people is missing' (*Cinema 2*, p. 216).
16. Deleuze, 'Coldness and Cruelty', p. 96.
17. Finelli, 'Abstraction versus Contradiction', p. 66.
18. Ibid. p. 66.
19. See Jameson, *Postmodernism* and *The Cultural Turn*.

20. Finelli, 'Abstraction versus Contradiction', p. 67, p. 70.
21. Benjamin, *Charles Baudelaire*, p. 71.
22. Benjamin, *Illuminations*, p. 289.
23. Žižek, *The Parallax View*, p. 114.
24. Althusser, *Lenin and Philosophy*, p. 210.
25. Ibid. p. 215.
26. Ibid. p. 215.
27. Ibid. p. 216.
28. Ibid. p. 217.
29. See Meillassoux, *After Finitude*.
30. Althusser, *Lenin and Philosophy*, p. 217.
31. Ibid. p. 218.
32. Ibid. p. 220.
33. Marx and Engels, *The German Ideology*, pp. 56–7.
34. 2 Thess. 2: 6–7.
35. Virno, *Multitude*, p. 60.
36. Ibid. p. 60.
37. Anderson, *Spectrum*, p. 26.
38. Virno, *Multitude*, p. 189.
39. See Löwy, *Fire Alarm*, pp. 66–7.
40. See Brennan, *Wars of Position* and Jameson, 'Lenin and Revisionism'.
41. Jameson, 'Lenin and Revisionism', p. 69.
42. Ibid. p. 69.
43. Postone (with Brennan), 'Labor and the Logic of Abstraction', p. 319.
44. I owe this point to Owen Hatherley.
45. Postone (with Brennan), 'Labor and the Logic of Abstraction', p. 324.
46. Perry Anderson, 'Jottings', p. 28.
47. On the geopolitical articulation of revolutionary subjectivity consult Alberto Toscano's 'Carl Schmitt in Beijing'.
48. Bull, 'The Limits, p. 19.
49. Badiou, *Logics of Worlds*, p. 50.
50. Postone (with Brennan), 'Labor and the Logic of Abstraction', p. 317.
51. See Noys, 'Separacija in reverzibilnost'.
52. Bull, 'The Limits', p. 20.

Bibliography

Adorno, Theodor W. *Negative Dialectics* [1966], trans. E. B. Ashton. London: Routledge & Kegan Paul, 1973.

Aeschylus. *The Oresteia*, trans. Ted Hughes. London: Faber and Faber, 1999.

Agamben, Giorgio. *Homo Sacer: Sovereign Power and Bare Life* [1995], trans. Daniel Heller-Roazen. Stanford, CA: Stanford University Press, 1998.

Agamben, Giorgio. *Potentialities: Collected Essays in Philosophy*, trans. and intro. Daniel Heller-Roazen. Stanford, CA: Stanford University Press, 1999.

Agamben, Giorgio. *Means without End: Notes on Politics*, trans. Vincenzo Binetti and Cesare Casarino. Minneapolis and London: University of Minnesota Press, 2000.

Agamben, Giorgio. *The Time That Remains: A Commentary on the Letter to the Romans* [2000], trans. Patricia Dailey. Stanford, CA: Stanford University Press, 2005.

Ahmad, Aijaz. *In Theory: Classes, Nations, Literatures*. London and New York: Verso, 2008.

Ahmad, Aijaz. 'Reconciling Derrida: Specters of Marx' and Deconstructive Politics'. In *Ghostly Demarcations: A Symposium on Jacques Derrida's Specters of Marx*, ed. Michael Sprinker. London and New York: Verso, 2008, pp. 88–109.

Alliez, Éric. 'Hegel and the Wobblies', trans. William Pagnotta, in Sylvère Lotringer and Christian Marazzi (eds), 'Autonomia: Post-political politics'. *Semiotext(e)* 3.3 (1980): 118–19.

Alliez, Éric. '*Anti-Oedipus* – thirty years on', trans. Alberto Toscano. *Radical Philosophy* 124 (March/April 2004): 6–12.

Alliez, Éric. 'Badiou: The Grace of the Universal'. In 'The Philosophy of Alain Badiou', ed. Matthew Wilkens. *Polygraph* 17 (2005): 267–73.

Alliez, Éric and Antonio Negri. 'Peace and War', trans. Alberto Toscano. *Theory, Culture & Society* 20.2 (2003): 109–18.

Althusser, Louis. *For Marx* [1966], trans. Ben Brewster. Harmondsworth: Penguin, 1969.

Althusser, Louis. *Lenin and Philosophy and Other Essays*, trans. Ben Brewster. London: New Left Books, 1971.

Anderson, Perry. *Arguments within English Marxism*. London: Verso, 1980.

Anderson, Perry. *English Questions*. London and New York: Verso, 1992.

Anderson, Perry. *Spectrum: From Right to Left in the World of Ideas*. London and New York: Verso, 2005.

Anderson, Perry. 'Jottings on the Conjuncture'. *New Left Review* 48 (November–December 2007): 5–37.

Arrighi, Giovanni. 'Hegemony Unravelling II'. *New Left Review* 33 (2005): 83–116.

Aufheben. 'Keep on smiling: Questions on immaterial labour'. *Aufheben* 14 (2006): 23–44.

Aufheben. 'The language of retreat: Paolo Virno's A grammar of the multitude'. *Aufheben* 16 (2008): 25–35.

Aufheben. 'Value struggle or class struggle?' *Aufheben* 16 (2008): 36–48.

Badiou, Alain. *Manifesto for Philosophy*, trans., ed. and intro. Norman Madarasz. Albany: State University of New York Press, 1999.

Badiou, Alain. *Deleuze: The Clamor of Being* [1997], trans. Louise Burchill. Minneapolis and London: University of Minnesota Press, 2000.

Badiou, Alain. *Ethics: an Essay on the Understanding of Evil*, trans. and intro. Peter Hallward. London and New York: Verso, 2001.

Badiou, Alain. 'Who is Nietzsche?'. *Pli* 11 (2001): 1–11.

Badiou, Alain. 'The Caesura of Nihilism'. Lecture given at the University of Cardiff, 25 May 2002.

Badiou, Alain. *Saint Paul: The Foundation of Universalism*, trans. Ray Brassier. Stanford, CA: Stanford University Press, 2003.

Badiou, Alain. 'Beyond formalisation: an interview with Alain Badiou'. *Angelaki* 8.2 (2003): 115–36.

Badiou, Alain. 'The flux and the party: in the margins of *Anti-Oedipus*' [1976], *Polygraph* 15/16 (2004): 75–92.

Badiou, Alain. *Being and Event* [1988], trans. and intro. Oliver Feltham. London and New York: Continuum, 2005.

Badiou, Alain. '*De la dialectique négative dans sa connexion à un certain bilan de Wagner*' (8 January 2005). Available from *Lacan.com*, http://www.lacan.com/badwagnerone.htm [consulted 8 February 2009].

Badiou, Alain. *Metapolitics* [1998], trans. and intro. Jason Barker. London and New York: Verso, 2005.

Badiou, Alain. *Polemics*, trans. and intro. Steve Corcoran. London and New York: Verso, 2006.

Badiou, Alain. *The Century* [2005], trans., with commentary and notes, Alberto Toscano. Cambridge and Malden, MA: Polity, 2007.

Badiou, Alain. 'Destruction, Negation, Subtraction – on Pier Paolo Pasolini', Lecture given at the Graduate Seminar, Art Center College of Design in Pasedena (6 February 2007). Available from *Lacan.com*, http://lacan.com/badpas.htm [consulted 18 August 2007].

Badiou, Alain. *The Meaning of Sarkozy*, trans. David Fernbach. London and New York: Verso, 2008.

Badiou, Alain. 'Of Which Real is this Crisis the Spectacle?', trans. Nina Power and Alberto Toscano. *Infinite Thought blog* (18 October 2008). Available from http://www.cinestatic.com/infinitethought/2008/10/badiou-on-financial-crisis.asp [consulted 23 February 2009].

Badiou, Alain. 'Rhapsody for the Theatre: A Short Philosophical Treatise' [1990], trans. Bruno Bosteels. *Theatre Survey* 49.2 (November 2008): 187–238.

Badiou, Alain. 'Roads to Renegacy', Interview by Eric Hazan, trans. David Fernbach. *New Left Review* 53 (September–October 2008): 125–33.

Badiou, Alain. 'Three Negations'. *Cardozo Law Review* 29.5 (2008): 1877–83.

Badiou, Alain. '"We Need a Popular Discipline": Contemporary Politics and the Crisis of the Negative'. Interview by Filippo Del Lucchese and Jason Smith. *Critical Inquiry* 34 (Summer 2008): 645–59.

Badiou, Alain. *Logics of Worlds* [2006], trans. Alberto Toscano. London and New York: Continuum, 2009.

Badiou, Alain. *Theory of the Subject* [1982], trans. and intro. Bruno Bosteels. London and New York: Continuum, 2009.

Badiou, Alain. 'On Simon Critchley's *Infinitely Demanding*: Ethics of Commitment, Politics of Resistance'. *Critical Horizons: A Journal of Philosophy and Social Theory* 10.2 (August 2009): 154–62.

Badiou, Alain and Slavoj Žižek. *Philosophy in the Present*, ed. Peter Engelmann, trans. Peter Thomas and Alberto Toscano. Cambridge and Malden, MA: Polity, 2009.

Balestrini, Nanni. *The Unseen*, trans. Liz Heron. London and New York: Verso, 1989.

Balibar, Étienne. 'Violence'. *Historical Materialism* 17.1 (2009): 99–125.

Baudrillard, Jean. *Forget Foucault and Forget Baudrillard* [1977], trans. Nicole Dufresne. New York: Semiotext(e), 1987.

Baudrillard, Jean. 'Anorexic Ruins'. In *Looking Back on the End of the World*, ed. Dietmar Kamper and Christoph Wulf, trans. David Antal. New York: Semiotext(e), 1989, pp. 29–45.

Baudrillard, Jean. *Symbolic Exchange and Death* [1976], trans. Iain Hamilton Grant, intro. Mike Gane. London: Sage, 1993.

Baudrillard, Jean. *The Transparency of Evil: Essays on Extreme Phenomena* [1990], trans. J. Benedict. London and New York: Verso, 1993.

Baugh, Bruce. *The French Hegel: from surrealism to postmodernism*. New York and London: Routledge, 2003.

Beckett, Samuel. *Proust and three dialogues with Georges Duthuit*. London: John Calder, 1999.

Benjamin, Walter. *Illuminations*, ed. and intro. Hannah Arendt, trans. Harry Zohn. New York: Schocken, 1968.

Benjamin, Walter. *Charles Baudelaire: A Lyric Poet in the Era of High Capitalism*, trans. Harry Zohn. London and New York: Verso, 1973.

Benjamin, Walter. 'Edward Fuchs, Collector and Historian' [1937]. In

One-Way Street and Other Writings, trans. Edmund Jephcott and Kingsley Shorter. London: New Left Books, 1979, pp. 349–86.

Bennington, Geoffrey. *Deconstruction is not what you think. . . and other short pieces and interviews* (e-book) 2005.

Bensaïd, Daniel. 'Alain Badiou and the Miracle of the Event'. In *Think Again: Alain Badiou and the Future of Philosophy*, ed. Peter Hallward. London: Continuum, 2004, pp. 94–105.

Bensaïd, Daniel. 'On a Recent Book by John Holloway'. *Historical Materialism* 13.4 (2005): 169–92.

Bensaïd, Daniel. '"Leaps Leaps! Leaps!"' In *Lenin Reloaded: Towards a Politics of Truth*, ed. Sebastian Budgen, Stathis Kouvelakis and Slavoj Žižek. Durham, NC and London: Duke University Press, 2007, pp. 148–63.

Bergson, Henri. *Creative Evolution* [1911], trans. Arthur Mitchell. New York: Dover Publications, 1998.

Berardi, Franco 'Bifo'. 'Communism is back but we should call it the therapy of singularisation'. *Generation Online*, 2009. Available from http://www. generation-online.org/p/fp_bifo6.htm [consulted 7 October 2009].

Berardi, Franco. *Precarious Rhapsody: Semiocapitalism and the pathologies of the post-alpha generation*, ed. Erik Empson and Stevphen Shukaitis, trans. Arianna Bove et al. London: Minor Compositions, 2009.

Bernstein, Eduard. *Evolutionary Socialism*, trans. Edith C. Harvey, intro. Sidney Hook. New York: Schocken, 1961.

Bhaskar, Roy. *Dialectic: The Pulse of Freedom*. London and New York: Routledge, 2008.

Bidet, Jacques and Stathis Kouvelakis (eds) *Critical Companion to Contemporary Marxism*. Chicago: Haymarket Books, 2009.

Blackburn, Robin. 'Finance and the Fourth Dimension'. *New Left Review* 39 (May–June 2006): 39–70.

Blackburn, Robin. 'Value Theory and the Chinese Worker: A Reply to Geoff Mann'. *New Left Review* 56 (March–April 2009): 128–35.

Boltanski, Luc and Eve Chiapello. *The New Spirit of Capitalism*. London and New York: Verso, 2007.

Bosteels, Bruno. 'Post-Maoism: Badiou and Politics'. *positions: east asia cultures critique* 13.3 (2005): 575–634.

Bosteels, Bruno. 'The Speculative Left'. *South Atlantic Quarterly* 104.4 (Fall 2005): 751–67.

Bosteels, Bruno. 'Radical Antiphilosophy.' *Radical Philosophy?* ed. Peter Klepec. *Filozofski Vestnik* 29.2 (2008): 155–87.

Bowring, Finn. 'From the mass worker to the multitude: A theoretical contextualisation of Hardt and Negri's *Empire*'. *Capital & Class* 83 (2004): 101–32.

Brassier, Ray. *Nihil Unbound: Enlightenment and Extinction*. Basingstoke: Palgrave Macmillan, 2007.

Brennan, Timothy. *Wars of Position: The Cultural Politics of Left and Right*. New York and Chichester: Columbia University Press, 2006.

Brown, Nicholas and Imre Szeman/Antonio Negri and Michael Hardt. '"Subterranean Passages of Thought": *Empire*'s Inserts', *Cultural Studies* 16.2 (2002): 193–212.

Bull, Malcolm. 'Where is the Anti-Nietzsche?' *New Left Review* 3 (2000): 121–45.

Bull, Malcolm. 'The Limits of Multitude'. *New Left Review* 35 (2005): 19–39.

Butler, Judith, Ernesto Laclau and Slavoj Žižek. *Contingency, Hegemony, Universality: Contemporary Dialogues on the Left*. London and New York: Verso, 2000.

Casarino, Cesare. 'Philopoesis: A Theoretico-Methodological Manifesto'. *boundary 2* 29:1 (2002): 65–96.

Casarino, Cesare and Antonio Negri. 'It's a Powerful Life: A Conversation on Contemporary Philosophy'. *Cultural Critique* 57 (2004): 151–83.

Chrissus and Odotheus. *Barbarians: disordered insurgence*. London: Elephant Editions, 2004. Available from http://alphabetthreat.co.uk/elephanteditions/pdf/barbarians.pdf [consulted 2 March 2010].

Clark, T. J. and Donald-Nicholson Smith. 'Why Art Can't Kill the Situationist International'. In *Guy Debord and The Situationist International: Texts and Documents*, ed. Tom McDonough. Cambridge, MA and London: The MIT Press, 2002, pp. 467–88.

Cohen, Sande. 'Science Studies and Language Suppression – A Critique of Bruno Latour's *We Have Never Been Modern*'. *Studies in History & Philosophy of Science* 28.2 (1997): 339–61.

Colletti, Lucio. *Marxism and Hegel*, trans. Lawrence Garner. London: NLB, 1973.

Comay, Rebecca. 'Dead Right: Hegel and the Terror'. *South Atlantic Quarterly* 103: 2/3 (Spring / Summer 2004): 375–95.

Connery, Christopher Leigh. 'The World Sixties'. In *The Worlding Project: Doing Cultural Studies in the Era of Globalization*, ed. Rob Wilson and Christopher Leigh Connery. Santa Cruz, CA: New Pacific Press. Berkeley, CA: North Atlantic Books, 2007, pp. 77–107.

Coole, Diana. *Negativity and Politics: Dionysus and Dialectics from Kant to Poststructuralism*. London and New York: Routledge, 2000.

Critchley, Simon. 'Comedy and Finitude: Displacing the Tragic-Heroic Paradigm in Philosophy and Psychoanalysis'. In *Ethics–Politics–Subjectivity: Essays on Derrida, Levinas and Contemporary French Thought*. London and New York: Verso, 1999, pp. 217–38.

Critchley, Simon. '"Fault Lines": Simon Critchley in Discussion on Alain Badiou', ed. Jon Baldwin and Nick Haeffner. Matthew Wilkens ed. and intro. for the issue 'The Philosophy of Alain Badiou'. *Polygraph* 17 (2005): 295–307.

Critchley, Simon. *Infinitely Demanding: Ethics of Commitment, Politics of Resistance*. London and New York: Verso, 2007.

Critchley, Simon. 'Mystical Anarchism'. *Critical Horizons: A Journal of Philosophy and Social Theory* 10.2 (August 2009): 272–306.

Croser, Caroline. 'Networking Security in the Space of the City: Event-ful Battlespaces and the Contingency of the Encounter'. *Theory & Event* 10.2 (2007).

Davis, Mike and Daniel Bertrand Monk (eds) *Evil Paradises: Dreamworlds of Neoliberalism*. New York and London: The New Press, 2007.

Day, Gail Ann. 'Strategies in the metropolitan Merz: Manfredo Tafuri and Italian Workerism'. *Radical Philosophy* 133 (2005): 26–38.

De Angelis, Massimo. *The Beginning of History*. London: Pluto Press, 2007.

Debord, Guy. *Society of the Spectacle*. Detroit: Black & Red, 1983.

Debord, Guy. *Comments on the Society of the Spectacle* [1988], trans. Malcolm Imrie. London and New York: Verso, 1990.

Debord, Guy. *Complete Cinematic Works*, trans. and ed. Ken Knabb. Oakland, CA and Edinburgh: AK Press, 2003.

Debord, Guy and Gianfranco Sanguinetti. "Theses on the Situationist International and Its Time" [1972], trans. Christopher Winks. *Not Bored!* 1998. Available from http://www.notbored.org/theses-on-the-SI.html [consulted 17 February 2009].

Deleuze, Gilles. *Nietzsche and Philosophy* [1962], trans. Hugh Tomlinson. London: Athlone, 1983.

Deleuze, Gilles. *Foucault* [1986], trans. Séan Hand. London: Athlone, 1988.

Deleuze, Gilles. *Cinema 2: The Time-Image*, trans. Hugh Tomlinson and Robert Galeta. London: Athlone, 1989.

Deleuze, Gilles. 'Coldness and Cruelty' [1967], trans. Jean McNeil, in *Masochism*. New York: Zone Books, 1989, pp. 9–138.

Deleuze, Gilles. *The Logic of Sense* [1969], trans. Mark Lester with Charles Stivale, ed. Constantine V. Boundas. New York: Columbia University Press, 1990.

Deleuze, Gilles. *Bergsonism* [1966], trans. Hugh Tomlinson and Barbara Habberjam. New York: Zone Books, 1991.

Deleuze, Gilles. 'Postscript on the Societies of Control' [1990]. *October* 59 (Winter 1992): 3–7.

Deleuze, Gilles. *Difference and Repetition* [1968], trans. Paul Patton. London: Athlone, 1994.

Deleuze, Gilles. *Negotiations, 1972–1990*, trans. Martin Joughin. New York: Columbia University Press, 1995.

Deleuze, Gilles. *Pure Immanence: Essays on a Life*, intro. John Rajchman, trans. Anne Boyman. New York: Zone Books, 2001.

Deleuze, Gilles. *Desert Islands and Other Texts 1953–1974*, ed. D. Lapoujade, trans. M. Taormina. Los Angeles and New York: Semiotext(e), 2004.

Deleuze, Gilles. *Francis Bacon: The Logic of Sensation*, trans. Daniel W. Smith. London: Continuum, 2005.

Deleuze, Gilles. 'Lecture Course on Chapter Three of Bergson's *Creative Evolution*', trans. Bryn Loban. *SubStance* 114.36.3 (2007): 72–90.

Deleuze, Gilles. 'Responses to a Series of Questions', ed. Robin Mackay, 'Unknown Deleuze'. *Collapse* III (2007): 39–43.

Deleuze, Gilles and Félix Guattari. *Anti-Oedipus* [1972], trans. Robert Hurley, Mark Seem and Helen R. Lane. Minneapolis: University of Minnesota Press, 1983.

Deleuze, Gilles and Félix Guattari. *Kafka: toward a minor literature* [1975], trans. Dana Polan, foreword Réda Bensmaïa. Minneapolis: University of Minnesota Press, 1986.

Deleuze, Gilles and Félix Guattari. *A Thousand Plateaus* [1980], trans. Brian Massumi. London: Athlone, 1988.

Deleuze, Gilles and Félix Guattari. *What is Philosophy?* [1991], trans. Graham Burchell and Hugh Tomlinson. London and New York: Verso, 1994.

Derrida, Jacques. *Of Grammatology* [1967], trans. Gayatri Chakravorty Spivak. Baltimore and London: The Johns Hopkins University Press, 1974.

Derrida, Jacques. *Writing and Difference*, trans. and intro. Alan Bass. Chicago and London: The University of Chicago Press, 1978.

Derrida, Jacques. *Spurs*, trans. Barbara Harlow. Chicago and London: The University of Chicago Press, 1979.

Derrida, Jacques. *Margins of Philosophy*, trans. Alan Bass. Brighton: Harvester, 1982.

Derrida, Jacques *Glas* [1974], trans. John P. Leavey Jr, and Richard Rand. Lincoln, NE: University of Nebraska Press, 1986.

Derrida, Jacques. *Positions*, trans. Alan Bass. London: Athlone, 1987.

Derrida, Jacques *The Postcard: From Socrates to Freud and Beyond* [1980], trans. Alan Bass. Chicago and London: The University of Chicago Press, 1987.

Derrida, Jacques 'Letter to a Japanese Friend' [1983]. In *A Derrida Reader: Between the Blinds*, ed. and intro. Peggy Kamuf. New York and London: Harvester Wheatsheaf, 1991, pp. 269–76.

Derrida, Jacques. 'Ulysses Gramophone'. In *Jacques Derrida, Acts of Literature*, ed. derek Attridge. New York and London: Routledge, 1992, pp. 256–309.

Derrida, Jacques. *Aporias*, trans. Thomas Dutoit. Stanford, CA: Stanford University Press, 1993.

Derrida, Jacques. *Specters of Marx* [1993], trans. Peggy Kamuf. New York and London: Routledge, 1994.

Derrida, Jacques. *The Gift of Death*, trans. David Wills. Chicago and London: The University of Chicago Press, 1995.

Derrida, Jacques. *Archive Fever: A Freudian Impression* [1995], trans. Eric Prenowitz. Chicago and London: The University of Chicago Press, 1996.

Derrida, Jacques. *Monolingualism of the Other; or, The Prosthesis of Origin*, trans. P. Mensah. Stanford, CA: Stanford University Press, 1998.

Derrida, Jacques. *Of Hospitality*, trans. Rachel Bowlby. Stanford, CA: Stanford University Press, 2000.

Derrida, Jacques. *On Cosmopolitanism and Forgiveness*, trans. Mark Dooley and Michael Hughes. London and New York: Routledge, 2001.

Derrida, Jacques. 'I'm Going to Have to Wander All Alone'. In *The Work of Mourning*, trans. Anne Pascale-Brault and Michael Nass. Chicago: The University of Chicago Press, 2001, pp. 192–5.

Derrida, Jacques. *Negotiations: Interventions and Interviews, 1971–2001*, ed., trans. and intro. Elizabeth Rottenberg. Stanford, CA: Stanford University Press, 2002.

Derrida, Jacques. 'Force of Law: The "Mystical Foundation of Authority"', trans. M. Quaintance. In *Acts of Religion*, ed. and intro. Gil Anidjar. New York and London: Routledge, 2002, pp. 228–98.

Derrida, Jacques. 'For a Justice to Come: An Interview with Jacques Derrida'. *Indymedia* (2004). Available from http://archive.indymedia.be/uploads/derrida_en.pdf [consulted 25 February 2008].

Derrida, Jacques. *Rogues: Two Essays on Reason*, trans. Pascale-Anne Brault and Michael Naas. Stanford, CA: Stanford University Press, 2005.

Derrida, Jacques. 'Marx and Sons'. In *Ghostly Demarcations, A Symposium on Jacques Derrida's Specters of Marx*, ed. Michael Sprinker. London and New York: Verso, 2008, pp. 213–69.

Derrida, Jacques and Maurizio Ferraris. *A Taste for the Secret*, trans. G. Donis. Cambridge: Polity, 2001.

Descombes, Vincent. *Modern French Philosophy*, trans. L. Scott-Fox and J. M. Harding. Cambridge: Cambridge University Press, 1980.

Eagleton, Terry. *The Illusions of Postmodernism*. Oxford and Malden, MA: Blackwell, 1996.

Eagleton, Terry. *Sweet Violence: The Idea of the Tragic*. Oxford and Malden, MA: Blackwell, 2002.

Eagleton, Terry. 'Marxism without Marxism'. In *Ghostly Demarcations, A Symposium on Jacques Derrida's Specters of Marx*, ed. Michael Sprinker. London and New York: Verso, 2008, pp. 83–7.

Edelman, Lee. *No Future: Queer Theory and the Death Drive*. Durham, NC and London: Duke University Press, 2004.

Elliott, Gregory. *Ends in Sight: Marx / Fukuyama / Hobsbawm / Anderson*. London and Ann Arbor, MI: Pluto Press, and Toronto: Between the Lines, 2008.

En Attendant. *John Zerzan and the Primitive Confusion*. London: Chronos Publications, 2004.

Fabbri, Lorenzo. 'Philosophy as Chance: An Interview with Jean-Luc Nancy'. *Critical Inquiry* 33 (2007): 427–40.

Finelli, Roberto. 'Abstraction versus Contradiction: Observations on Chris Arthur's *The New Dialectic and Marx's 'Capital'*', trans. Peter Thomas. *Historical Materialism* 15.2 (2007): 61–74.

Foucault, Michel. *The Order of Things: An Archaeology of the Human Sciences* [1966], trans. Alan Sheridan. London and New York: Tavistock/Routledge, 1970.

Foucault, Michel. *The History of Sexuality vol.1. An Introduction*, trans. Robert Hurley. London: Penguin, 1979.

Foucault, Michel. *The Care of the Self: The History of Sexuality*, vol. 3, trans. Robert Hurley. New York: Vintage, 1986.

Foucault, Michel. *The Use of Pleasure: The History of Sexuality*, vol. 2, trans. Robert Hurley. Harmondsworth: Penguin, 1987.

Foucault, Michel. 'Maurice Blanchot: The Thought from Outside', trans. B. Massumi. In *Foucault / Blanchot*. New York: Zone Books, 1987, pp. 9–58.

Fox, Dominic. *Cold World: The Aesthetics of Dejection and the Politics of Militant Dysphoria*. Winchester and Washington, DC: Zero Books, 2009.

Freud, Sigmund. 'Negation' [1925]. In *PFL 11 On Metapsychology*, ed. Angela Richards. Harmondsworth: Penguin, 1984, pp. 435–42.

Galloway, Alexander R. *Protocol: How Control Exists after Decentralization*. Cambridge, MA and London: The MIT Press, 2004.

Galloway, Alexander R and Eugene Thacker. *The Exploit: A Theory of Networks*. Minneapolis and London: University of Minnesota Press, 2007.

Garo, Isabelle. 'Deleuze, Marx and Revolution: What It Means to "Remain Marxist"'. In *Critical Companion to Contemporary Marxism*, ed. Jacques Bidet and Stathis Kouvelakis. Chicago: Haymarket Books, 2009, pp. 605–24.

Gibson, Andrew. *Beckett & Badiou: The Pathos of Intermittency*. Oxford and New York: Oxford University Press, 2006.

Gillespie, Sam. *The Mathematics of Novelty: Badiou's Minimalist Metaphysics*. Melbourne: re.press, 2008.

Graeber, David. *Fragments of an Anarchist Anthropology*. Chicago: Prickly Paradigm Press, 2004.

Haar, Michel. 'The Play of Nietzsche in Derrida'. In *Derrida: A Critical Reader*, ed. David Wood. Oxford and Cambridge, MA: Blackwell, 1992, pp. 52–71.

Haar, Michel. 'The Politics of Prescription'. *South Atlantic Quarterly* 104 (2005): 769–89.

Hägglund, Martin. *Radical Atheism: Derrida and the Time of Life*. Stanford, CA: Stanford University Press, 2008.

Hallward, Peter. *Out of this World: Deleuze and the Philosophy of Creation*. London and New York: Verso, 2006.

Hallward, Peter. 'Order and Event: On Badiou's *Logics of Worlds*'. *New Left Review* 53 (September–October 2008): 97–122.

Hallward, Peter. 'The Will of the People: Notes towards a dialectical voluntarism'. *Radical Philosophy* 155 (May/June 2009): 17–29.

Hallward, Peter ed. *Think Again: Alain Badiou and the Future of Philosophy*. London and New York: Continuum, 2004.

Hardt, Michael. 'Today's Bandung?'. *New Left Review* 14 (March–April 2002): 112–18.

Hardt, Michael and Antonio Negri. *Empire*. Cambridge, MA: Harvard University Press, 2000.

Hardt, Michael and Antonio Negri. *Multitude*. London: Penguin, 2004.

Harman, Graham. 'DeLanda's Ontology: Assemblage and Realism'. *Continental Philosophy Review* 41.3 (2008): 367–83.

Harman, Graham. *Prince of Networks: Bruno Latour and Metaphysics*. Melbourne: re.press, 2009.

Harvey, David. *Justice, Nature and the Geography of Difference*. Oxford: WileyBlackwell, 1996.

Hatherley, Owen. *Militant Modernism*. Winchester and Washington, DC: Zero Books, 2009.

Hegel, G. W. F. *Phenomenology of Spirit* [1818], trans. A. V. Miller. Oxford: Clarendon Press, 1977.

Heidegger, Martin. *The Question Concerning Technology and Other Essays*, trans. and intro. William Lovitt. New York: Harper, 1977.

Heidegger, Martin. '"Only a God Can Save Us": *Der Spiegel*'s Interview with Martin Heidegger' [1966]. In *The Heidegger Controversy*, ed. Richard Wolin. Cambridge, MA and London: The MIT Press, 1993, pp. 91–116.

Héritier, Françoise. *Two Sisters and Their Mother: The Anthropology of Incest*, trans. Jeanne Herman. New York: Zone Books, 1999.

Hirschman, Albert O. *The Rhetoric of Reaction: Perversity, Futility, Jeopardy*. Cambridge, MA and London: Harvard University Press, 1991.

Hobson, Marion. *Jacques Derrida: Opening Lines*. London and New York: Routledge, 1998.

Holloway, John. 'Why Adorno?'. In *Negativity and Revolution: Adorno and Political Activism*, ed. John Holloway, Fernando Matamoros and Sergio Tischler. London: Pluto Press, 2009, pp. 12–17.

Jameson, Fredric. *Marxism and Form: Twentieth-Century Dialectical Theories of Literature*. Princeton, NJ: Princeton University Press, 1971.

Jameson, Fredric. *Postmodernism, or The Cultural Logic of Late Capitalism*. London and New York: Verso, 1991.

Jameson, Fredric. *The Cultural Turn: Selected Writings on the Postmodern, 1983–1998*. London and New York: Verso, 1998.

Jameson, Fredric. 'Lenin and Revisionism'. In *Lenin Reloaded: Towards a Politics of Truth*, ed. Sebastian Budgen, Stathis Kouvelakis and Slavoj Žižek. Durham, NC and London: Duke University Press, 2007, pp. 59–73.

Jameson, Fredric. 'Marx's Purloined Letter'. In *Ghostly Demarcations, A Symposium on Jacques Derrida's Specters of Marx*, ed. Michael Sprinker. London and New York: Verso, 2008, pp. 26–67.

Jensen, Casper Bruun. 'A Nonhumanist Disposition: On Performativity, Practical Ontology, and Intervention'. *Configurations* 12 (2004): 229–61.

Kerslake, Christian. *Deleuze and the Unconscious*. London and New York: Continuum, 2007.

Kerslake, Christian. 'Becoming Against History: Deleuze, Toynbee and Vitalist Historiography'. *Parrhesia* 4 (2008): 17–48. Available from http://www.parrhesiajournal.org/parrhesia04/parrhesia04_kerslake.pdf [consulted 19 August 2008].

Klossowski, Pierre. *Such a Deathly Desire*, trans. and with an afterword by Russell Ford. Albany: State University of New York Press, 2007.

Kordela, A. Kiarina. *$urplus: Spinoza, Lacan*. Albany: State University of New York Press, 2007.

Lacan, Jacques. *The Four Fundamental Concepts of Psycho-Analysis*, trans. Alan Sheridan. Harmondsworth: Penguin, 1979.

Latour, Bruno. 'The Enlightenment Without the Critique: A Word on Michel Serres' Philosophy'. In *Contemporary French Philosophy*, ed. A. Phillips Griffiths. Cambridge: Cambridge University Press, 1987, pp. 83–97.

Latour, Bruno. *The Pasteurization of France*, trans. Alan Sheridan and John Law. Cambridge, MA and London: Harvard University Press, 1988.

Latour, Bruno. *We Have Never Been Modern*, trans. Catherine Porter. London and New York: Harvester Wheatsheaf, 1993.

Latour, Bruno. 'Socrates' and Callicles' Settlement – or, The Invention of the Impossible Body Politic'. *Configurations* 5.2 (1997): 189–240.

Latour, Bruno. 'Never too late to read Tarde'. *Domus* (October 2004), Bruno Latour's Web site. Available from http://www.bruno-latour.fr/presse/presse_art/GB-DOMUS%2010-04.html [consulted 22 October 2009].

Latour, Bruno. 'Why Has Critique Run out of Steam? From Matters of Fact to Matters of Concern'. *Critical Inquiry* 30 (2004): 225–48.

Latour, Bruno. *Reassembling the Social*. Oxford: Oxford University Press, 2005.

Latour, Bruno. 'Let the dead (revolutionaries) bury the dead'. For a special issue of the Turkish journal of sociology *Birikim*, edited by Koray Caliskan (2006), Bruno Latour's Web site. Available from http://www.bruno-latour.fr/poparticles/poparticle/P-121_REVOLUTION.html [consulted 14 October 2007].

Latour, Bruno. 'Turning Around Politics: A Note on Gerard de Vries' Paper'. *Social Studies of Science* 37.5 (October 2007): 811–20.

Latour, Bruno. 'We are all reactionaries today: interview to Konstantin Kastrissianakis'. *Re-public re-imaging democracy* (2007). Available from http://www.re-public.gr/en/?p=129 [consulted 8 November 2007].

Latour, Bruno. 'Response'. The Harman Review: Bruno Latour's Empirical Metaphysics, ANTHEM Group Symposium, London School of Economics, Tuesday, 5 February 2008. Available from http://www.lse.ac.uk/collections/informationSystems/newsAndEvents/2008events/HarmanLatour.htm [consulted 15 July 2008].

Latour, Bruno and Michel Callon. '"Thou shall not calculate!" or How to Symmetricalize Gift and Capital', trans. Javier Krauel, from '*Comment peut-on être anticapitaliste?*', La Découverte, *La revue du MAUSS* 9 (1997), Bruno Latour's Web site. Available from http://www.bruno-latour.fr/poparticles/poparticle/p071-en.html [consulted 19 March 2009].

Linebaugh, Peter. *The Magna Carta Manifesto: Liberties and Commons for All*. California: University of California Press, 2008.

Lotringer, Sylvère and Christian Marazzi. 'The Return of Politics'. In 'Autonomia: Post-Political Politics'. *Semiotext(e)* 3.3 (1980): 8–21.

Löwy, Michael. *Fire Alarm: Reading Walter Benjamin's 'On the Concept of History'*, trans. Chris Turner. London and New York: Verso, 2005.

Lukács, Georg. *History and Class Consciousness* [1923], trans. Rodney Livingstone. London: Merlin Press, 1971.

Lyotard, Jean-François. *Peregrinations: Law, Form, Event*. New York: Columbia University Press, 1988.

Lyotard, Jean-François. *Duchamp's Transformers* [1977]. Venice, CA: The Lapis Press, 1990.

Lyotard, Jean-François. *Heidegger and "the jews"* [1988], trans. Andreas Michel and Mark Roberts, intro. David Carroll. Minneapolis: University of Minnesota Press, 1990.

Lyotard, Jean-François. *Libidinal Economy* [1974], trans. Iain Hamilton Grant. London: Athlone, 1993.

Mandarini, Matteo. 'Not Fear but Hope in the Apocalypse'. *ephemera* 8.2 (2008): 176–81. Available from http://www.ephemeraweb.org./journal/8-2/8-2mandarini.pdf [consulted 31 July 2008].

Mandarini, Matteo. 'Beyond Nihilism: Notes Towards a Critique of Left-Heideggerianism in Italian Philosophy of the 1970s'. In *The Italian Difference: Between Nihilism and Biopolitics*, ed. Lorenzo Chiesa and Alberto Toscano. Melbourne: re.press, 2009, pp. 55–79.

Mann, Geoff. 'Colletti on the Credit Crunch: A Response to Robin Blackburn'. *New Left Review* 56 (March–April 2009): 119–27.

Marcuse, Herbert. *Eros and Civilization*. London: Allen Lane The Penguin Press, 1969.

Martin, Stewart. 'The absolute artwork meets the absolute commodity'. *Radical Philosophy* 146 (November/December 2007): 15–25.

Martin, Stewart. 'Artistic Communism – A Sketch'. *Third Text* 23.4 (2009): 481–94.

Marx, Karl. *Critique of the Gotha Programme* [1875]. Moscow: Progress Publishers, 1971.

Marx, Karl. *Grundrisse*, trans. Martin Nicolaus. Harmondsworth: Penguin, 1973.

Marx, Karl. *Capital vol. 1*, intro. Ernest Mandel, trans. Ben Fowkes. Harmondsworth: Penguin, 1976.

Marx, Karl. *Capital vol. 3*, intro. Ernest Mandel. Harmondsworth: Penguin, 1981.

Marx, Karl. *Early Writings*, intro. Lucio Colletti, trans. Rodney Livingstone and Gregor Benton. London: Penguin, 1992.

Marx, Karl and Friedrich Engels. *The German Ideology* [1845], ed. and intro. Chris Arthur. London: Lawrence and Wishart, 1970.

Marx, Karl and Friedrich Engels. *The Communist Manifesto*, intro. and notes Gareth Stedman Jones. London: Penguin, 2002.

May, Todd, Benjamin Noys and Saul Newman. 'Democracy, anarchism and radical politics today: An interview with Jacques Rancière', trans. John Lechte. *Anarchist Studies* 16.2 (2008): 173–85.

Mayer, Arno J. *The Furies: Violence and Terror in the French and Russian Revolutions*. Princeton, NJ and Oxford: Princeton University Press, 2000.

Meillassoux, Quentin. *After Finitude*, trans. Ray Brassier. New York and London: Continuum, 2008.

Mitchell, Timothy. 'Dreamland'. In *Evil Paradises: Dreamworlds of Neoliberalism*, ed. Mike Davis and Daniel Bertrand Monk. New York and London: The New Press, 2007, pp. 1–33.

Monk, Daniel Bertrand. 'Hives and Swarms: On the "Nature" of Neoliberalism and the Rise of the Ecological Insurgent'. In *Evil Paradises: Dreamworlds of Neoliberalism*, ed. Mike Davis and Daniel Bertrand Monk. New York and London: The New Press, 2007, pp. 262–73.

Morin, Edgar. 'Approaches to Nothingness', trans. David Antal. In *Looking Back on the End of the World*, ed. Dietmar Kamper and Christoph Wulf. New York: Semiotext(e), 1989, pp. 81–95.

Murphy, Timothy S. and Abdul-Karim Mustapha (eds) *The Philosophy of Antonio Negri Volume Two: Revolution in Theory*. London and Ann Arbor, MI: Pluto Press, 2007.

Nancy, Jean-Luc. *Being Singular Plural* [1996], trans. R. D. Richardson and A. E. O'Byrne. Stanford, CA: Stanford University Press, 2000.

Nealon, Jeffrey T. 'Post-Deconstructive? Negri, Derrida, and the Present State of Theory', *symplokē* 14 (1–2) (2006): 68–80.

Negarestani, Reza. *Cyclonopedia: Complicity with Anonymous Materials*. Melbourne: re.press, 2008.

Negarestani, Reza. 'The Corpse Bride: Thinking with Nigredo', ed. Robin Mackay, 'Concept Horror'. *Collapse* IV (2008): 129–60.

Negri, Antonio. *Marx Beyond Marx*, trans. Harry Cleaver, Michael Ryan and M. Viano. New York: Autonomedia, 1991.

Negri, Antonio. *Insurgencies: Constituent Power and the Modern State* [1992], trans. Maurizia Boscagli. Minneapolis and London: University of Minnesota Press, 1999.

Negri, Antonio. '*Kairòs*, Alma Venus, Multitudo' [2000]. In *Time for Revolution*, trans. and intro. Matteo Mandarini. New York and London: Continuum, 2003, pp. 139–261.

Negri, Antonio. *Books for Burning: Between Civil War and Democracy in 1970s Italy*, trans. and ed. Timothy S. Murphy, trans. Arianna Bove, Ed Emery, Timothy S. Murphy and Francesca Novello. London and New York: Verso, 2005.

Negri, Antonio. *The Political Descartes*, trans. and intro. Matteo Mandarini and Alberto Toscano. London and New York: Verso, 2007.

Negri, Antonio. 'Art and Culture in the Age of Empire and the Time of the Multitudes', trans. Max Henninger. *SubStance* 112.36.2 (2007): 48–55.

Negri, Antonio. *Reflections on Empire*, trans. Ed Emery. Cambridge and Malden, MA: Polity, 2008.

Negri, Antonio. 'Metamorphoses', trans. Alberto Toscano. *Radical Philosophy* 149 (May/June 2008): 21–5.

Negri, Antonio. 'The Specter's Smile'. In *Ghostly Demarcations, A Symposium on Jacques Derrida's Specters of Marx*, ed. Michael Sprinker. London and New York: Verso, 2008, pp. 5–16.

Negri, Antonio. *The Labor of Job: The Biblical Text as a Parable of Human Labor*, trans. Matteo Mandarini, foreword by Michael Hardt, commentary by Roland Boer. Durham, NC: Duke University Press, 2009.

Negri, Antonio and Gabriele Fadini. 'Materialism and Theology: A Conversation'. *Rethinking Marxism* 20.4 (October 2008): 665–72.

Nietzsche, Friedrich. *Twilight of the Idols / The Anti-Christ* [1889], trans. and intro. R. J. Hollingdale. London: Penguin, 1968.

Nietzsche, Friedrich. *The Will to Power*, trans. W. Kaufmann and R. J. Hollingdale, ed. W. Kaufmann. New York: Vintage, 1968.

Nietzsche, Friedrich. *On the Genealogy of Morals/Ecce Homo*, ed. W. Kaufmann. New York: Vintage Books, 1969.

Nietzsche, Friedrich. *Ecce Homo* [1888], trans., intro. and notes R. J. Hollingdale. London: Penguin, 1979.

Noys, Benjamin. '"The Powers of the Negative": Review of Sam Gillespie, *The Mathematics of Novelty* (re-press 2008)'. *S: Journal of the Jan van Eyck Circle for Lacanian Ideology Critique* vol.2 (2009): 102–8. Available from http://www.lineofbeauty.org/index.php/s/article/viewFile/24/81 [consulted 9 October 2009].

Noys, Benjamin. '"Monumental Construction": Badiou and the Politics of Aesthetics'. *Third Text* 23.4 (2009): 383–92.

Noys, Benjamin. 'Separacija in reverzibilnost: Agamben o podobi' ['Separation and Reversibility: Agamben on the Image'], trans. Rok Benčin (Slovenian), *Filozofski Vestnik* 30.1 (2009): 143–59.

Perez, Gilberto. *The Material Ghost: Films and their Medium*. Baltimore and London: The Johns Hopkins University Press, 1998.

Piccone, Paul. 'The Changing Function of Critical Theory'. *New German Critique* 12 (Autumn 1977): 29–37.

Polanyi, Karl. *The Great Transformation* [1944]. Boston: Beacon Press, 1957.

Polkinghorne, John. *Quantum Theory: A Very Short Introduction*. Oxford: Oxford University Press, 2002.

Pope, Alexander. 'An Essay on Man'. In *The Oxford Authors Alexander Pope*, ed. Pat Rogers. Oxford and New York: Oxford University Press, 1993, pp. 270–309.

Postone, Moishe. 'Critique and Historical Transformation'. *Historical Materialism* 12.3 (2004): 53–72.

Postone, Moishe (with Timothy Brennan). 'Labor and the Logic of Abstraction: An Interview'. *South Atlantic Quarterly* 108.2 (Spring 2009): 305–30.

Power, Nina. 'He's Not Beyond Good and Evil'. *Mute: Culture and Politics After the Net* 2.11 (March 2009): 28–35.

Power, Nina. 'Non-Reproductive Futurism: Rancière's rational equality against Edelman's body apolitic'. *borderlands e-journal* 8.2 (2009). Available from http://www.borderlands.net.au/vol8no2_2009/power_futurism.pdf [consulted 9 November 2009].

Power, Nina and Alberto Toscano. 'The Philosophy of Restoration: Alain Badiou and the Enemies of May', ed. Christopher Connery and Hortense J. Spiller, 'The Sixties and the World Event'. *boundary 2* 36.1 (Spring 2009): 27–46.

Power, Nina and Alberto Toscano. 'Aesthetics, Inaesthetics, Anti-Aesthetics'. In *Think Again: Alain Badiou and the Future of Philosophy*, ed. Peter Hallward. London: Continuum, 2004, pp. 218–31.

Roberts, John. *Philosophizing the Everyday: Revolutionary Praxis and the Fate of Cultural Theory*. London: Pluto Press, 2006.

Roberts, John. 'On the Limits of Negation in Badiou's Theory of Art'. *Journal of Visual Arts Practice* 7.3 (2008): 271–82.

Roberts, John. 'Productivism and Its Contradictions'. *Third Text* 23.5 (2009): 527–36.

Roberts, John. 'Art and its Negations' (unpublished).

Rorty, Richard. 'Philosophy as a Kind of Writing: An Essay on Derrida'. *New Literary History* 10.1 (Autumn 1978): 141–60.

Said, Edward 'Opponents, Audiences, Constituencies, and Community', *Critical Inquiry* 9.1 (September 1982): 1–26.

Saussure, Ferdinand de. *Course in General Linguistics*, trans. Roy Harris. London: Duckworth, 1983.

Serres, Michel with Bruno Latour. *Conversations on Science, Culture, and Time*, trans. Roxanne Lapidus. Ann Arbor, MI: The University of Michigan Press, 1995.

Seymour, Benedict. 'Drowning by Numbers: The Non-Reproduction of New Orleans'. *Mute Magazine* (2006). Available from http://www.metamute.org/Drowning-by-Numbers [consulted 11 September 2009].

Situationist International. *Situationist International Anthology*, ed. Ken Knabb. Berkeley, California: Bureau of Public Secrets, 1981.

Smith, Jason. 'Jacques Derrida, "Crypto-Communist?"'. In *Critical Companion to Contemporary Marxism*, ed. Jacques Bidet and Stathis Kouvelakis. Chicago: Haymarket Books, 2009, pp. 625–45.

Sontag, Susan. 'Under the Sign of Saturn' [1978]. In *Under the Sign of Saturn*. London: Vintage, 1996, pp. 109–34.

Sprinker, Michael ed. *Ghostly Demarcations: A Symposium on Jacques Derrida's Specters of Marx*. London and New York: Verso, 2008.

Stites, Richard. *Revolutionary Dreams: utopian vision and experimental life in the Russian Revolution*. New York and Oxford: Oxford University Press, 1989.

Stolze, Ted. 'Marxist Wisdom: Antonio Negri on the Book of Job'. In *The Philosophy of Antonio Negri Volume Two: Revolution in Theory*, ed. Timothy S. Murphy and Abdul-Karim Mustapha. London and Ann Arbor, MI: Pluto Press, 2007, pp. 129–40.

Sweeney, Marvin A. 'Pardes Revisited Once Again: A Reassessment of the Rabbinic Legend Concerning the Four Who Entered Pardes'. *Shofar: An Interdisciplinary Journal of Jewish Studies* 22.4 (2004): 43–56.

Thompson, E. P. 'Time, Work-Discipline, and Industrial Capitalism'. *Past and Present* 38 (December 1967): 56–97.

Toscano, Alberto. 'Factory, Territory, Metropolis, Empire'. *Angelaki* 9.2 (August 2004): 197–216.

Toscano, Alberto. 'The Bourgeois and the Islamist, or, The Other Subject of Politics'. In *The Praxis of Alain Badiou*, ed. Paul Ashton, A. J. Bartlett and Justin Clemens. Melbourne: re.press, 2006, pp. 339–66.

Toscano, Alberto. 'Religion and Revolt'. */seconds* 4 (2007). Available from http://www.slashseconds.org/issues/001/004/articles/04-atoscano/index.php [consulted 9 September 2008].

Toscano, Alberto. 'Carl Schmitt in Beijing: partisanship, geopolitics and the demolition of the Eurocentric World'. *Postcolonial Studies* 11.4 (2008): 417–33.

Toscano, Alberto. 'In Praise of Negativism'. In *Deleuze, Guattari and the Production of the New*, ed. Simon O'Sullivan and Stephen Zepke. London: Continuum, 2008, pp. 56–67.

Toscano, Alberto. 'Review Essay: Beginnings and Ends: For, Against and Beyond '68'. *New Formations* 65 (Autumn 2008): 94–104.

Toscano, Alberto. 'The Culture of Abstraction'. *Theory, Culture & Society* 25.4 (2008): 55–73.

Toscano, Alberto. 'The Open Secret of Real Abstraction'. *Rethinking Marxism* 20.2 (April 2008): 273–87.

Toscano, Alberto. 'Partisan Thought'. *Historical Materialism* 17.3 (2009): 175–91.

Toscano, Alberto. 'The Sensuous Religion of the Multitude: Art and Abstraction in Negri'. *Third Text* 23.4 (2009): 369–82.

Tronti, Mario. 'Lenin in England' [1964], *Marxists Internet Archive*. Available from http://www.marxists.org/reference/subject/philosophy/works/it/tronti.htm [consulted 18 May 2008].

Tronti, Mario. 'Workers and Capital', *Texas Archives of Autonomist Marxism*, originally translated in *Telos* 14 (Winter 1972): 25–62, and originally published as 'Poscritto di problemi', in Mario Tronti, *Operai e Capitale*. Turin: Einaudi, 1966, 1971, pp. 267–311. Available from https://webspace.utexas.edu/hcleaver/www/TrontiWorkersCapital.html [consulted 2 March 2010].

Turchetto, Maria. 'The Empire Strikes Back: On Hardt and Negri'. *Historical Materialism* 11:1 (2003): 23–36.

UCFML (Group for the Foundation of the Union of Communists of France Marxist-Leninist). 'Maoism: A Stage of Marxism'. *positions* 13.3 (2005): 515–21.

Valentin, Jérémie. 'Gilles Deleuze's Political Posture'. In *Deleuze and Philosophy*, ed. Constantin V. Boundas. Edinburgh: Edinburgh University Press, 2006, pp. 185–201.

Vaneigem, Raoul. *The Book of Pleasures* [1979]. In *Collection of Desires*. Richmond: Paper Street, n.d., pp. 4–50.

Villani, Arnaud. '"I Feel I Am a Pure Metaphysician": The Consequences of Deleuze's Affirmation', Robin Mackay ed. 'Unknown Deleuze'. *Collapse* III (2007): 45–62.

Virno, Paolo. *A Grammar of the Multitude: For an Analysis of Contemporary Forms of Life*, trans. Isabella Bertolleti, James Cascaito and Andrea Casson, foreword by Sylvère Lotringer. Los Angeles and New York: Semiotext(e), 2005.

Virno, Paolo. *Multitude: Between Innovation and Negation*, trans. Isabella Bertoletti, James Cascaito and Andrea Casson. Los Angeles and New York: Semiotext(e), 2008.

Virno, Paolo. 'Natural-Historical Diagrams: The 'New Global' Movement and the Biological Invariant', trans. Alberto Toscano. In *The Italian Difference: Between Nihilism and Biopolitics*, ed. Lorenzo Chiesa and Alberto Toscano. Melbourne: re.press, 2009, pp. 131–47.

Wade, Robert. 'Financial Regime Change?'. *New Left Review* 53 (September–October 2008): 5–21.

Waite, Geoff. *Nietzsche's Corps/e: Aesthetics, Politics, Prophecy, or the Spectacular Technoculture of Everyday Life*. Durham, NC: Duke University Press, 1996.

Weizman, Eyal. *Hollow Land: Israel's Architecture of Occupation*. London and New York: Verso, 2007.

Wright, Steve. *Storming Heaven: Class composition and struggle in Italian Autonomist Marxism*. London and Sterling, VA: Pluto Press, 2002.

Zerzan, John. *Elements of Refusal*. Columbia, MO: Columbia Alternative Library, 1999.

Žižek, Slavoj. *The Sublime Object of Ideology*. London and New York: Verso, 1989.

Žižek, Slavoj. 'The Spectre of Ideology'. In *Mapping Ideology*, Slavoj Žižek. London and New York: Verso, 1995, pp. 1–33.

Žižek, Slavoj. 'Repeating Lenin' [1997]. *Lacanian Ink*, Lacan.com (2001). Available from http://www.lacan.com/replenin.htm [accessed 28 September 2009].

Žižek, Slavoj. *Organs without Bodies: On Deleuze and Consequences*. London and New York: Routledge, 2004.

Žižek, Slavoj. *The Parallax View*. Cambridge, MA and London: The MIT Press, 2006.

Žižek, Slavoj. *The Indivisible Remainder: on Schelling and Related Matters*. London and New York: Verso, 2007.

Žižek, Slavoj. 'Divine Violence and Liberated Territories: SOFT TARGETS talks with Slavoj Žižek'. *Soft Targets* (March 14 2007). Available from http://www.softtargetsjournal.com/web/zizek.php [accessed 29 April 2009].

Žižek, Slavoj. 'Mao Tse-Tung, The Marxist Lord of Misrule'. In *On Practice and Contradiction*, Mao Tse-Tung. London and New York: Verso, 2007, pp. 1–28.

Žižek, Slavoj. *In Defense of Lost Causes*. London and New York: Verso, 2008.

Žižek, Slavoj. *Violence: Six Sideways Reflections*. London: Profile Books, 2008.

Žižek, Slavoj. *First as Tragedy, Then as Farce*. London and New York: Verso, 2009.

Zournazi, Mary. 'Navigating Movements: An Interview with Brian Massumi'. *21C Magazine* 2 (2003). Available from http://www.21cmagazine.com/issue2/massumi.html [consulted 20 April 2008].

Index